LINCOLN CHRISTIAN COL
W9-CAE-271

A great harvest will be reaped when prayer seeds are sown in the dynamic way *Prayerwalking* demonstrates. Here's a vital, joy-filled plan for practical, uplifting intercession. It's based on balanced principles in God's Word and loaded with stories which give rise to a sense of wonder and expectation: What is God about to do, and where do I fit into it?

Jack Hayford
Pastor, The Church on the Way

Prayerwalking gives you eyes and feet and heart for one of the most exciting prayer adventures you may ever have. And, coming as it does in the midst of the most strategic prayer movements in the history of the church, it brings a creatively compelling new dimension to the whole idea of concerted prayer. I know of no resource on prayer that is as original and as creative — and yet so biblical and so kingdom-centered. Walk its pages and see for yourself.

David Bryant
Founder/president, Concerts of Prayer International

I believe that *Prayerwalking* has the potential for being one of the most significant books of this decade in mobilizing Christians for strategic praying for the expansion of Christ's church around the world.

Paul A. Cedar
President, Evangelical Free Church of America

Steve and Graham have given us biblical foundations, practical guidelines and encouraging anecdotes concerning prayerwalking. This is a stimulating, exciting book which makes you want to get out there and do it, preparing the way for evangelism and church planting.

Roger Forster
Ichthus Christian Fellowship, London

Praying On-Site With Insight

Steve Hawthorne
and Graham Kendrick

Foreword by John Dawson

PRAYERWALKING by Graham Kendrick and Steve Hawthorne
Published by Charisma House
A Strang Company
600 Rinehart Road
Lake Mary, FL 32746
www.charismahouse.com

This book or parts thereof may not be reproduced in any form, stored in a retrieval system, or transmitted in any form by any means—electronic, mechanical, photocopy, recording, or otherwise—without prior written permission of the publisher, except as provided by United States of America copyright law.

Unless otherwise noted, all Scripture quotations are from the New American Standard Bible. Copyright © 1960, 1962,1963, 1968, 1971, 1972, 1973, 1975, 1977 by the Lockman Foundation. Used by permission.

Scripture quotations marked NAS revised are from the New American Standard Bible. Copyright © 1960, 1962, 1963, 1968, 1971, 1972, 1973, 1975, 1977, 1993 by the Lockman Foundation. Used by permission.

Scripture quotations marked KJV are from the King James Version of the Bible.

Scripture quotations marked NKJV are from the New King James Version of the Bible. Copyright © 1979, 1980, 1982 by Thomas Nelson, Inc., Publishers. Used by permission.

Copyright © 1993 by Graham Kendrick and Steve Hawthorne
All rights reserved

Library of Congress Catalog Card Number: 92-74603
International Standard Book Number: 0-88419-268-7

05 06 07 08 09 — 21 20 19 18
Printed in the United States of America

ACKNOWLEDGMENTS

Hundreds of people helped with this book. We are grateful to them all, although it is not possible to mention them all. We honor the scores of our prayerwalking friends who readily contributed their proven wisdom. We thank God for the grace upon our church families, Hope Chapel and Ichthus Christian Fellowship. These churches have been a steady fountain of nurture and vision.

The format of a practical manual did not easily lend itself to extensive referencing, so we did not use a standard academic pattern of footnotes. We are greatly indebted to dozens of fine leaders and writers who have shaped and clarified our thinking. Many have contributed to this volume in significant ways.

Warm thanks to James Foreman, Mike O'Quin and Rosemary Phillips, for their superb assistance. Thanks to Deborah Poulalion, Walter Walker and the others at Creation House. The teams of people serving the March for Jesus movement in the United Kingdom and America helped in significant ways. We especially honor the special group of intercessors who agreed to pray for us through the months of research and writing.

Our wives and daughters walked with us through the challenge of completing this book. How we appreciate and delight in each of them.

Steve Hawthorne, Austin, Texas
Graham Kendrick, London, England

685

112840

CONTENTS

FOREWORD

This is one of the few times that I have strongly promoted a book before it was published. That's because we need this book. I have watched the growth of the manuscript with increasing excitement. Its strategy is revolutionary because it is so simple.

As I travel from city to city addressing pastors' gatherings, I see four dynamic activities emerging within the church worldwide. Each one is simple in execution but profound in implications. Each one complements the other within the rising tides of revival.

1. Public praise, exemplified by the worldwide marches for Jesus.

2. Corporate repentance and confession, a growing trend at citywide prayer gatherings, often leading to new levels of reconciliation between the races and subcultures of a city.

3. United pastoral prayer. Examples include six hundred pastors from seventy denominations praying all morning in Los Angeles and thirty pastors from Portland taking a three-day retreat together at the coast. Our leaders are meeting each other with respect and appreciation as they unite around the essentials. This must be the most united generation since the early church.

4. Prayerwalking, the subject of this book. It could be as simple as an individual going for a walk around the block while he prays or as complex as a citywide campaign where united pastors get out maps, divide up the neighborhoods between churches and systematically walk every street in the course of a year.

Prayerwalking fits the restless culture of the nineties. Let's face it. It's hard to pray for your city while imagining it from a "prayer closet." We need the exercise, and we need to see what is really going on. So let's go!

Authors Steve and Graham are veterans involved in all four of the strategies I have mentioned. They have given us a book filled with inspiration and wisdom, but above all else it is practical. It is a book that gives us the big picture but anchors everything in the possibilities of daily life. Every life can be an adventure. After all, what matters is not our dream or our journey but who walks with us on the road. Jesus is beckoning right now. Come on — let's follow him.

John Dawson
International director of urban missions
Youth With A Mission
Los Angeles
March 1993

PART I

How to Prayerwalk

1

Praying On-Site With Insight

Across the globe God is stirring ordinary believers to pray persistently while walking their cities street by street. Some use rather well-arranged plans. Others flow with Spirit-given prompts. Their prayers run the gamut from lofty appeals to pinpoint petitions, ranging beyond their own homes to their neighbors. It's hard to stop there, so most of them eventually burst into prayers for the entire campus or city or nation. No quick fix is envisioned. But expectancy seems to expand with every mile. Most of these pray-ers don't imagine themselves to be just bravely holding flickering candles toward an overwhelming darkness. Rather, long fuses are being lit for anticipated explosions of God's love.

Everyday believers are praying every day, house by house, in their neighborhoods.

> When my husband and I first moved in, we began to walk through the streets every day, praying for every one of the twenty-eight homes in our neighborhood. We prayed for every family, eventually learning their names and knowing some of their needs. Within six months we started a small Bible study in our home with the folks we had been praying for. It wasn't long before we saw four of our neighbors commit their lives to the Lord. Other neighbors have joined us walking and praying. We've got a reputation now because of how close people have come to each other. New people moving in are welcomed by four or five believers who reach out to them. The new people don't know it, but they have been prayed for long before they moved in.
>
> —*Cynthia Long, mother of three and member of Hill Coun-*

> *try Bible Church of Cedar Park, Texas. Since the Longs started prayerwalking four years ago, they have seen Bible study groups emerge in three different homes involving thirty people from their neighborhood.*

Churches are coming together and spreading out to diverse neighborhoods.

> At that first prayerwalk we had all the churches from the north side of the city begin at a north position and all the churches from the south begin at a south position. And we began walking toward city hall. It was quite a moment when both sides met and we turned into city hall.
>
> —*Bob Gal, pastor of First Assembly church of Calgary, Alberta, Canada. Once the group, consisting of five to six thousand people, came together at city hall, leaders of local churches led the crowd in praying for families, their congregations, their city, their province and their nation.*

Students are marching in quiet prayer throughout their high schools and college campuses.

> In 1989 we gathered the teenagers from several different youth groups because they wanted to do a praise and prayer march. About eighty of us went to a high school on a Saturday morning and marched around the perimeter of the school singing praise songs. At the end of the walk we had them get in groups of four or five and pray for the school. Later that very night a youth pastor from one of the churches had a knock on his door. There was a student who had started a satanist cult in that high school and had about forty kids following him. He said that his house had burnt down that evening, and he was tired of this life and wanted out of it. He gave his life to Christ and proceeded to lead many of the teenagers he had led into satanism into Christianity.
>
> —*Tom Pelton, director of the March for Jesus, U.S.A., office in Austin, Texas. After that prayerwalk, Tom helped organize a prayer and praise march around every high school in the city over the next six months. The ex-satanist later carried a wooden cross during a citywide March for Jesus as his first public profession of faith.*

Groups of intercessors are praying across counties, whole countries and even continents.

We walked approximately eight hundred miles from London to Berlin, along a carefully planned route through northern France, Belgium and on into Germany, arriving in Berlin five weeks later. The team prayed every step of the way, six to eight hours a day.

Eight men and women formed the basic core team who walked the whole way, joined by dozens of others who walked segments with us for a week or two. Two of the core team were men who had served in the British military, ages seventy and seventy-eight. One was in the Royal Air Force, and the other had seen many of his friends killed at Dunkirk. Their presence became a kind of catalyst for the issue of reconciliation between Great Britain and Germany. There are deep things within both of our histories that need to be dealt with. I felt the prayerwalk was a vehicle for both nations to face up to the past and to repent of some of the carnage of the last war. With every step we felt that we were forming a prophetic linking of our nations.

—John Pressdee, of Ichthus Christian Fellowship in London, telling of the special prayer expedition which concluded on May 23, 1992. On that day the British prayer team joined more than sixty thousand German believers in the national March for Jesus.

A New Word: *Prayerwalking*

Many people have begun to use a new word to describe the recent burst of citywide intercession. Yet to walk while praying is probably not a new activity, though it seems different from the well-known formats of prayer. The rising interest is so substantial that it can only help to add a new word to our vocabulary: *prayerwalking*. We define prayerwalking simply as *praying on-site with insight.*

How Does Prayerwalking Help?

Learning to pray on-site with insight can help you in at least four ways.

• **Thaw the ice** in your neighborhood. Most Christians sincerely want to serve their neighbors. But many feel frozen from extending their witness or service for fear that neighbors might be offended. Prayerwalking provides a quiet way to help people while gradually coming to understand and care for them. The climate of steady prayer can warm the atmosphere of friendship. Hearts opened by prayer can lead to doors opened for God's healing touch.

• **Overcome fear** of the troubled parts of your city. Most believers are genuinely concerned about their city but find themselves inhibited by fears and habits of isolation. Why endure the unsettled feeling that you don't belong in your own city? Or the nagging guilt that you should do something? We all sense that God's healing for wounded cities won't come from quarantining ourselves away from our own towns, but most believers don't know where to start. Prayerwalking provides a way to re-enter your inner city with godly confidence. Prayerwalkers find that they belong to the places they pray for.

> I can never go past that place without remembering when I was there, kneeling and praying with my friends. It changed my view of the city forever. It was overwhelming. Fourteen years of living in fear in the suburbs, and one day swept it away.
> —*A woman from Boston, speaking of a day of prayer called Pray For Boston '92. She was among hundreds of believers who prayed according to planned routes throughout central sections of Boston.*

• **Contend with evil.** Many Christians feel besieged by evil. Rising crime and open hostility to Christ appear to be energized by stubborn spiritual evil. Prayerwalking provides a way to wage some of the necessary spiritual war with your feet literally on the ground. It makes biblical sense to step out from a defensive, fortress mentality and come physically near to the people whom we know God longs to redeem.

• **Progress in prayer.** Most Christians sincerely desire to pray more. But who hasn't found it hard to build a life of prayer? Prayerwalking offers struggling intercessors one stimulating way to stretch themselves in prayer. One leader who organizes dozens of young Christians in regular prayerwalks said, "It's one of the few ways we've found to break the boredom people feel trying to stay alone in the prayer closet. If they prayerwalk awhile, they get stirred up to go after every sort of prayer."

Prayerwalking is just what it sounds like: walking while praying. Because there are many kinds of walks and several sorts of prayer, it will help to define the word *prayerwalk* in a sharp, narrow sense. We make our attempt in this chapter, taking into consideration the reported experiences of hundreds of walking intercessors.

A Phenomenal Move of God

We are amazed to find that there has been an explosion of prayerwalking in the last twenty years. Though our research only amounts to informal polling, we have made efforts to track prayerwalking on every continent and through diverse streams of Christianity. While we make no claim to scientifically defensible findings, three items stand out significantly.

1. Independent start-ups. We found hundreds of independent initiatives. We can find no father of this movement. It's unlikely that we'll ever find an original prayerwalker who stimulated the idea years ago. There has been a healthy cross-pollination of ideas, but God apparently has authored the idea of prayerwalking in the hearts of hundreds of pioneers who have quietly gotten on with the job and have passed on the idea to countless others.

2. Recent exploding movements. Initiatives appear to be clustered on the timeline. Our informal queries have surfaced very few reports of prayerwalking, as we understand it, before the mid-seventies. During the late seventies we found several reports about deliberate, corporate, intercessory walks. Some of them started on university campuses, many in everyday residential settings. In the mid-eighties scores of diverse initiatives popped up with very little connection with one another. Many initiators of prayerwalks can remember little influence from other prayerwalking efforts. The instigation points seem to be independent of one another, scattered unevenly across the globe.

3. Diverse styles with a common agenda. The beginnings of prayerwalking movements and mutations from them have been marvelously diverse, yet feature common themes of prayer. There appears to be a common agenda echoing through the prayers of prayerwalkers. Prayerwalkers tend to call for Christ's lordship to be enacted more fully on earth. When Christians pray on the common ground of the streets, prayers tend to gravitate to true biblical bedrock. As the Bible is used as an essential prayer source, Scripture provides a sound doctrinal core for a diverse movement of praying Christians from many denominational backgrounds.

Prayerwalkers typically encompass wide neighborhoods and sometimes entire cities in prayer, virtually blanketing whole regions with a cloud of prayer. But at the same time prayerwalking tends to bring intercessors up close with laser-like focus on specific names and homes. The alarm clocks of God are being set to go off in specific neighborhoods, household by household, as prayerwalkers pass by, appealing to heaven for great spiritual awakenings.

The prayers have a common theme, but there has been no standardizing of style. Prayerwalks have at times drawn attention with flaming torches, Day-Glo uniforms, billboard-size signs or choreography. Prayerwalkers may have tried out every conceivable way of carrying, wheeling or forming the symbolic shape of a cross. Most prayerwalks take place quietly — perhaps three students walking daily around dormitories they want to see evangelized. Sometimes pairs of factory workers walk through their plants during lunch break. Parents can be seen walking around their children's schools after-hours. Or missionaries pace the slums of their adopted cities in the early morning before dawn. Prayerwalkers have walked while aboard trains encircling the perimeter of huge cities. Prayerwalkers often climb to elevated viewpoints, pouring out prayer for the towns in view below.

The phenomenon is so beautifully diverse, so suddenly widespread, with so many instigation points, that it appears to us to be an authentic move of God. His Spirit is simply doing more of what he loves to do for all believers: He is helping us pray.

Because there is no authoritative, original method of prayerwalking, it is our conviction that everyone who has ever prayerwalked has only learned a valuable variation. We don't approach the writing of this book as experts or originators. We have attempted to craft this guide as a composite of the prayer wisdom God has endowed to many different parts of Christ's body. Throughout the book we recount the stories and statements of dozens of Christians involved in prayerwalking. A few of their names have been changed because of the opposition they face in the communities they serve.

In all matters of prayer it is wise to turn with the early disciples to the only one who can "Teach us to pray" (Luke 11:1). Jesus is enrolling his church afresh in the school of prayer. Churches of many streams and cities have much to gain and much to give as we literally walk together with Jesus.

Clarifying the Concept of Prayerwalking

Prayerwalking is just what it sounds like it would be: walking while praying. But since there are many kinds of walks and several sorts of prayer, it will help to define the word *prayerwalk* in a sharp, narrow sense which fits the experience of most practicing prayerwalkers around the world. As stated previously, we define prayerwalking as *praying on-site with insight.* Let's consider this definition in each of its parts.

Praying

Prayerwalking is genuine prayer — God working with and through people, on earth and in heaven. While there are technical lessons to be learned, prayerwalking is essentially relationship with God — talking and walking with God himself through Jesus.

• **Directed, intercessory praying.** Prayerwalking helps pray-ers learn how to pray for others, deferring urgent matters in their own lives from the top of their prayer agendas. While many believers enjoy communing with God during private walks, we are not including such devotional walks in our definition of prayerwalking. Prayerwalking focuses intercessory prayer on the neighborhoods, homes and people encountered while walking.

> I often walk around my neighborhood in the early morning for twenty minutes. My prayer usually comes from the Scripture I've been memorizing, but it's not really a devotional time. It's a time of intercession and claiming this neighborhood for God. I remember in the beginning I started in part because I needed to exercise, and I would pray for my [own interests]. It was much more self-centered at first. But as I began to look around and pray for the people around me, I learned to enjoy praying for others. Now I pray for my neighbors from the time I start out the door.
>
> — *Candy Spears, member of First Evangelical Free Church, Tempe, Arizona*

• **Intentional praying.** Although believers enjoy the privilege of filling extra moments with short bursts of intercession, even while afoot, we encourage you to pursue prayerwalking as a deliberate activity. Try to walk in order to pray, rather than praying only at the extra moments when you find yourself walking. In the long run, quality intercession is not incidental.

Sincere pray-ers are learners. Most of what we will ever learn about prayer is still ahead of us. For busy, preoccupied urbanites, it may not really help to encourage prayer-jogging or even prayer-driving (Americans usually think of this!) as maximal intercessory efforts. Tossing up quick requests while waiting encapsulated in one's car at red lights is a poor way to learn on-site prayer. Learn how to pray at your best by setting aside time to deliberately intercede for others.

On-Site

Prayerwalking is on-site prayer. On-site praying is simply praying in the very places where you expect your prayers to be answered.

Walking is the best way to place yourself on-site, but exceptions to walking are almost the rule. Prayerwalkers routinely break from walking to take a deliberate stance at special spots or station themselves at elevated viewpoints.

Why walk? Walking works best for more than one reason. Walking helps sensitize you to the realities of your community. Sounds, sights and smells, far from distracting your prayer, engage both body and mind in the art of praying. Better perception means boosted intercession.

> We enter a world hitherto hidden from our busy Christian lives. It is the world of powerful praying while on the move — total body praying. We begin to experience a new freedom in prayer. Moving at a slower pace we find we have more time to hear and to observe. We feel in touch with reality. Even an awareness of the weather teaches us that life is not controlled by fast cars, satellite links and computers. These things are only the toys with which children play, while God's great plans roll by unhindered.
>
> —*John Houghton, leading pastor of Hailsham Christian Fellowship, Hailsham, Great Britain, describing an extended prayer expedition. Excerpted from* Prayerwalking *by Graham Kendrick and John Houghton (Kingsway Publications, 1990, p. 27).*

Walking also connects Christians with their own neighborhoods. By regularly passing through the streets of their cities, walkers can present an easygoing accessibility to neighbors. Walking seems to create opportunities to help or to pray for new friends on the spot, right at the times of great need. Some streets present risks, but vulnerability yields valuable contact with those who have yet to follow Christ.

> I started praying through our neighborhood of about sixty-six homes. We prayed for every home a couple of times a week. When we first started, my family and I handed out letters to every house, inviting them to give us prayer requests. I'm still not sure this was the best idea. Very few responded. But one Mormon woman gave us a list of requests. She had family problems, health problems, and she was infertile. So as a family we prayed for her health, her salvation and that she would bear children.
>
> About this time, a second woman and her husband who lived on that street started attending our church. These two gals just "happened" to be best of friends. After a few months of coming to church, the second neighbor accepted Christ. Now as she grows in the Lord, she's constantly telling her Mormon friend about her new faith in Christ and all that he is doing for her. This Mormon woman is becoming much more open to the possibility that Christianity is true. She's pleased to have us continue to pray for her and her family, and, in fact, we're going over to her house soon to see their new *baby*!

> *—Tim Wainwright, pastor of an Evangelical Free church in greater Phoenix, Arizona. Tim said he recognized the Lord's wisdom in using a new believer to reach his Mormon neighbor because she would have never trusted and opened up to a Christian pastor and his wife at first.*

Every step becomes an acted prayer. Walking embellishes spoken petitions with an undeniable body language that can be read in the heavenlies. The act of walking emboldens pray-ers to push through feelings of futility and intimidation. Entrenched evil can post spiritual "No Trespassing" signs which seem to enforce the misery of the status quo. Prayerwalkers gently defy such fraudulent claims of darkness over their community.

With Insight

When praying within sight of a community, many find that they pray with insight they would not have had otherwise. Insight for prayer can come in three ways: responsive insight, researched insight and revealed insight.

1. Responsive insight. Prayerwalkers do their work with their eyes open, allowing the sights of people, objects, events and entire communities to flood their prayers with significance. Ordinary powers of observation yield abundant insights about the best focus of prayer.

> People from our church have been prayerwalking for about a year now. Five teams choose their own timing during the day. Six other teams move out once a week in the evening as part of a home meeting. We find enough to pray about as we walk. On one occasion we were outside the home of a guy we knew was involved in the occult. The house was in total darkness. As we prayed for light to come to this guy, all of a sudden nearly all of the lights in the house came on, and his girlfriend popped out of the house. We really felt we had hit something. We began to pour blessings on the house and ask God to reverse what these people had gotten into. Later on that same walk, as we passed by another house, we heard an enormous row going on inside. A woman was screaming, "Go on and hit me." We stopped and prayed outside the home that the spirit of violence and anger would be removed. Things quieted down. We stayed there and asked God to fill the house with his peace. I'm due to visit that troubled home again shortly.
>
> *—John Allister, a pastor in Mount Pleasant, South Wales, United Kingdom*

Prayerwalkers at times view ordinary scenes of life as if they were wearing filtering lenses. They see the present moment with the compassionate longing of Jesus. Overlapping their view of the present situation can appear thrilling futurescapes of what God might do, or at times, the dreadful ramifications if people refuse his love. Ordinary people sometimes stand out like long-lost relatives when seen by praying eyes. Routine events take on a crucial importance. On the scene, prayer finds its own natural urgency.

> A few years ago I was walking through an industrial city north of here. It suddenly struck me that there are all these busy people going about their busy lives, missing the point. I was grief-stricken for all these lovely family people on their way to destruction. Ever since then, even when I'm walking to work I can't help but pray and intercede for the area I'm walking through.
>
> —*Allie Staples, member of Ichthus Fellowship of London*

2. Researched insight. Some prayerwalkers have ventured out informed beforehand about the people or predicaments of particular communities. Examining the history of what has taken place at select settings often directs prayerwalkers to significant spots and informs potent prayers. Others have used research which emphasizes the present-hour social structure blockading the gospel. When research uncovers sources of persistent crime, injustice or occult practices, prayerwalkers can often find a useful direction for their praying.

> We [found] the words that God has already put into the land and prayed them back in, like inscriptions over universities and buildings. The motto of Boston is derived from 1 Kings 8:57: "May the Lord God be with us as he was with our fathers." That was our theme, and it goes all the way back to the roots of the city.
>
> —*David MacAdam, pastor of New Life Community Church in Concord, Massachusetts*

Mary Lance Sisk of Charlotte, North Carolina, reported that a statewide gathering of intercessors was planned to take place on Roanoke Island near the site of one of the first colonies of America (actually at a place called Kill Devil Hills!). To pray better at that location, different volunteers prepared simple background reports on topics in the state's history, such as the Native Americans, early European settlers, the first churches and even the notorious pirate named Blackbeard. The research fueled a weekend of prayer, but, more important, it encouraged intercessors to find out the history of the land before praying over it.

3. Revealed insight. This source of awareness needs to be based firmly on the revelation of the Bible, corroborated by the revealing work of the Spirit, who comes alongside as believers pray.

When believers pray according to the Bible, very often God's Spirit illumines his Word with extra candlepower. It's no secret why. When Christians discipline their minds to follow the thoughts and truths of Scripture, they subject their total beings to the Spirit of truth, who delights to reiterate enscriptured promises. By keeping our minds trained according to God's thoughts revealed in Scripture, we are more likely to pray the largest and most needful prayers.

Speaking to God with the phrases of Scripture helps open our ears to the whispered prayer promptings of God's Spirit. Prayerwalkers find that God seems to draw their attention to certain people or homes or places. Prayerwalkers find themselves in a position to meet divine appointments, in which the timing of encounters or events points toward a direction for prayer.

> A lady walked outside while we were praying for homes. I felt the Lord say to go over and talk to her. I walked over there and talked with her. I said, "Has anyone ever told you about Jesus?" She said, "I can't believe you're standing here with me. I almost died in surgery last week. I had a terrifying vision. I knew I didn't have a relationship with God, but I didn't know how to go about it. Can you tell me more?" I went into the house and shared with her about Jesus, and she gave her heart to Jesus.
>
> —*Jimmy Siebert, college pastor of Highland Baptist Church in Waco, Texas, who does regular prayerwalking with others throughout the neighborhood surrounding the church*

Sometimes God's Spirit divulges information about a community that could be known in no other way but that it was revealed. When God energizes spiritual gifts such as discernment, he often illuminates what seems cloudy, unknowable or even unprayable.

> The Lord led us to have a prayer time at the gates of our old city walls in Sarajevo because we believe whoever controls the gates of the city controls the city. Someone felt they had a word from God that we were supposed to write out blessings on small pieces of paper and then place them in the walls after we prayed. We actually felt rather silly going out to the walls with pockets full of Bible verses and prayers. We worshipped and prayed at

the walls, then we went to place our "blessings" in the cracks.

To our great surprise, we found that the walls were already stuffed with little pieces of paper! We opened up the papers and found curses that the Islamic *hojas* [spiritists] had written and stuffed in the walls. When people go to the *hojas* with requests for prayer and fortune-telling, they are given curses written in Arabic, and these are put in the city walls. We quickly pulled these curses out of the walls, stuck in the blessings as God had instructed and prayed for repentance in our city.

We previously had a problem with witchcraft in the church, but in the weeks to follow we had a great increase in people coming into the church, confessing witchcraft and being delivered from it. It was quite a breakthrough.

—Robert Haris Jurjevic, pastor of Biblijska Vjerska Zajednica "RAFAEL," Sarajevo

Responsive, researched and revealed insights often blend to fortify prayer with a starkly relevant authenticity. Up-close and personal prayer becomes an adventure.

A Refreshment — Not a Replacement — for Prayer Meetings

Some of our standard prayer meetings wobble between trivial matters of self-concern and topics of remote interest. Superficial prayer meetings can bore believers before they get a chance to taste the joy which flows from diligence in prayer. The experience of prayerwalking can rejuvenate believers to gather in homes and church buildings to pursue their full privilege of prayer, of which prayerwalking is only a part.

Prayerwalking Does Not Stand Alone

The great value of prayerwalking is that it leads to dozens of other kingdom activities, not the least of which is more prayer of every kind. Evangelism and church-planting efforts often spring up from prayerwalks. Prayerwalking should never be an end in itself.

Christians often yearn to be more vitally involved in serving and evangelizing their city, but sometimes they aren't sure where to start. God mobilizes his people into ministry in at least two ways. First, people tend to pursue what they have prayed for. Second, people tend to be involved with what they have seen. These two motivational activities are brought together in prayerwalking. Who knows what God may do in our lives as we behold our cities with praying eyes?

How to Use This Book

The special focus on on-site prayer means that we have left out many important items about prayer in general. Use this book in conjunction with many of the superb prayer resources available today (see appendix B). You will need more than you will discover here, but don't try to do everything you find suggested between the covers all at once. We've stuffed this guide with a wealth of practical ideas which apply to all kinds of situations.

Don't wait to finish the entire book before setting out on your first prayerwalk. Get through the next chapter and then step out into your city right away, using what you learned from Part I. All you need is another believing friend with a couple of hours to spend praying. Having begun prayerwalking, you will then have a background of experience which will help the rest of the book be of more value.

Part II gives some biblical basis for prayerwalking. Part III enlarges on basic prayerwalking, offering more practical ideas. In Part IV we have selected instructive stories and presented guidelines appropriate for walking through entire cities or regions in distant lands.

This is more of a menu than a manual. Pick and choose between the ideas to find what is timely and fitting for what God is already doing in your city.

Begin in the community where God has placed you. Prayerwalkers grow literally a step at a time. Who knows what God may unfold for you?

Christ as Guide and Goal

Prayerwalking is abundantly simple: You are walking with Jesus. Our prayer is that you would not be moved from this simplicity. May God set the compass of your heart to keep you fixated on Christ himself. Christ is your guide, and Christ is your goal. And Christ is the Father's gift. All that you might seek for your community the Father gives freely, but only with Christ himself (Rom. 8:32).

As you set your heart's direction to seek Jesus, you will find freedom to enjoy your privilege in prayer. If the program of prayerwalking distracts you from Jesus, your steps will fall leaden to the ground, and your busy life will be encumbered by yet another wearisome complication. But you won't be disappointed if you walk with the simple desire for more of Christ for your city.

You are walking in promised places with the Lord of all the earth. As you go with him in prayer, confidence grows that he will soon fulfill all the purpose in his heart for your city. Jesus is waking your city for God.

2

BASIC PRAYERWALKING

We emerged from the church into the San Diego sunshine and began walking in clumps of two and three. We were seven new acquaintances who had set aside time to learn how to prayerwalk. We had met in the facilities of Mount Soledad Presbyterian Church, which perches near the peak of the highest promontory overlooking virtually all of greater San Diego. I (Steve) was guiding them on their first prayerwalk.

I watched them take tentative steps at first, almost as if they were trying to walk without making any sound. Their eyes wandered as if they didn't know where to focus them while they were praying. Soon they felt comfortable with their eyes at work, lifting and moving their gazes from one house to another. They seemed to walk with their eyes, scanning the neighborhood with a blend of bewildered curiosity and confidence.

Their opening prayers were a bit stilted, beginning with familiar prayer phrases. Some of them found that their customary opening prayers didn't seem to apply. Yet some standard prayers seemed to lift in the breeze as if the prayer itself had been waiting for wind in its wings. Soon they were almost interrupting each other with prayers that wouldn't have even occurred to them fifteen minutes earlier. Within a few hundred yards of walking, it was as if ducklings had found water.

Some were almost fighting the sense of surprise that so suddenly they were praying with simple, direct faith for one of the wealthiest and yet neediest areas of the city. As we beheld the entire cityscape below us, some of the new prayerwalkers offered sizable prayers with the self-conscious hesitancy of someone trying on new shoes. But these shoes fit.

After a few early prompts, they knew they could do this. And they were eager to continue in the neighborhoods closer to their homes. They hadn't started out as legendary prayer warriors. In the ninety minutes they hadn't learned all that they needed to know. They were a band of ordinary believers — housewives, students, engineers — who knew God well and were learning more about how to pray.

Simple to Learn

My friends in San Diego were like most other prayerwalkers I have known: They picked up prayerwalking rapidly. Their short exploit wasn't the standout exhilaration of their lifetimes. They didn't expect it to be. While enjoyable, it was still a challenge, stretching muscles both physical and spiritual. But they could easily sense the rightness of it, as if it were built into them instinctively.

Most Christians learn how to prayerwalk quickly. Why? Once we get beyond habits of housing our prayers in stained-glass confinement, we experience a simple truth of prayer: Intercession need not be long-distance prayer. *We instinctively draw near to those for whom we pray.* Prayerwalking is as basic as caring for others and crying for help. It may actually be a more elementary format for prayer. It is easier to direct our hearts with genuine concern for what fills our eyesight.

Hard to Pursue

Even though prayerwalking is simple to learn, it can be difficult to pursue for at least three reasons.

1. Prayerwalking is spiritual battle. Prayer of any kind is a struggle. Even though we were created for communing with God, and even though we are mandated to speak his blessings on earth, every prayer seems contested in forceful ways.

When we step beyond the boundaries of our own homes, the struggle to pray escalates. The spiritual war has always been raging, but when you step into your neighborhood with redemption in mind, you might experience an indirect onslaught from the enemy, pestering your mind and daunting your heart. These subtle intimidations should give you more than a hint that prayerwalking is considered spiritual trespassing by ensconced evil powers.

2. Prayerwalking requires patience. Prayerwalking can be tough to continue because of our ingrained impatience. We want to see immediate results. There are plenty of dramatic stories of prayerwalking. But most prayerwalkers report that prayerwalking is a fairly quiet affair without a lot of hubbub and thrills.

The city will go to the persistent. There is a slow-burn significance to prayerwalking. Generations of harm are being undone. Seeds of new life are being planted, germinating beneath the surface of everyday life. Prayerwalkers need to be patient because God is patient. He is unfolding, step by step, something glorious for his Son in every community.

> It's hard, week after week, going through different neighborhoods, praying the same things, trying to be disciplined and deliberate about it, just to proclaim the kingdom. Sometimes the heart didn't mesh with what the mind said was the right thing to do. But we could see how right and needful it was to prayerwalk the city, so we just pressed on. I'm glad we did. The difficulty of praying helped stretch our faith that God was going to do great things in quiet ways.
>
> —*Jack Ryan, speaking of praying through a mostly Muslim city in Southeast Asia*

Perhaps our impatience has roots in self-concern. How much does self-interest fuel our fascination with crime patterns? Certainly crime rates indicate disintegration of righteousness and the flourishing of evil. But prayerwalking will always disappoint us as a device for merely making bad things go away. If all we want is to reduce the chances of our home being robbed, eventually our self-concern will divert us from prayer to short-term defensive solutions such as burglar alarms. But if our hearts turn to God's highest desire for our communities, perseverance becomes more than possible. Well-done prayerwalking can nurture an expectation of large measures of his kingdom.

> Sometime last year, for the first time ever in Cedar Rapids, Iowa, there had been a black/white confrontation among youth in a particular area. Black and white churches got together and went to that area to do prayerwalks. We planned three of them to take place over a period of about ten months. Black leaders had set up the last one about three months before the Rodney King trial occurred. So on the very weekend that the riots erupted, black and white churches in Cedar Rapids had already scheduled a prayerwalk together. Black and white churches walked through town together. Sometimes we sang, but most of the time we prayed. We gathered at two or three strategic spots along the way and ended up in a picnic area on the other side of town where we spent the rest of the day. We ate ribs and played football. The last few hours different people got up and spoke for five or fifteen minutes, giving exhortations about the Lord and his healing of the city. Of course, we felt the timing was significant. The riots were still going on in other cities the same

day we were meeting. There was peace in our city almost like God provided an antidote for the poison of this thing. The Lord had great mercy on us.

—*Francis Frangipane, pastor of River of Life Church, Cedar Rapids, Iowa*

3. Prayerwalkers need the freedom of well-learned fundamentals. Much of the pleasure of prayerwalking is the joy of discovering hundreds of ways to pray for the same neighborhood. It's even more fun to be on the scene as God answers prayer in surprising ways. The most persistent prayerwalkers are the ones who seek always to grow in the basic foundations of praying according to the Word of God and with the Spirit of God. As prayerwalkers seek these two essentials of prayer, a nonstandardized newness fills each day's venture in prayer. On the other hand, prayer habits form fast. Without learning the fundamentals of prayerwalking, some have too quickly developed rigid routines, which get tedious. They unwittingly forfeit many of the almost infinite variations of outdoor intercession.

Basic Prayerwalking

Prayerwalkers launch out in a variety of styles that fit their backgrounds and communities. We have examined a wide variety of prayerwalking efforts in order to distill prayerwalking to its simplest format. This chapter covers what we will call *basic prayerwalking*. Later chapters will build on basics, giving new ways to plan effective prayerwalks and to further your skills in on-site prayer.

This chapter serves as a practical menu of opening ideas. It's not really a list of sequenced steps or ironclad rules. Some experienced prayerwalkers skip items mentioned in this chapter. But most healthy prayerwalking efforts with sustained life find a way routinely to do just about everything described here.

Feel free to pick and choose what fits your group and community. But if you are just starting out, you would do well to attempt most of what follows. We have organized this catalog of primary ideas under three sequential phases of prayerwalks: preparing, walking, reporting.

Before the Walk: Preparing

Get ready before you hit the streets. Prayerwalking comes so naturally to most believers that they often fail to prepare adequately before setting out. Why spend time preparing for something that seems to come naturally? To enhance effectiveness. We pray better when we launch out freshly invigorated and focused.

Prayerwalking can magnify the hassles and hazards of everyday spiritual war. Even so, it shouldn't be approached with an unhealthy anticipation of demonic encounter. Some prepare by seeking fresh cleansing from known sin. Others take great care to put on the whole armor of God, piece by piece. Where should you begin? What should you never leave out? Preliminaries can easily degenerate into compulsive personal traditions or even be tainted with a tad of superstition.

Whatever your approach may be, beware of performing dead formulas. God is ready to bestow an abundance of forgiveness as well as every needed fortification. It would take days to begin to consciously appropriate all that God is granting. Exercise all due discipline, but avoid ritualizing that which is relational.

1. Refresh Yourself in God.

You are about to become a bridge of blessing between heaven and earth. You are adequate for the task, provided you give your whole self — body, mind, heart and spirit. It makes sense to begin every prayerwalk with a time of worship before God.

• **Prepare your heart.** Open your mouth in order to open your heart. Whether you sing, shout or whisper, warm up your vocal cords with praise before setting out. Put the name of Jesus on your lips. Dismiss, for the time being, other desires or affections, however legitimate they may be. Seek to position your heart before God in fresh gratitude and blessing.

• **Gather your mind.** Take charge of the directions your mind will go. Fix your attention on the purposes and ways and thoughts of God before you launch out. The simplest way to direct your train of thought is to read Scripture audibly. There may be pressures weighing upon you, demanding your attention: Leave them with God.

What can you do to keep your mind clear of distracting pressures during the prayerwalk? Some prayerwalkers bring along a small piece of paper on which they can jot down ideas or reminders of urgent affairs that may occur to them.

• **Seek God for guidance.** Be still before him for a short while at least, with a readiness to sense special instructions regarding where you should walk or what you should pray.

> We felt from the start that we should only take prayers into those areas that God wanted us to pray for. You could spend your whole life praying all over the place, but you may not get anywhere until you've got people praying in the areas that God is telling them to pray in.

—*Mark Pritchard relocated from his native land of New Zealand to encourage prayer efforts in Boston, Massachusetts.*

Relax regarding guidance. The whole idea of guidance is that you have a guide. Perhaps no more guidance is needed than was received on the last occasion of prayerwalking. Go with the plans you have formed unless you clearly sense otherwise.

Guidance can be a distracting game. Pursuing new guidance can even be a subtle excuse for a failure to persevere. Don't get trapped into thinking that every prayerwalk session is to be different or that God must give you additional communiques at every street corner. Expect some happy surprises, but most of prayer is persistence.

2. Refresh Relationships.

Perhaps the strongest argument against prayerwalking by yourself is that you miss out on making the unassailable prophetic statement of believers literally walking together. It is a portrait of love, an enactment of God's kingdom family on earth. Loving relationships become Christ's "body language" to the heavenlies. You can imagine the havoc when there is estrangement and sinful friction between prayerwalkers. The foremost issue of spiritual battle is our love for one another.

> Before we set out prayerwalking, we had a very strong sense of the fear of God, that we were to get our hearts right before each other. If there was any unforgiveness among our team, we should get that out in the open and set our hearts right before God before we ever left our property.
>
> —*James Foreman, elder at New Covenant Church of Austin, Texas, speaking of his experience leading some on-site prayer efforts of Youth With A Mission workers in Japan*

• **Receive each other.** Before setting out, take the trouble to greet and meet others as you gather. Be sure partners are acquainted by name. Talk before you walk. It is an efficient use of time in which to make sure prayerwalkers have connected with each other. Consider preliminary time spent in friendly conversation a shortcut; otherwise, the first half mile may be spent chatting to develop an adequate sense of friendship. Try to reserve the walk for prayer.

• **Forgive each other.** Preferably, prayerwalkers will have repaired relationships with each other before the appointed hour for prayerwalking. Be a wise family. Sometimes brothers or sisters lack wisdom or encouragement to rectify relationships. If the spiritual family ties are in a particularly odious state, it is better to postpone the prayerwalk than to try to stumble through it. Rancorous relationships can open prayerwalkers to significant vulnerability. Prayerwalkers with refreshed relationships step out from high ground.

• **Approach God.** As Scripture makes abundantly clear, our stance in prayer is ever before the throne of grace, though our feet may be traversing terra firma (Heb. 4:14-16). Take your stance before the Father, enthroned in highest heaven. The way is opened for us forever by the blood and priestly excellence of Jesus.

3. Brief the Team.

Gather prayerwalkers before setting out. Encourage them to act and pray as a team by briefing them about five basic parameters of the day's prayerwalk: who, where, what, when and why.

• **Who? Organize prayer teams.** Who will pray at your side as you walk? Any group larger than three can be helped by organizing them further into pairs or "triplets." Different groupings have been tried and have advantages. But realize that teams greater than three get cumbersome and fail to draw out the fullest participation of every prayerwalker.

Teams of four and five call for louder prayers so that all can readily agree. Such groups present a higher profile to the community, which in some situations is desirable, yet in other settings is not as appropriate. Without experienced leadership, groups larger than seven often break down after walking a few hundred yards into pairs and trios with a few individuals straggling in distant orbits from the group.

Partners can be allowed to find each other spontaneously as they leave the room. Some experienced leaders, when considering the specific challenges of the community, choose to assist the mixing and matching of partners with respect to experience, capabilities or physical strength.

Why form prayer teams? Why not spread out in solo mode? Prayerwalking needs to be seen as a team activity fundamentally because intercessory prayer is fortified when believers agree. Prayerwalking is a continual response to the community and how God is leading. As teams pray together, one person's wisdom reinforces another person's vision, resulting in solid, confident praying.

• **Where? Designate areas, routes or sites.** Locate where prayerwalkers will go to work. Sometimes all that needs to be stipulated is a roughly defined area of town. For other situations prayerwalkers do well if a specific route is delineated. Routes can be vaguely defined, although some require precise direction to the point of suggesting certain street crossings.

Maps can help a great deal. One large map can be adequate. Other groups distribute sketched map portions to every prayer team. Frequently teams spare themselves the trouble of maps by setting out with a guide who is acquainted with the neighborhood.

Prayerwalkers can set out depending entirely on the Spirit of God for place-to-place guidance. However, when terrain is assigned, people focus more attention on praying and less on matters of their next steps. On the other hand, if routes are too tightly designated, walkers can lack freedom for God to escort them divinely to prayer appointments. Find an appropriate balance between spontaneity and structure.

Prayerwalks frequently focus prayer at specific sites. Consider routing to special sites which may add to the significance of the walk. You may want to anticipate particular schools, homes and church buildings along the way.

If more than one pair or trio is setting out, you don't necessarily need to prayerwalk in different locations. You can even follow the same route in an opposite direction or plan to start from different points and meet at a central location.

There's no limit to creative ways to cover the ground. Try zigzagging your large urban tracts. Or you can pass meticulously up and down every street. Some take care to systematically bless every home. Why not blanket the area with prayer from a few designated sites?

Prayerwalkers never fail to grasp the significance of tracking along the perimeter of an area so as to encircle it. Be forewarned: Outer edges of cities are tough to find and even trickier to walk.

Of course, exercise due caution with regard to traffic. Unless a highway is important for prayer, opt for residential areas and routes. Respect legalities pertaining to pedestrians. Where places are off-limits, creative ways can be found to pray effectively without having to intrude.

Prayerwalkers do not incessantly walk. Prayerwalking includes praying while standing at select places. Elevated viewpoints are favorite prayerwalk spots. Elevated places can be bridges, mountains or top floors of buildings.

- **When? Agree on timing.** Budget your time together. Are you in agreement about how long you have to spend during the day's prayerwalk? Come to agreement about an appointed time to regather. It's difficult to gauge how long it will take to navigate urban terrain, so allow reasonable flex in the schedule.

- **What? Review topics of prayer.** Remind the team that in their praying they need to pursue a balance between *worship*, *warfare* and bringing about a *welcome* for Christ. One simple maxim to bring balance: Make sure God is addressed and people are blessed.

Fortify prayer with information. The right amount of background data can help prayer teams to stick to the point with resilient, expansive prayers. You may summarize research pertinent to the area, people or site. A review of prayers offered or answered on previous prayerwalks can help. God's best stimulant for prayer is his Word. Without sermonizing, share passages of Scripture which are expected to factor into the day's prayer.

Good leadership is called for in reviewing topics of prayer. Touch on what needs clarity, but beware of elaborating prayer requests more than is needed. Why not bring up requests by praying them on the street?

• **Why? Emphasize the significance of prayerwalking.** Put the day's prayerwalk on the map and the calendar. Particular dates or times may have special significance. Recount the significance of a particular site. Are prayerwalking efforts linked with further hopes for church planting or other forms of ministry? Hold back the hype, but encourage each other to grasp the importance of what you are about to do by considering the larger picture.

Find ways to make briefings brief! For example, comments covering the above briefing items could all be reduced to a few easy-to-remember headings on a flip chart.

During the Walk: Praying

Keep prayerwalking simple by keying in on the fact that you are walking with Jesus. Jesus your Lord has long considered the places and people for whom you are just beginning to pray. You are stepping into his city, over which he has utmost authority and boundless compassion. So walk where he walks; pray with his prayers.

• **Open your eyes.** Most of prayerwalking is vision, which has been described as "the art of seeing what you are looking at." On a normal day, a "For Sale" sign on a house may turn your mind to consider land values or property tax rates. During a prayerwalk, seeing the same sign may stimulate you to pray for those who have moved away or to bless the family that will soon move in.

A practical way to use "the eyes of your heart" (Eph. 1:18) is to ask God to help you see the city with his eyes.

> When I came to the city of Amsterdam, I spent six months simply walking the streets of every major neighborhood in the city. I rode trams and metros and buses, getting a feel for the city. I asked God to let me see the city through his eyes. I asked him to help me understand her culture. I read every book I could get my hands on about Amsterdam. I sat in coffee shops and "brown cafes," listening to the people. I developed a fondness for the openhearted, humor-loving, sea-faring Amsterdamer. It was out of those many months of walking her streets that I grew

to love the city of Amsterdam. In fact, now I not only love her, I like her!

—*Floyd McClung, in his book* Seeing the City With the Eyes of God *(Chosen Books, 1991, p. 113). Floyd serves as international executive director of Youth With A Mission.*

Your job is not to rake revelation out of the sky. Don't imagine that you should turn off a mental switch as if you were trying to go into some kind of clairvoyant mode. You are simply walking and talking with God almighty. He is well able to show you whatever you need to see.

Open your ears so that two-way prayer transpires. Every silent moment need not be nervously filled with verbiage. Listen for God's whispered cues. Expect him to highlight the truths you have hidden in your heart and apply them to what is around you.

• **Open your mouth.** Enjoy Spirit-directed silence, but for the most part pray aloud. Prayer is not telepathy. God certainly knows what you are thinking, but your faith is bolstered as you verbalize your prayer.

Praying aloud doesn't mean praying loudly. Though some occasions call for dramatic, outspoken praying, most prayerwalking takes place in a quiet, unobtrusive way.

Don't wait for impassioned feelings to float your prayers. Choose to begin voicing what needs to be prayed. You may experience moments of spontaneous overflow, but prayerwalkers find themselves praying very deliberately most of the time.

• **Pray together.** Seek to consciously follow and reinforce prayers lifted by others in your prayer team. One prayer multiplies with another as you learn to agree in your requests. Pursue conversational style so that you can develop cogent themes and topics together. Sticking to the subject can prove challenging with so many prayer-provoking sights surrounding you. It's usually best to press a few points of prayer as far as you can, rather than hoping your team will cover every need with every prayerwalk. Learn to enjoy praying through the most important matters again and again. The best prayers seem to improve every time they are prayed.

It's perfectly in order to break out of intense intercession for short times to discuss what you are feeling, where you will go next, what prayers should be lifted and so on.

• **Pray with Scripture.** Sometimes prayerwalkers behold obvious needs but fail to sense how to pray. Lack of a practiced prayer vocabulary hushes others. Take along bits of Scripture or a small Bible when you walk. You can turn just about any verse or phrase into a prayer. If this proves difficult at first, start out with some of the prayers found in Scripture. With minimal adaptation, these prayers virtually pray themselves. You can be confident of praying the will of God when you pray the Word of God.

• **Pray with relevance.** Allow the community you are prayerwalking to preoccupy your prayer. Leave your personal "laundry lists" of prayer needs behind. Pray with sensitivity to the people and places you are actually encountering. Prayerwalkers can often feel overwhelmed in trying to care equally for every person they pass. Extend your empathy unevenly, perhaps praying for only a few of the families or children you may meet.

Mix compassion with curiosity as you pass homes, shops and schools. Rouse your interest in familiar settings and faces by considering how their stories may unfold in soon-coming years. What have they experienced to bring them to this point? What does God desire for them?

After the Walk: Reporting

Assemble prayerwalkers soon after walking to report to each other significant prayers and insights. Tell the stories of answered prayers, but avoid creating an expectation that each prayerwalker will have a dramatic story to tell. Be ready for any who may return heavy-hearted or exultant.

It is wise to keep a record of important matters to help in future prayerwalking. Some prayerwalkers maintain a journal to keep track of prayers prayed. Memories of what areas were covered quickly fade. Those inclined to systematically prayerwalk their city often trace accomplished routes on a master map.

Evaluate your prayerwalking session. How can you make changes that will enrich later prayerwalks?

Consider what your prayers and insights might mean for various ministry efforts. Has God spoken in such a way that a word should be wisely shared with others? Decide how, when and where to continue prayerwalking.

Getting Started

Three essential planning points for first-time prayerwalkers

1. Pray with others.

The partner you choose does not have to be experienced in prayerwalking. The important thing is not to begin alone or with people who have not yet committed their lives to Christ.

2. Start near home.

Begin in your own city, but preferably *not* in your own neighborhood. Why not start in the immediate vicinity of your home? Experience shows that it's easier to learn the art of prayerwalking in an unfamiliar place. For opening attempts, many find that familiarity with houses, families and faces deters them from stretching their faith to pray large, visionary prayers for the lasting transformation of entire neighborhoods. Stored-up memories can daunt the most sincere prayerwalker from asking for substantial changes in the lives of specific people.

You don't need to travel far from home. One block away may take you into a realm of fresh faces. Of course, you will quickly bring back your newly exercised and strengthened faith to your own neighborhood.

3. Allow time.

We recommend setting aside at least two hours for your opening experience. That will allow you adequate time for a sturdy learning experience. Start with an appropriate preparation session but avoid extensive lecturing. Map out a comfortable route that is not overly ambitious. After the prayerwalk, spend some time discussing concerns, hopes and ideas for next steps. Subsequent prayerwalks can easily be streamlined to take less time.

PART II

The Purpose of Prayerwalking

3

BEYOND TECHNIQUE

Prayerwalkers may sometimes ask themselves, "Is this just a gimmick to get God's attention? God can hear me from my living room or church hall, so why am I meandering around town muttering prayers?" It is a fair question. Why pray in proximity? What is really going on when people walk and pray?

God at Work Through Prayer

We should probably avoid speaking of prayerwalking as a useful technique because it is so easy to trivialize the wondrous glory of prayer. Prayerwalking doesn't "work" any more than any other form of prayer "works." When people pray, it is God himself who works all things according to his will. The mysteries of why and how he involves his children with him by their praying has never been fully comprehended. Though hard to grasp, it's wonderfully true: God is at work with us when we pray.

The conspicuous activities that go with prayerwalking can sometimes obscure the simple dynamic of prayer. We all know that the Lord hears our hearts and responds to our faith. However, fascination with steps and gestures can divert our attention away from him just enough to trap us into trusting our habits. Attention to techniques can even take a subtle superstitious twist. If repeated rotely they can become little better than a sort of spiritual magic, as if demonic powers can be intimidated by people merely walking around the block. Or, worse yet, some may behave as if God can be induced to act when he is pressured with the proper formulas.

Prayerwalking Is God Helping Us to Pray

That God hears prayer at all is wondrous. Have you considered how remarkable it is that he also helps us pray? Think of prayerwalking as a simple help to intercession. Prayerwalking helps intercession in three specific ways.

1. Prayerwalking helps us agree in prayer.

Prayer is not a voice vote. God doesn't suddenly bend his attention if a large enough assembly makes enough noise.

Jesus said, "If two of you agree on earth about anything that they may ask, it shall be done for them by My Father who is in heaven" (Matt. 18:19). When intercessors pray in agreement, they aren't generating power by some mathematical formula. Jesus teaches that it is the Father's prerogative to exert power. If we read one verse further we see why: "For where two or three have gathered together in My name, there I am in their midst." When Jesus is in the midst of agreeing pray-ers, we can be sure that the Father is doing his work by his power — because of Jesus.

Take note of one simple proviso of agreeing in prayer: "where two or three have gathered in My name." Whatever else this gathering may mean, it must have something to do with physical nearness to each other. Incidentally, most prayerwalking happens to be done in bands of two or three.

Prayerwalking is not a special extravagance for some sort of spiritual elite. Anyone who can pray can also prayerwalk (including those who are disabled). Somehow walking together evens the field so that long-standing lay/clergy splintering almost disappears. Those who may not feel eloquent can still join in the prayer fully by silently walking, using their faith with every step.

Focusing on the same subject can be tough while sitting in a circle in a room. When walking a street together, prayerwalkers are surrounded by prayer needs, and it becomes easier to share the same concerns and the same level of intensity.

2. Prayerwalking helps focus your faith.

God is never coerced by repeated formulas of words, however loud or eloquent the display of human verbiage. In the same way, God is unmoved by attempts to manipulate him by physical maneuvers. Our walking does not wake him up. God instead delights to respond to the requests of people as they extend themselves to him in sincere faith.

Who of us has not had the uneasy experience of trying to squeeze his or her heart toward an elusive sensation of faith? Some have guessed wrongly that faith amounts to vague twinges of religious sentiment which make you feel that you have contacted "the other side." Not at all. Faith is a personal reliance on God expressed in actions. Faith expressed physically rarely evaporates to mystical sentiment.

Faith is simple in that there is but one object of our trust: the person of God in Christ. But faith is also a complex act in that it involves the different parts of your person acting together, as if they weren't at all separate. Prayer in faith is the gathered involvement of your heart, mind, soul and body. Just as prayer becomes more powerful as individuals gather together and agree, so too when every member of your being is gathered and exerted in a singular act of prayer, you will notice a greater vitality.

> The actual movement of the body helps empower prayer. I found this out in my earliest years as a Christian. I was tucked away in a barracks room. There wasn't much room to pray, even if I had tried to kneel by the bed. You get out into the hills and start walking and you come alive to God in the whole motion of your body. It's a stimulus for prayer.
>
> *—Roger Forster has led innumerable prayerwalking efforts in the course of planting and pastoring house churches. He is the founder and pastor of Ichthus Christian Fellowship, London.*

Faith exerted in prayer can be likened to the dynamic of leverage. Through prayer we lift matters of concern to God with our faith. Prayerwalking simply provides a stronger leverage point. When we draw closer to who we are praying for, somehow our little faith can go a long way to lift our requests to God.

3. Prayerwalking helps guide your prayers.

We have already pointed out that walking amidst scenes of unanswered prayer spotlights specific prayer needs. Prayers can be razor sharp for specific families with names and faces. Perception is heightened, and thus prayer can be far more directed by the Spirit of God.

The Triple Dynamic of Fruitful Prayerwalks

As visible as prayerwalks can be, more takes place than meets the eye. We can categorize the effect of prayerwalking by seeing its influence in three directions: before the throne of God, amidst the realm of evil powers and throughout the communities of people. These three aspects suggest three different dynamics of most fruitful prayerwalks:

worship of God, *warfare* against evil and a *welcome* to Christ's kingdom in people's hearts. The interplay between worship, warfare and welcome is so fluid that the distinction may seem contrived. We mention them separately so as to better grasp what happens during prayerwalks.

1. Worship

Some prayerwalks emphasize bringing pleasure to God's heart. Sincere intercessory prayer leans hard on the promises of God and thus invariably proclaims the excellencies of God. Prayerwalkers often give themselves entirely to the work of magnifying God, offering him praises from the places they stand. The concern for his pleasure almost eclipses all other concerns.

> On some Saturday mornings we take about five hundred worship tapes recorded at our church and take about fifteen teams and distribute those tapes to every house. We knock on the door and give them a free praise tape and say something like, "Tomorrow we're going to do this same music live in Central Park, and you're welcome to come." After the big praise rally we direct the believers to divide up in teams, walk out across the neighborhood praying and see what happens. The people learn how to pray from the modeling of others. We try to do one of these once every two months. We've tried different things, but for us the best thing is to give the praise tapes, then rally openly for praise and worship, and then fan out. Praise gets all over everybody.
>
> —*Terry Teykl, pastor of Aldersgate United Methodist Church, College Station, Texas*

> As we were praying through the neighborhoods of Turkey, we felt the Lord speak to us: "I'm calling forth worshippers from this place, and you are to prophetically foreshadow and forecast this worship." It was a bit scary because open declaration of the gospel is severely restricted. But our little team pushed through the cloud of intimidation and began to worship out loud. People were drawn to the worship in the plazas. I think they were drawn to the spirit of worship more than the crazy Americans. That's the first time I realized that Christian worship is inclusive: "Guys, come on in here. Even if you don't fully understand the theological concepts of these songs, join in the party, join in the celebration, join in the worship. We're singing songs about Jesus." We even had people joining in and singing some of the songs.

—Duane Blackburn, a short-term worker to Turkey. During their prayer journey, Mark and the team scheduled intercessory prayerwalks every morning and spent many afternoons in public worship. The team enjoyed many fruitful conversations during the worship events.

2. Warfare

Many prayerwalks aim to expose, limit or displace the power of evil forces. They seek to bring healing in order to interrupt sinful cycles which feed entrenched evil. Malevolent powers are restrained so that good things may come forth.

Over fifteen thousand believers gathered in London for praise and prayer on a cold rainy morning in May 1988. A program had been prepared so that groups of praise marchers could pause before significant landmarks of the city and pray intelligently into the very roots of London life. Graham reports:

> We felt we should pray particularly concerning issues of righteousness and justice in the financial dealings of the city. We did not want to make an issue of any particular injustice, but research on the spiritual history of the city made it clear that it had been built upon greed and unrighteous trade. We prayed with that in mind, asking that God would deal with greed in the city.
>
> That particular year was quite a boom time. The deregulation of 1986 had meant that every bank and investment house in the world had wanted to set up in the square mile. Those were heady days on London's money markets, with fortunes waiting to be made. Millions were changing hands at the press of a computer button. The city wine bars were crowded with twenty-five-year-olds taking home £250,000 a year (equal to about $500,000), their Porsches parked outside. The boomers were arrogant and self-confident with an accompanying disregard for justice and righteousness.
>
> We had prayed more from historical and spiritual insight than from inside knowledge of the financial world, but having prayed along these lines, we were fascinated to read the newspapers in the following months, especially on Black Monday in October 1987 when the global stock market collapsed. Business slumped to record lows. In the following months many new and even well-established companies went bankrupt. An estimated twelve thousand whiz kids lost their jobs. The party was over.
>
> Alongside this, insider dealing was exposed. Something called the Guinness Affair broke and began its long journey

through the courts, exposing dishonest trading by seemingly respectable establishment figures.

Had our prayers contributed to these events which changed the course of the nation? It is impossible to prove a cause-and-effect connection, and these questions can only truly be answered in eternity. But we took note that the city had been shaken around the very issues of greed and unrighteous trade. Whatever else had combined to cause it, the mercy of God was checking the runaway materialism which was claiming the soul of the nation at that time

— *Graham Kendrick, as quoted from his book* Public Praise *(Creation House, pp. 35-36, used by permission)*

On one small island we were challenged about a particular tree that the people worship there. The Christian worker lived near that tree, so the people were trying to have him expelled from the island because he was coming against their tree. Since he was [already] being hassled, we felt we hadn't fired the first shots. We felt we had authority to join in prayer around that tree and curse it. We remembered that Jesus had cursed a tree. Two days later a tremendous tropical storm came across there. I was back there six months later, and the tree had literally dried up from the root. It was rotting, with no leaves on it. The branches are gone, and they have it held up with wires. That spoke to the islanders. We made a subsequent trip back. This time we took worshippers with us and four guitars. We went around the island and worshipped. We went around to many of the homes, and many people gave their lives to Christ. Notably among them, one of the Buddhist temple leaders was converted. Now that Christian worker has more to work with.

—*Mark Geppert, relating a story from a prayer expedition around an island in South Asia. Mark, based in Pittsburgh, Pennsylvania, travels frequently on prayer expeditions.*

3. Welcome

At times prayerwalkers pronounce blessings upon the community, sometimes demonstrating their expectation of God's coming kindness by offering to pray with hurting people. As God brings prayed-for results, people of the community often turn their hearts expectantly toward God, welcoming the further work of Christ in their city. A climate of receptivity increases. People are stirred with a holy hunger for God, awakened to a gentle yearning for the kingdom of God. The Holy Spirit engenders a welcome for the Son of God.

Begin by praying blessing over the entire area. Pray for everyone in a global way. Pray for salvation, healing and spiritual freedom over each block, lot, house, office and apartment.

—John Huffman, of Latin America Mission. Adapted from his handbook "Manual of Participatory Missionary Prayer" (Latin America Mission). John has designed "Christ for the City," an adaptable program for comprehensive prayer to advance the gospel in specific neighborhoods. He has designed two-week, ten-day or one-week plans for prayer. In each of them, the first endeavor of prayer on the streets is what he calls "general blessing for the entire area."

Why do we get all covert and secretive? Just tell them what you're doing. We're here walking in your neighborhood, praying for you. We're praying that God would bless you. How many times have people ever heard that? They think God is against them. We're content to leave it at just praying for them in Jesus' name, but if they want to know more, we'll tell them more.

—Maury Millican, associate pastor of Mission Hills Church in Austin, Texas. Maury walks with a partner through apartment complexes near the place where the church gathers. During these walks they have seen people choose to follow Jesus.

Integrating Worship, Warfare and Welcome

Any healthy prayerwalk will include all three — worship, warfare and welcome. At any given moment one dimension or another may be the dominant dynamic. This is normal. But a wholesome blend is essential.

As we have studied a wide diversity of prayerwalks, we have found that some seem to be more well-rounded and perhaps more powerful than others. Prayerwalkers who blend worship, warfare and welcome tend to continue in the vision with less intimidation and more joy. The prayerwalking efforts which have reported dramatic results — many people coming to Christ, churches being planted or withering crime rates — featured each of these three dynamics in some way. However, do not think of these three dynamics as independent ingredients. You can't fully practice any one of them without in some way doing them all.

There are instances of stressing one dynamic too greatly with a resulting loss of effectiveness. One way of overdoing one of the three dynamics could be described as a "warfare walk." In this case the demonic realm seems to occupy full attention. There seems no end to invective against evil. Hell seems unshaken in response, happy for the extra attention, content to allow such a prayer filibuster to preoccupy the church. Not only that, but the believers generally grow weary of it.

Other prayerwalks so eagerly target their communities in an evangelistic mode that prayerwalks degenerate into what might be called mere "witness walks." Direct testimony can be practiced so strenuously that the work of prayer is sidclined. Some parades have even appeared to be in combat with the community itself. If this happens, the walk turns into an attention-getting device or a forgettable preaching ploy. There may be better means of evangelism than using the prayerwalk format.

It's hard to imagine that the worship dynamic could be overdone. Perhaps a public worship event, such as March for Jesus, can be considered a worship walk (see appendix C). At these events believers from many denominations and traditions gather in one grand worship procession. The integrity of the entire event lies in the single common factor of all participants: a committed, worshipful love for Jesus. On special days of public worship festivals, such as the March for Jesus, praise fills the soul of the city as the church gathers to God.

4

ABRAHAM: PIONEER PRAYERWALKER

Abraham begins the long journey of God's praying people. Many of Abraham's forefathers had worshipped and "walked with God," such as Enoch (Gen. 5:22), but Abraham was first to walk by God's command through a land of promise. That walk opened a series of on-site prayer events. He established public worship amidst new neighbors. His friendship with those neighbors led to an even greater worship extravaganza involving several nearby nations. After this he prayed the first city-size prayer while viewing the city of Sodom. The long record of Abraham's on-site praying gives an ample mandate for prayerwalking.

Abraham's Vision Expedition

God beckoned Abraham to examine the land heritage he was granting him. At this point Abraham (still named Abram, but for simplicity we'll call him Abraham throughout this chapter) had been living in the land God promised for some time, ranging short distances with his herds from a place he had named Bethel. When that camp proved inadequate to sustain the entire extended family, Lot and Abraham parted. Lot picked out the most attractive territory. Scripture uses the telling phrase that Lot "chose for himself" the watered valley of the Jordan (Gen. 13:1-11).

God had another process for Abraham than choosing "for himself." God ordered Abraham to do a far-reaching survey, taking in the entire horizon, "northward and southward and eastward and westward" (Gen. 13:14). Abraham did more than spin around a few times, squinting into the distant hills. God told him to find his feet and thoroughly walk the land: "Arise, walk about the land through its length and breadth" (Gen. 13:17).

It wasn't a big deal for Abraham to go for long hikes. Walking was a large part of his job description at the time as a nomadic herd-keeper. But this particular excursion was not a routine nomadic move. It was a specific walk of vision.

> And the Lord said to Abram, after Lot had separated from him, "Now lift up your eyes and look from the place where you are, northward and southward and eastward and westward; for all the land which you see, I will give it to you and to your descendants forever. And I will make your descendants as the dust of the earth; so that if anyone can number the dust of the earth, then your descendants can also be numbered. Arise, walk about the land through its length and breadth; for I will give it to you" (Gen. 13:14-17).

Prayerwalking Is a Matter of Vision

God directed Abraham to examine thoroughly a huge portion of land. Abraham dutifully walked, inspecting the land. But as he went, God turned his attention in a different direction, far down through time and generations to envision what God would grant to his family.

Abraham was not just surveying real estate, as Lot did. Lot had only seen some of the attractive features of the land that were present at that hour. Abraham was directed to value the land because of the people who would live there. "I will make your descendants as the dust of the earth."

Try to walk with Abraham for a few steps in your mind. We have no idea how many miles or days Abraham spent walking, but he certainly encountered a great deal of dust and sand. He was not working out real estate subdivisions on the map of his mind. Abraham was told to envision his offspring. God was stretching his mind and heart to focus on the vast people that would somehow come to regard Abraham as their father.

Seeing Is Receiving

The main thing required of Abraham was to use his eyes: "Lift up your eyes and look from the place where you are" (Gen. 13:14). And again in verse 15 God was giving him all the land "which you see."

As Abraham scanned the horizon, he came to grasp the main thing that God was doing. God was in the act of giving: "I will give it [the land] to you and to your descendants." And again, "Walk about the land...for I will give it to you." God was giving. Abraham was seeing.

This is the fundamental dynamic of prayerwalking: God is giving.

And somehow in our seeing we can begin to receive what God is giving. Some may say seeing is believing. In this case seeing is receiving.

We don't really know what Abraham asked for, if anything. But prayer is as much listening to God as it is speaking with God. Abraham let God's promise soak into his soul: "I will give it to you." God prompted him not just to seek a place to live but to find his family. He was cued to see millions of his children.

The most notable of all Abraham's descendants tells us of the significance of being "seen" by Abraham long years beforehand. That preeminent one of all Abraham's children is Jesus, who said, "Abraham rejoiced to *see* My day, and he *saw* it and was glad" (John 8:56, italics added).

According to Jesus, the significance of Abraham's vision lies in the doubly-noted act of rejoicing while seeing. Rejoicing is a deliberate endeavor. The receiving of Abraham's vision was made certain by his intentional act of rejoicing in God's promise. Abraham received what he could dimly envision by rejoicing in what he clearly understood of God's promise. The second half of John 8:56 is open-ended, with no immediate object to the verb of seeing — "he saw [it?] and was glad." That implies Abraham beheld more than just one person. Perhaps he saw entire nations sprinkled with multitudes of people in Christ in a coming day, which Jesus himself calls "My day."

The biblical fact is that Abraham heard God speak. We don't know whether God spoke audibly or in some other whispered way. But Abraham's listening was anything but a mystical, out-of-body experience. God wanted to capture Abraham's full attention by involving his whole person. By his physical, walking presence, Abraham was beginning an act of receiving that would continue with Joshua generations later and continue even further in the person of Jesus. In a powerful way God's people today can continue the same walk as their faith-father, Abraham, in full confidence that God plans to expand Abraham's family in every place of the earth.

Implications for Today's Prayerwalkers

- **Prayerwalking is an affair of vision.** Physical sight boosts spiritual vision to sense God's future for a city. We walk to see. We see in order to pray more powerfully. The vision God wants us to anticipate is the many millions of people in God's family. As we have an eye for God's yet-to-be-adopted children, we will see the preeminent one of Abraham's seed: Christ himself. Vision is an act of stretching our expectations of Christ, to see Him exhibited in the family of Abraham's faith. If Abraham rejoiced to see what Jesus called "My day" (John 8:56), shouldn't we rejoice in anticipation of an even greater fullness of God's family yet to come?

• **Prayerwalking is a matter of receiving from God.** The primary person in prayerwalking is God. Lean more on his intent to give than on the worthiness of anyone to receive. Prayerwalkers should expect prayerwalking to be a relational affair with the God of Abraham. It is not blind, fervid requesting or pleading according to a set list of perceived problems.

• **Petitions catch up with promises.** The prayer during the walk was not petitionary. God was doing the talking, giving answers far more than Abraham was making requests. Abraham heard a reiteration of the promise God had made to him earlier (Gen. 12:1-3,7), but Abraham's walk solidly anchored his soul to the soil (Gen. 24:7) and tethered his hopes to God's huge promise. "With respect to the promise of God, he did not waver in unbelief, but grew strong in faith, giving glory to God" (Rom. 4:20). He learned what prayerwalkers are still learning by prayerfully walking the places God is giving them: Standing in the *location* of God's promise helps strengthen faith to wait for the *fulfilling* of God's promise.

Prayerwalking is one way to get a glimpse of God's promises and learn to pray and praise "with respect to the promise of God."

> When we prayed Scripture, it was like God had loaned us the lenses of heaven to help us believe him for new churches in this huge megalopolis of Bombay. The slums and pollution and injustice could seem so ancient and changeless. But it all took on a different light when we saw it through our prayers from Isaiah or Romans or the Psalms. We felt we could best grip India's godly future by praying Scripture promises for the children we would meet. Some of the kids really stood out. Many are incredibly poor, but when we cried out for the blessing of Abraham's family to come on them, we felt confidence that we were helping to graft many of them into that ancient family. We knew God had each one of them in his heart. Surely he wouldn't leave them orphans. Surely God would raise up church families for them — churches which didn't yet exist. But we saw those churches coming. We saw them as sure as Abraham saw Isaac coming. It got so that we felt we had long-lost relatives all over this foreign city.
>
> —*Steve Chism, a student from Pasadena, California, describing the sense of vision which emerged during prayerwalks in India in 1989*

Establishing Worship and Forming Friendships

Abraham's ongoing story suggests some of the results of prayerwalking. Just after his prayerwalk Abraham "moved his tent and came and dwelt by the oaks of Mamre" (Gen. 13:18). This is a major change of location for nomadic Abraham. The implication is strong that he had discovered God's choice of a dwelling place as a result of his prayerwalk.

His choice of dwelling was named after Mamre, a leading man of the Amorite people. Abraham befriended Mamre's brothers, who were Eshcol and Aner (Gen. 14:13). The language of this verse indicates that Abraham had established a covenant for the families to help each other.

Abraham did more than build friendships in his new neighborhood. He "built an altar to the Lord" (Gen. 12:7-8). We can safely assume that he "called on the name of the Lord" at this altar as he had done at the previous altar he had built near his fixed place of residence (Gen. 13:4). To call on the name of the Lord is to worship God openly, declaring the name of God with praise.

God's name is more than how he might list himself in the phone book. God's name here means the entire body of truth God has revealed about himself. This means that Abraham established public, ongoing worship of the only holy God.

Abraham had not lived long in his new community before he was called on to rescue Lot, his own relative. His new friends helped out on the rescue operation (Gen. 14:24), which recovered far more than Lot's stuff. Abraham was able to restore the goods and families of some entire towns. This was no small feat. No one argued at all when the Most High was acknowledged publicly as having accomplished a miraculous rescue. Abraham reinforced the matter of giving God specific glory by refusing to take any reward for himself. He put his family on display as the family who would be blessed by God rather than by an earthly king (Gen. 14:18-15:1).

Prayerwalking led to disciplined worship, which, in turn, led to redemptive friendships, which opened opportunity for yet another event of worship on an even larger scale. God arranged events so that they led to a grand occasion of thanksgiving to himself. People of several nations were gathered, worshipping the God of Abraham. Attention was given to Abraham, but he deferred all glory to God.

Take note of who Abraham was helping: Sodom, the city of legendary evil. Was the redemptive war and the following event of worship a last-chance opportunity for Sodom to repent? We can't really say. But, as we will see, Abraham found himself positioned to serve his degenerate neighbors even more.

Implications for Today's Prayerwalkers

• **Open key friendships.** Prayerwalking leads to redemptive relationships with the community. It can also open ways of serving our neighbors besides prayer. As we develop relationships in the community, we are sure to wage war on behalf of the people of the city, not against them. Our warfare may be spiritual — or quite tangible — as we take on areas of redemptive service.

> Kindness opened one man's heart to God when we were doing free lawn care. We had loaded a couple of mowers and rakes into a truck and drove around until we saw long grass. We approached his house and knocked on the door to tell him what we were up to. Through the screen door this man barked, "What do you want?" We gave him the brief explanation; without even looking up, his response was simply, "Yeah, whatever...."
>
> He sat motionless in front of the TV watching a Reds baseball game. We mowed enthusiastically — we sometimes call it "power mowing" in the Vineyard — and finished in about thirty minutes. We stopped by to tell him we were done and ask if we could pray for any needs in his life. He said he didn't have any needs. As we stepped away from the door, one young man in the group said he was sure this man was in great emotional need and that we ought to insist on praying for him. We turned around and prayed a simple little prayer: "Come, Holy Spirit, and touch this man's pain, whatever it is." The response was instant and surprising — he erupted in deep sobbing, grabbing the nearest person in the circle and wetting his shoulder with tears for some minutes. As the crying died down, he told us his son had been arrested the night before for stealing a car to support a drug habit. That day God's presence and power penetrated this man's pain and isolation in a tangible way...because we were willing to cut a little grass.
>
> —*Steve Sjogren, adapted from the book* A Conspiracy of Kindness *(Vine Books, 1993, Ann Arbor, Mich.). Steve is pastor of the Vineyard Christian Fellowship of Cincinnati North.*

• **Find your way home.** Prayerwalking can be an important part of the process of choosing where to live. Abraham wasn't hunting for the most pleasing parcel of land to own. He was receiving the entire land. But in the process of walking the whole area, it became clear where he was to set up his family's dwelling.

> We basically walked through an area to pray and ask the Lord to

come through the area to open up the hearts of the people, to allow us to have inroads to minister to them. Soon after that one couple that prayed with us bought a house in that area. They had been looking at houses, but not in that area until that time. We prayed for bigger things, but I sensed this as an immediate answer to our prayer.

— Greg Sandman, pastor of The Vineyard Christian Fellowship in Littleton, Colorado. A home fellowship group now meets in the newly purchased house. Members of the group are beginning to do more prayerwalking in their neighborhood and throughout Littleton.

• **Establish open altars.** As Abraham found, prayerwalking can lead to establishing public praise. God may impress you to stop walking and to worship him right out in the open, or he may lead you to plan a more elaborate celebration.

It seems a little silly, but we used to do Israeli folk dances. We'd do it as worship dance, and we felt like demonic strongholds were actually pushed back by praising God openly in public right on the mall of a campus where hundreds of students passed by during the change of classes. We would get out guitars, sing, dance and worship God. It opened doors for conversation. It's hard to measure things in the spiritual realm, but we saw a more receptive climate on campus.

— Chris Meredith, of Elkton, Maryland, speaking of public worship on the University of Delaware campus during 1986. Ten to fifteen students regularly participated in public worship sessions. Several of the same students quietly prayerwalked their campus as well.

We have decided it's our responsibility to go and take the streets back, to reclaim the streets. The streets in large portions of our area of East Austin, an African-American, Hispanic area, [are] infested with drug deals. They are lined up with drug users, prostitutes and those who make money off illicit gain. We felt it was our responsibility as a church to do more than just come between the four walls on Sunday...[we wanted] to move the church onto its feet, if you will, by marching and praying, preaching and praising. That's what we do at midnight on Friday night and Saturday night and sometimes during the week. We go at midnight because that's when the people we want to affect are on the streets.

If we know there is a problem with a group of young people out on the street, we like to go and get right in the middle of that. We gather people together; we sing praise songs at that very point. After having prayer for that night's mission, we form columns of twos and fours, depending on the number of people, and we march a predesignated route. We stop at various corners where the traffic is very heavy, and we have prayer for all of those individuals who are there, prayer for the community, prayer for the city, and we trust God to reclaim that area [for] its rightful inhabitants. Although we do pray and we do have a word, we mainly praise up and down the streets. It's jubilant praise because there's no reason for solemn praise. We are not grieving and mourning. We are excited about what God is doing and what he's getting ready to do.

—Sterling Lands II, pastor of Greater Calvary Baptist Church in Austin, Texas. Anywhere from ten to one hundred people participate in the marches. Lands' church has helped bring substantial healing to some of the troubled people they have met on the midnight marches.

• **Stand ready to serve.** Your open worship will be heard louder when you corroborate your song with service, as Abraham did in helping rescue his friends in trouble. Such acts of kindness and healing are received by God as gifts of worship (Acts 10:4; Heb. 13:16). Jesus taught us to do good deeds in such a way that people see and expressly glorify the Father in heaven (Matt. 5:16). Look for God to open ways for entire communities to observe your worship and be served by Christ's kindness.

A non-Christian called our church and asked us to come and exorcise the neighborhood, about four to five blocks from the church. That neighborhood was riddled with drug dealers, so we were reluctant to do it, but we did it. Our church had been in this community a long time. We had not fulfilled our mission. The area had become inner city, and we were like an island to ourself. But with this invitation we went into that neighborhood, and we blocked off the streets, took in prepared food, cleaned up graffiti, planted trees. We had a meeting in the streets to pray that the drug dealing would cease in the neighborhood. We had the mayor come. We had live music along with our prayer.

Frankly, after the day was over, I was exhausted and somewhat happy it was over. I had to go home and write my message on mercy and compassion and love for my congregation. I would prefer to preach to my congregation in the church within the four walls. The idea of speaking in the streets was pretty ridiculous, which now seems pretty shameful. But that's where we were at that time, all doing our religion within the four walls of the church. After that the police department of Oakland called me up, and within about thirty days we were told that drug dealing was cleared from the neighborhood, and we were asked to continue the block party effort.

—David Kiteley, pastor of Shiloh Christian Fellowship in Oakland, California. His church continues to hold block parties in high-crime areas about twelve times a year. At the parties, Christians pray for the neighborhood, choirs sing, ex-drug addicts tell their stories and social program directors offer help.

Interceding for Whole Cities

Some years later Abraham was visited by angels who disclosed the task God had sent them to accomplish. They were to investigate the evil and execute God's destructive judgment. The angels went on to Sodom. But Abraham turned to God and prayed (Gen. 18:22-23).

Consider the place from which Abraham prayed. It was a place away from his home (Gen. 18:33). Abraham apparently didn't use the newly built public altar to pray for Sodom and Gomorrah. The record says that he was "before the Lord," but he physically stood at a place of some height from which he could clearly see the entire valley of the cities of Sodom and Gomorrah (Gen. 19:27-28).

Look again at Abraham's prayer which he argued "before the Lord" while he had the city in his view (Gen. 18:22-23). Abraham first argued that God should hold back destruction from a city in which there are both righteous and wicked. God agreed. From that established premise Abraham cried out for God to reduce the number of people to be regarded as a sufficient righteous presence to restrain judgment on a city. Abraham argued successfully to the number of ten before God broke off the prayer session. We will never really know whether Abraham had intended to negotiate for five (counting Lot's future sons-in-law, five may have been enough).

Abraham carefully pursued his prayer according to what he had heard the angels say about his special place in the destiny of nations.

> Shall I hide from Abraham what I am about to do, since Abraham will surely become a great and mighty nation, and in him all the nations of the earth will be blessed? For I have chosen him, in order that he may command his children and his house-

> hold after him to keep the way of the Lord by doing righteousness and justice; in order that the Lord may bring upon Abraham what he has spoken about him (Gen. 18:17-19).

The angels spoke of righteous living and God's purpose to bless all peoples. They wanted Abraham to know that future generations of Abraham's faith family would excel in living out righteousness and justice. Somehow this righteousness and justice, as demonstrated by Abraham's children, would be pivotal in the fulfillment of God's supreme purpose that all the nations be blessed.

Certainly the people of Sodom represented one of the world's peoples God intended to bless. Indeed, they had just experienced tangible blessing at the hand of Abraham's household. Abraham pressed God to extend further blessing upon the city and all of its people because of the presence of a righteous few.

Abraham's experience should tell us that we walk with a generous God, who holds all cities in his hands. He is a God who himself hears the cumulative cry of nations and walks among them looking for righteousness. As we walk through the cities of earth, it may well be that angels walk with us, assessing what they find. God's judgments are moving toward culmination.

There is much we cannot know, but if we are to pray in keeping with the way in which this story presents the affairs of God with cities, it would appear that in some way God's coming judgments remain contingent. Our prayers for cities are heard with great seriousness by a listening "Judge of all the earth" (Gen. 18:25). Let us not fail to pray with sober urgency.

Implications for Today's Prayerwalkers

• **Pray city-size prayers.** We need to adopt the wide-ranging scope of Abrahamic intercession: Pray for entire cities and peoples. We may have people in mind who are dear to us, as Lot was important to Abraham. Let us name them. But let us go on to pray as we are privileged: Make bold requests on behalf of entire cities.

• **Grasp the basic prayer agenda given to Abraham.** Angels spoke of the righteousness and justice of God's people, which will ultimately bless all nations. Abraham has forever established that God can be willing to restrain judgment from a city because of the presence of righteousness in it. Can we not build on Abraham's prayer today? Surely we can humbly ask God to extend his mercy even further. God is willing to hold back punishing judgment so that he can increase the number of righteous people in our cities.

5

JOSHUA: PRAYER WARRIOR

Most Christians realize they are being spiritually opposed as they serve God. The fight we each face is part of a global war that has been rampaging through cities, churches and minds throughout earth for thousands of years. While understanding that spiritual powers are real, some may feel they have enough stress in the course of daily living without picking street fights with demons. Others have been turned off by cartoonish caricatures of evil powers or by what appears to be superstitious speculations about what is haunting the neighborhood.

How can we go beyond waging spiritual war as a one-on-one defensive duel to keep evil from encroaching on our home? We must either overcome in the battle for whole cities or practically concede to house arrest, isolated in cocoon-like dwellings.

This guide does not attempt to provide an adequate introduction to all of the significant dimensions of spiritual war. Several other recent resources do an excellent job of giving a much more detailed understanding of God's war and what to do in dozens of different circumstances (see appendix B). Our goal in this chapter is to learn from the life of Joshua important lessons about the tactic of prayerwalking.

Walking for Strategic Vision

Joshua's first footsteps on the land were not with the Israelites as they crossed the Jordan and began to encircle Jericho. Forty years earlier Joshua, Caleb and ten other leaders had surveyed the land afoot. Moses later pointed to the faith expressed on that foray as crucial for the entire future: "To him [Caleb] and to his sons I will give the land on which he has set foot, because he has followed the Lord fully" (Deut. 1:36).

Surveying Value and Opposition

Twelve select leaders were given their assignment: to get a strategic preview of the land and the people. Their job of exploring, evaluating and reporting could be called the work of vision. The list of what they were to discover boils down to two things: the land and the people.

First, they were to assess the value of the land God was giving them. "See what the land is like...And how is the land in which they live, is it good or bad?...Is it fat or lean? Are their trees in it or not? Make an effort then to get some of the fruit of the land" (Num. 13:18-20).

Second, they were to survey the people. They were to discover the resistance arrayed against the advance of God's people. "See...whether the people who live in it are strong or weak, whether they are few or many....And how are the cities in which they live, are they like open camps or with fortifications?" (Num. 13:18-19).

They went on an exploratory prayerwalk that lasted for forty days. At least two of them prayerwalked. Ten of them were perhaps just walking. We will see how their report suggests what happened as they walked the land.

They categorized their initial report in the two areas they were assigned to research: The first area of vision was the land. Regarding the land, they at first had a very good report: "The land...certainly does flow with milk and honey, and this is its fruit" (Gen. 13:27). They had brought back samples of the fruit to give evidence of the abundant heritage God was giving them.

Finding Early Fruit

They strained their muscles to exhibit the distinctive wealth of the land. Their orders were to "make an effort" to get some fruit of the land. (Gen. 13:20. A literal rendering of the Hebrew might be "use your strength.") It was early in the season for the first grapes. They didn't expect to find a full range of fruits, or even any at all in ripeness. Nevertheless they were to bring evidence of the abundant yield of the land.

They brought home more than one kind of fruit, but the showpiece was a massive bunch of grapes that took two men to carry. The surprise increased as people realized that the grapes had developed out of season.

The fruit was so phenomenal that the scouts named an entire valley after this cluster. (They named it *Eshcol*, which means "cluster.") Why the new name? The men surely sensed that this discovery was a divinely given sign of the abundance to come. They renamed the entire region as a way of recognizing the lavish bounty of God that was about to burst forth as they labored in the land.

Assessing the Enemy

Regarding the second area of vision, that of the people arrayed against them, they brought a factual, but still rather intimidating, report.

> The people who live in the land are strong, and the cities are fortified and very large; and moreover, we saw the descendants of Anak there. Amalek is living in the land of the Negev and the Hittites and the Jebusites and the Amorites are living in the hill country, and the Canaanites are living by the sea and by the side of the Jordan (Num. 13:28-29).

Two features of their report stand out: First, the enemy had ranged the entire terrain, and all territory was already claimed. There were no unoccupied places, no niches in which to gain easy access. Second, they had perceived, with some degree of accuracy, that there had been a long history of spiritual evil reinforcing the defensive might of the cities. The city walls loomed so tall that they seemed to be "fortified to heaven" (Deut. 1:28). The institutions were imbued with ancient evil.

The descendants of Anak that they saw were offspring of the Nephilim (Num. 13:33). We cannot be sure who these beings were. The text of Numbers does not mention details. Some Jewish traditions have considered the gigantic Nephilim to be descendants of the illicit union of "the sons of God" with "the daughters of men" recorded in Genesis 6, a sort of angelic bastard race of evil. These beings supposedly acted as portal points of hell, giving entrance to demons who would possess or afflict people throughout later ages. Once again, we cannot be sure what they saw, but we do see the intimidation they brought.

Intimidation by Exaggeration

In the back-and-forth discussion about what to do next, the despairing ten scouts ended up changing their report of both the land and the people. The people of Canaan were declared to be "too strong for us" (Num. 13:31). How much of the intimidation resulted from exaggeration? They accurately reported the presence of the oversized sons of Anak. But how accurate were their reports that they had actually sighted the ancient, gigantic Nephilim (Num. 13:33)?

When the ten scouts described themselves as grasshoppers next to the sizable enemy, intimidation overwhelmed the rest of the people, even driving the scouts to rashly reverse their good report about the land. The land was suddenly regarded as worthless. No one could hold back the hysteria. Weeping went through the night (Num. 14:1).

A Vision of Victory

Joshua and Caleb made a final effort to communicate vision. The outline is familiar: the land and the people. Regarding the land, they insisted that it was "exceedingly good land" (Num. 14:7). Regarding people, Joshua probably acknowledged that the people and their cities were indeed allied with great evil when he described them as functioning under a shadow. Such a description could apply to an imperial governmental power, but because he contrasts their shadow with the Lord of the Israelite people, it is likely that he is describing a spiritual force that extended over several named peoples, many cities and much territory. "Their [referring to the people, such as the Anakim] protection [literally 'shadow'] has been removed from them, and the Lord is with us; do not fear them" (Num. 14:9).

Joshua acknowledged that darkness was somehow akin to the people, strengthening them greatly. Yes, they were mighty. But he had kept his viewpoint high and wide enough to see the overwhelming greatness of God. He had seen what was crucial to the battle: that the opposing force had been disarmed at the highest level.

Joshua's final plea is for the people not to fear. He read the situation well. The people refused to obey, not because of sinful pride or idolatry, but because of the terror triggered by the overblown report and their stubborn unbelief. Caleb said later, "My brethren who went up with me [his fellow scouts] made the heart of the people melt with fear..." (Josh. 14:8). The distinct feature of Caleb and Joshua's report was their focus on God's power. "If the Lord is pleased with us, then He will bring us into this land, and give it to us" (Num. 14:8). Joshua and Caleb had been searching for more than a census of what was wrong and evil. They had been looking for what God was accomplishing in the land.

Implications for Today's Prayerwalkers

- **Vision is an act of war.** Spiritual reconnaissance is best accomplished by pursuing a vision of God. Walk to see something about God more than you walk to say something about evil. Intimidating "grasshopper vision" can result from looking through the wrong end of the telescope first. Allow your view of Christ to almost eclipse your study of hell's corruption. Basic Bible study will yield a rudimentary knowledge of God's purposes throughout history. Without such an awareness of God's work throughout the ages, it might be hard to pick up the dealings of God in the present hour. So school yourself, as no doubt Joshua did, in the unfolding purposes of God as revealed in Scripture.
- **Discern evil carefully.** Prayerwalkers often report a heightened sensitivity to spiritual battle as they intercede on the streets. Avoid the two extremes of ignoring evil or inventing phantoms. Brace yourself to

behold what's wrong with your city without expecting to hear the clash of angelic swords. At the same time, don't hide your eyes from seeing the evident aftermath of evil or what may have given rise to it.

We can't know all that our curiosity demands about spiritual war. For our sakes God hinders our voyeurism of spiritual violence. Be very cautious in seeking out evil powers. They love attention. Mapping the spiritual terrain is still a new art. Work with other wise leaders from various local churches, or your picture of evil can be enormously flawed by demonic disinformation. Why believe the author of all lies and the prince of pride regarding his power? Don't assume that you have perceived evil adequately to describe it sufficiently. We really wouldn't understand the name and address of an evil being were it to tell us the truth. Perhaps this is why those with gifts of discernment have sometimes identified evil powers by the effect they may have had in human affairs. Thus we have evil powers referred to as the spirit of lust or a spirit of unrighteous trade.

Your observations are valuable, even though they are likely to be subjective impressions. Blend and balance insights with others who are prayerwalking the same area.

Recognize when you are going beyond the reconnaissance that is truly necessary. Precise naming of powers may not be needed to wage adequate battle. In most situations, knowing only one name is sufficient — the name of Jesus, whose name is far above every other name.

• **Discover the fruit of the future.** Remember the muscle-straining effort Joshua had made to demonstrate an important feature of their task: to discover the fruit of the future. Joshua's enthusiasm for the land God was giving never failed. He could see that the land was virtually pregnant with God's future blessing. The lesson for prayerwalkers at war is to make top priority of discovering the future fruit of a city.

God does not extend empty blessings. To those who look, God is pleased to give "grape-cluster" evidence of his highest intentions. Look for the fruit as if all that you find were just early sproutings, out of season, first specimens of what God can bring. What unique implanting of goodness is from God's hand, preserved and purposed to explode into a great harvest?

> When we first started prayerwalking, we had a couple come up to us and say, "We've just become Christians. We've met the Lord in our home, and not by going to church or any outside means. We just came to Christ." We told them that we had been prayerwalking past where they lived. They soon became foundation people in the new church. We saw them as first fruits of others that would come.

> —*Jeff Lawton of Norwich, Norfolk, in England. Members of Jeff's church meet every Wednesday morning at 6:30 to prayer-walk seven different routes.*

You may be moved during prayer to give a place or neighborhood an additional name with prophetic significance. The prophetic name *Eshcol* (meaning "cluster") was a good sample of prophetic renaming that spoke of a magnitude of fruitfulness. Try giving anticipatory names to areas as a form of spiritual blessing. Expect great numbers of new believers but anticipate a harvest of the gospel beyond what can be quantified. Prophetically taste the goodness of God. What will be the distinct flavor of obedience that can come to Christ's glory from this city? What fruit that grows nowhere else rises to God from this land?

> Every city you go to has its own personality. And as beautiful as that personality may be on one side of the coin, on the flip side that very same attribute in one way or another has become distorted or poisoned and has become destructive.
>
> —*Jack Hayford, pastor of Church on the Way in Van Nuys, California, from a message entitled "Touching Your Town Through Prayer." Hayford has urged Christians in Los Angeles to "take the city" by redemptive blessings which are filled with fresh understanding about the city.*

Lift your stated blessings to God in sincere prayer. Like Joshua, use wisdom and lift your report of the goodness of God to other warriors so that the battle will be directed beyond the expulsion of evil to the cultivation of God's abundant glory, flourishing like fruit.

• **Give a useful, balanced report.** Tremendous ministry opportunities can alternately thrill you or overwhelm you with false pressure to make things happen. God may indeed impart to you a sense of divine assignment. But if you are praying on a large enough scale, you are probably anticipating matters well beyond your power to enact. Carry out your responsibility before God to encourage others to faithful action.

Your communication to others is incomplete if it amounts to a satanic damage report. It may be wise to limit your statements with this revised maxim: If you can't say something about what God is doing, don't say anything at all. Major on the great value of the faith-future. Display samples of the fruitfulness that is already visible. Of course, be faithful to give the dark side of the picture, but use caution in speaking about evil powers that hold sway over cities or territories. If you do speak of the enemy, follow Joshua's example. He spoke without exaggeration or excessive detail. Enemy powers were described, but not apart from speaking of the vastly superior power of God triumphing over them. Please don't fabricate feelings or circulate rumors when speaking of what you sense God doing in your city. Recall Caleb's words about a worthwhile report: "I brought word back to him as it was in my heart" (Josh. 14:7).

Stepping Into the Story

If there is a key to spiritual war it is given in the life summary of Caleb and Joshua: They followed God. It is so profound that it may slip our notice.

> None of the men who came up from Egypt...shall see the land...for they did not *follow Me fully*, except Caleb...and Joshua...for they have *followed the Lord fully* (Num. 32:11-12, italics added).

Scripture mentions their footsteps on the soil, but the key was not in their feet. Other people who were with them set foot and laid eyes on the land. The difference was that Joshua and Caleb followed God fully.

Follow God Personally and Purposefully

The Scriptures twice reiterate that Caleb followed the Lord fully (see Deut. 1:36; Josh. 14:9).

What did it mean to follow the Lord fully? What was this "different spirit" (Num. 14:24)? The original Hebrew expression is rare, used once to describe Joshua and five times for Caleb (Num. 14:24, 32:11-12; Deut. 1:36; Josh. 14:8-9,14). This phrase is used only one other time, of King David (1 Kin. 11:6).

Literally translated, the expression says that Joshua and Caleb "fulfilled after the Lord." To *fulfill* probably means to complete a task in a maximal way. *After the Lord* suggests a holy friendship. Combining the word *fulfill* with the phrase *after the Lord* gives Joshua's way of following a dimension of passionate intimacy united with a determined pursuit to complete God's mission. Joshua's following was personal as well as purposeful.

Joshua's understanding of his part in God's purposes helped him order his steps strategically. The Israelites were not a horde of homesteaders, just warfaring for the fun of grabbing land. They knew that the advance into the land helped extend God's glory among the nations, "that all the peoples of the earth may know that the hand of the Lord is mighty" (Josh. 4:24).

Implications for Today's Prayerwalkers

• **Make your prayerwalking humbly historic.** Joshua recognized his day as a crucial juncture of history. God may choose to pivot his great plans upon your small steps, plans he has been unfolding for centuries. Recognize the significance of your walking without taking yourself too seriously. You aren't the first to pray for your city, and you won't be the last. Make a balanced attempt to place your city and your generation in the history of God's purposes. Without such reference, prayers can sag into the tiresome right-now demands of over-privileged children.

Keep pace with God's relentless patience through many generations. Think of your day's prayerwalk as a significant, but brief, item on a heavenly calendar that marks time in generations. Finding God's footsteps through the centuries isn't as difficult as it may seem. Everyone can join in by actively remembering what God has done and what he has promised to do. Step into the story by soaking in the entire saga of the Bible. Frame prayers for your day from the stories of Scripture.

• **Get ready for the surprise God has in store.** Exercise the power of looking forward in patient anticipation. As clear as his promises are, God delights in surprising us beyond what we could have ever asked or thought (Eph. 3:20). Joshua prepared his comrades to be God-followers with a forward-looking attitude: "Go after it [the ark of God]...that you may know the way by which you shall go, *for you have not passed this way before*" (Josh. 3:3-4, italics added).

Break away from retrograde wishing to get back to the "good old days." A few sincere spiritual warriors have glibly deputized themselves as the spiritual police of their hometowns. Intentions are good, but with a short horizon of history some would-be vigilantes might do little more than perform citizen arrests on a few interloping demons who are disturbing the peace. Restoring the quietude of bygone days is too small a goal. In doing so we may be missing God's heart to lead our cities to where they have never been before.

Encountering the Councils of God

Joshua didn't storm Jericho right away. He had completed gathering needed intelligence to form a workable strategy, but he hadn't yet put any plan into action (Josh. 2). At this time of waiting we find him doing something similar to what we know as prayerwalking. The record says that he was "by Jericho" with his eyes open (Josh. 5:13). His mind was no doubt occupied with the coming battle. He was very likely seeking God in prayer for the best approach. While gazing at Jericho he suddenly encountered a figure like a warrior with a drawn sword. Coming closer to discern the allegiance of the mysterious soldier, Joshua saw that he was standing before someone of angelic order, or perhaps even greater, the "captain of the host of the Lord" (Josh. 5:14).

Upon learning the warrior's immense identity, Joshua dropped to the dirt and ceremonially bowed. This probably was not the customary salute to a superior officer. Joshua's gesture is one of worshipful subservience. Most angelic messengers quickly deliver whatever message they have and depart. No angel of God would demand or accept the kind of worship given by Joshua. Was this an early manifesting of our Lord Jesus? Many believe so. In any case, Joshua submitted himself with decorum befitting a servant: "What has my lord to say to his servant?" (Josh. 5:14).

The angelic figure gave no orders for battle but rather a surprising word that the spot on which Joshua stood had been deemed "holy." Why was it regarded as holy? It was just an obscure, uninhabited patch of the Jordan valley. From what we know, it was not sought as a religious holy place before that time or after.

In this case the word *holy* probably means that the ground had been exalted for a session of divinely royal business. Biblical visions of the way in which God surrounds himself with angelic councils "in the splendor of holiness" are very similar with ancient patterns of throne room protocols (Ps. 96:5-9, see margin note on v. 9; Job 1:6-12; Dan. 7:9-14 and others). Appropriate etiquette in such ancient throne rooms of human kingdoms often demanded the removal of shoes and ceremonial bowing (Gen. 42:6; 1 Kin. 1:16-31; Esth. 4:11, 5:1-2). The biblical accounts of God's assembly in the heavens indicate that assignments and orders regarding the affairs of kingdoms are discussed and decreed before an entourage of angelic servants (1 Kin. 22:19-22; Is. 6:1-11; Rev. 5). We don't trivialize the glory of God's "holy place" on high to understand it, in some of its functions, in a way similar to the earthly sessions of high-level human military strategy which we have dubbed "war rooms" or "situation rooms."

For all we know, Joshua's physical sight only disclosed one person of heavenly origin. But the messenger's word requiring bare feet in a holy place hints that Joshua was about to come within earshot of the throne room councils of the heavenlies. Though he had not been transported to heaven, heaven's councils had come near to him. Joshua quickly took the posture appropriate for obedient listening. As he waited attentively before God, Joshua was given specific orders for the battle ahead.

He could never have guessed the scheme of battle which was given to him. It was a unique plan, never done before or exactly repeated since.

Implications for Today's Prayerwalkers

• **Seek guidance beyond strategic information.** As Joshua sent scouts to gather helpful information, we need to do our homework for entering new areas to advance the kingdom by getting pertinent research accomplished. On the other hand, prepare yourself with a holy hesitancy to seek God for his unique orders. He may well augment your plans about how to reach your city.

• **Take your shoes off before you put them on.** Build worship into the tactical plans of any prayerwalk. Warriors must be worshippers, not just to get divine data for battle plans and not just because praise "works," but because of God's great worthiness.

• **Cultivate lifelong disciplines of worship.** In God's ways, it may not be possible to learn war without practicing a life-style of worship. The confusing noise of battle is not the place to learn the potent intimacy of worship.

Joshua learned the practice of worship from Moses, from whom he also learned the arts of war. Joshua consistently lingered in the tent of meeting, learning the grandeur and fear of God in his holy place (Ex. 33:11). Today those who worship through Jesus by faith come before God through the torn veil to his dwelling place on high. This holy place is the very throne room from which all spiritual war takes place (compare Hebrews 8:1-2 and 12:22-27 with Psalms 2, 29 and 93, in which God is enthroned in the heavens, commanding his judgments upon rebellious enemies. Psalms 76, 82 and 110 and Revelation 5-11 enlarge the same picture more).

Your prayerwalk can be an encounter time for you to meet heaven's wisdom. There is no need for the Lord to take you into heavenly councils, amaze you with armed angels or astound you with any other mystical experience. You know better than to struggle to lift yourself heavenward by mystical mental acrobatics, as if it were even possible. Simply and earnestly love and listen to God. He is well able to bring heaven near you.

Prayer by Action: Prophetic Symbolism

The instructions Joshua obtained for taking Jericho were a series of bizarre actions. Try to picture the daily parade that encircled Jericho for a week: carefully positioned soldiers, priests, the ark of God and then more soldiers. Their commanded silence was hardly noticed because of the incessant blast of priestly trumpets. Every person of Israel was involved somehow, especially the final day with its resounding climactic shout (Josh. 6).

God had not disclosed a secret, fail-safe plan for city-taking. Instead he had given Israel a way to exert faith for that particular battle. Hebrews 11:30 says, "By *faith* the walls of Jericho fell down, after they had been encircled for seven days" (italics added). The parade was not designed to be a war dance to intimidate enemies or psych up the warriors. The marches, the shouts, the trumpets were in fact demonstrative prayers, enacted statements of faith.

In every battle that Joshua won there is indication that God was sought for wisdom (Ex. 17:8-16; Josh. 8:1, 10:8, 11:6; Joshua 9:14 indicates a notable exception to seeking God's counsel). God often gave Joshua specific ways to display his faith. For example, at Ai, "the Lord said to Joshua, 'Stretch out the javelin that is in your hand toward Ai, for I will give it into your hand' " (Josh. 8:18). Conventional tactics of war contributed to the victory, but Joshua knew the crucial matter of symbolically acting out his faith in a way God gave him: "Joshua did not withdraw his hand with which he stretched out the javelin until he had utterly destroyed...Ai" (Josh. 8:26).

These dramatic prayers have been called *prophetic symbols* or *prophetic acts*. They aren't devised by human minds to make prayers peppy. Authentic prophetic symbols are always granted by God. Although they anticipate God's work, they neither force nor foretell the future. Somehow our praying in genuine trust opens the affairs of earth to the will of God in heaven. When we pray according to his will, God delights to answer in a marvelous sort of joint endeavor which no one yet has fully explained. Heaven is never coerced, and human will on earth is never violated.

In the battle where Joshua commanded the sun to stand still, God had already made his will in the matter evident with signs from heaven. Joshua was inspired to speak prophetically. He directly "spoke to the Lord," but the words came out as if directed to the sun and moon (Josh. 10:12). Prophetic actions have double direction. They are addressed to God as prayers, but they become instruments in God's hands on earth. "The Lord listened to the voice of a man; for the Lord fought for Israel" (Josh. 10:14).

Prophetic Action Is a Normal Way to Pray

Prophetic actions are commonplace in Scripture. People of every generation of faith utilized gesture and demonstrative action. God rolled back the Red Sea, but He put a rod in Moses' hand as a bridge to heaven's power. God parted the Jordan River but with the prophesying footsteps of the leading priests.

Jesus himself, though fully God, prayed as a full human being and exerted faith as he prayed. None of Jesus' miracles took place by magic. Every one was an act of faith involving some kind of prayer, and many of them involved actions of prophetic significance. Why else did Jesus pray with his hands extended (Luke 5:13,14:4) or breathe on his friends (John 20:22) or send a blind man to wash in a pool (John 9:6-7)?

Prophetic Action Is Not Magic

It is surprising to realize that, after Jericho, Joshua never ordered another march around a city. Why not repeat the method if it worked so well? Joshua knew that prophetic actions were not to be repeated with false reliance on the act itself.

There is one time in biblical record in which the prophetic symbols commanded at Jericho were repeated as if they had been mere battle tactics. It happened generations after Joshua, when faith in Israel sagged to all-time lows. At a point of military crisis, a faithless group of elders rallied priests to carry the ark amidst soldiers. They even raised a shout that shook the earth. But no walls fell. Instead, the ark was taken, the priests were slain along with many soldiers and God lifted his glory from Israel (1 Sam. 4).

Implications for Today's Prayerwalkers

- **Every step a prayer.** The act of walking is perhaps the simplest prophetic symbol. You can express faith with your feet.
- **Do as God gives.** Seek God for his unique battle plan. Be content if he gives you no particular physical prayer, but don't hesitate to carry out his will as you know it. You do not need to fully understand what prophetic actions mean in order to do them in faith.
- **Don't fight by formula.** Resist and engage evil powers only with the captain of hosts, using the means he gives us for every distinctive battle. Prayerwalkers may come to surmise that their steps in themselves have power. Attention on walking can skew our focus away from talking with God. Recipes for vaporizing evil too easily become magic formulas devoid of the power of the person of Jesus. Satan is always as ready to enchant us with our supposed power as we are to believe that our actions coerce the very heavens into compliance. A good rule of thumb is to assume that most prophetic actions are intended for one-time use.

> Some of my friends have done some crazy things, praying in the purist simplicity of faith, and God honors it. And I honor them. But we don't absolutize their actions or support that they are patterns to be followed any more than we would suggest that all prophets should dig holes in walls like Ezekiel or bury their undergarments down by the river like Jeremiah once did. The principle here is childlike obedience, not the presumptuous imi-

tation of somebody else's path to victory.

—*John Dawson, of Los Angeles, California. John has encouraged thousands to pray for their communities through his book* Taking Our Cities for God *(Creation House, 1989). John serves as the international director of urban missions for Youth With A Mission.*

Magic is the performance of rituals that are thought to wield power over affairs of people or invisible entities. Steer clear from an extra-biblical fascination with invisible realms that supposedly correspond with realms that we see. Some prayer regarding the natural and the supernatural lies on the margin of biblical truth and lends itself to an unhealthy dualism (a rigidly divided universe of two exclusive realms). Use biblical language about the very real domains of heaven and earth.

Discerning the Battle Lines for Cities

Let's go back to Joshua's encounter with the heavenly warrior. Joshua demanded that the soldier announce his identity by declaring his loyalties in the battle ahead: "Are you for us or for our adversaries?" The first word of the reply must have rung like a bell in Joshua's mind for years: "No" (Josh. 5:13-14).

What did this person mean by saying no to the basic question of allegiance? Did he lack all diplomatic courtesy? His drawn sword was evidence that he was on the scene for the purpose of war. How could he avoid taking sides? Was he from a distant place, perhaps putting up his military services for hire? Who was this person?

"Rather I indeed come now as captain of the host of the Lord" (Josh. 5:14). This heavenly leader owed no allegiance to any people or city. He served the Most High. He outranked all skirmishing factions of earth. Joshua's encounter with the heavenly warrior helped him wage war with a noble humility. Although Joshua was fighting in league with angelic majesties, he had not recruited God to fight on his side. In fact, Joshua had been enlisted himself to serve God's greater purposes.

Know Your Leader

God jolted Joshua into proper alignment regarding spiritual war. No battle plan could be given without a basic wisdom about the war. Joshua's question showed his tendency to define the battle as an us-vs.-them struggle. He was defining the battle in terms of himself instead of God: Are you for *us* or for *our* adversaries?

Perhaps we express the same tendency to oversimplify the battle as a two-sided tussle, particularly when walking our own neighborhoods.

Spiritual war is never truly staged as if it were a sporting event with two opposing sides neatly uniformed in black and white. The very nature of God's war is to redeem beloved people who are presently in vicious rebellion against him.

For a simple conquest, "know your enemy" might suffice as a maxim for war strategy. But for spiritual war, to know your leader is the basic requirement. "The people who know their God will display strength and take action" (Dan. 11:32).

The Unique Battle of Jericho

The battle of Jericho stood out as different from any other battle that the Israelites ever fought. First, heavenly powers were manifest. The captain of the host of the Lord was made visible. The host of angelic powers at his command was unseen except for the fallen walls. Something pushed down those walls with incredible precision. No human power could have done it. There is no mention of any manifestation of evil angelic forces. But presumably the drawn sword of the heavenly warrior was used against enemy powers.

Second, Jericho stood out as the watershed battle that shook the defensive might of the entire land. Israel had fought other battles, but those were usually defensive skirmishes against attacking tribes. This was the first battle against an entrenched enemy. It marked their entry into an entire territory. With the stronghold of Jericho devastated, the remaining inhabitants of the land were forced to fall-back stratagems or hurried alliances that actually exposed the enemy more greatly (Josh. 9:1-3; 10:1-8).

Third, the battle of Jericho was for God alone. The people were to "Shout! For the Lord has given you the city" (Josh. 6:16). But God gave them the city in order to give it back to him again. The very next sentence of Joshua's orders: "And the city shall be under the ban, it and all that is in it belongs to the Lord..." (Josh. 6:17).

An item "under the ban" was something God reserved as a ceremonial gift of worship to himself (Lev. 27:28). The Hebrew words for *under the ban* are sometimes translated "devoted" as in Micah 4:13. "That you may devote to the Lord their unjust gain and their wealth to the Lord of all the earth." The entire city of Jericho was to be burned except for the precious metals. They were consecrated as being "holy to the Lord" and carefully placed in the "treasury of the house of the Lord" (Josh. 6:19,24).

When Achan took gold, silver and clothing from Jericho, his sin was not a simple case of covetousness. He had violated the purity of the victory at Jericho. The victory was entirely for the Lord. God did not place a ban on the goods of Jericho because they were more defiled than the items found in other cities. God wanted to make the point that the purpose of the battle was not to facilitate wild looting but to mark in every Hebrew heart and every Canaanite mind that God was Lord of all the earth.

As desirable as the location of the city might have been, it was not conquered so that it could be inhabited by the tribes of Israel. Joshua pointedly cursed the very site of the city. "Cursed before the Lord is the man who rises up and builds this city Jericho" (Josh. 6:26).

Other cities were burned, but they were not cursed from being inhabited again. (Ai was cursed, probably to complete what had been compromised by Achan's violation of the ban at Jericho [Josh. 8:26-28].) At the outset of the entire campaign, God made clear that this was not a pillage party by a ruthless, marauding horde. God was advancing his plan to glorify himself. God had made his purpose clear at the people's first attempt to enter the land years before. "As I live, all the earth will be filled with the glory of the Lord" (Num. 14:21).

The result of the battle of Jericho was God's glory among distant nations. "So the Lord was with Joshua and his [God's] fame was in all the land" (Josh. 6:27; a literal translation would be "all the earth"). The reputation of God's name is of utmost concern in the context. In the next chapter Joshua asks God what he would do for his "great name" if Israel's memory were cut off from the earth (Josh. 7:9). Later in the book travelers supposedly came from distant lands telling the tale that the fame (or more literally, *name*) of the Lord had been heard in a very far country (Josh. 9:9). The battle was God's — for *his* glory, against *his* enemies.

Joshua's Assignment

God's ultimate purpose was to be honored and glorified by the nations of earth. What was Joshua's assignment to make that happen?

When the Israelites conquered cities the way God told them to, two things were accomplished. First, God was destroying systems of false worship. Every idol, shrine, temple, altar, high place of worship or instrument of sorcery was to be utterly obliterated (Deut. 12:1-3). God's goal was to subdue every enslaving spiritual force at work in the idols. God knew the people to be weak and easily seduced into subjugation to spiritual forces. Yet Joshua was never commissioned to come against any spiritual entities (Josh. 23:6-7; Deut. 12:29-30). There is no reference which would suggest that the spiritual forces alive in the practiced idolatry were destroyed or even dealt with directly. Joshua was assigned to destroy the devices of false gods which had held people captive and would certainly ensnare the Israelite people. No doubt evil spiritual powers were vastly curtailed by the demolition of demonic worship.

God had a second objective in calling for the annihilation of the people throughout the land: He was punishing the sin of the Canaanites which had taken centuries to come to a "filled up" point where it could get no worse (Gen. 15:16, literal translation). God had allowed sin to run its full course.

God's retribution was just. We might wonder how the Canaanites felt about God's wrath. The only statement recorded from a Canaanite regarding the justice of the conquest came from a king who acknowledged the justice of God's action. "As I have done, so God has repaid me" (King Adoni-bezek, found in Judg. 1:7).

Same War, Different Battle

Unless we take the battle of Jericho at face value, we are likely to make sloppy use of it as a battle map for our cities. Reading the Jericho story figuratively sometimes results in a misperception of spiritual battle lines as the bad guys against the good guys. Unwise allegorizing of Joshua's battles makes faceless Canaanites represent the evil demonic powers of today as if they were dark pieces on a chessboard. It's easy to raise a war cry with such imagery, but we are likely to misfire.

Take Jericho seriously. Jericho does not stand as an old legend vaguely suggesting some kind of never-ending conflict between good and evil in urban settings. The battle at that city was just as real as the struggle for God's glory in your city today. It's not idle speculation to say that we fight in the same war as Joshua, only we're in a much later battle.

We are not involved in war games. God is not recycling old battles as training maneuvers for eternity. In any war there are different phases. Establishing a beachhead precedes mop-up operations. What God accomplished at Jericho set the stage for furthering his purposes. The battle of Jericho indicates the contours of later battles, but it will never be fought again.

How do we know that we now stand at a later stage of God's purposes? Because God has exalted Jesus to his right hand. The Father has promised to bring the earth under the headship of his Son. The very name Jesus in Hebrew is Joshua. Jesus has inherited complete leadership in God's war. He has brought the entire conflict very close to its culminating victory.

If we follow Jesus we will be shaken into alignment with God's purposes of the hour. Consider the rebuke Jesus gave to two close friends. An idea for on-site prayer had occurred to the brothers Jesus had nicknamed the "Sons of Thunder" (James and John, see Mark 3:17). The brothers were ready to add lightning as well.

Jesus had sent them ahead to arrange an overnight stay. The whole group was rejected in an ugly but common incident of religious racism. "And when His disciples James and John saw this, they said, 'Lord, do You want us to command fire to come down from heaven and consume them?' But He turned and rebuked them" (Luke 9:54-55).

Jesus could see that they were playacting in a two-sided war of pitting God against their own enemies. Their desire to promote Jesus had degenerated into a sort of vendetta evangelism. Jesus did not quietly dismiss the suggestion. He rebuked them: "You do not know what kind of spirit you are of; for the Son of Man did not come to destroy men's lives, but to save them" (Luke 9:55-56, recorded in many ancient texts).

What was this alien spirit that they did not know? A spiritual force had been at work fooling them into recycling old hatreds. They quickly classified people who had dishonored Jesus as condemnable enemies.

Jesus refused to make or destroy enemies. He did not seek or avoid those who opposed him. Emphatically, Jesus turned and continued his walk to the next village, possibly another Samaritan town.

Jesus had advanced God's war for salvation beyond the days of Joshua's battle. James and John had not yet understood the change. Jesus was already exposing and shaming demonic powers which had remained hidden in Joshua's battles. Jesus had set his course resolutely to go to his death. By his dying he would entirely disarm "the rulers and authorities" by making "a public display of them, having triumphed over them" (Col. 2:15).

We saw that Joshua's assignment was to destroy structured evil and to punish sin. Jesus was bringing forgiveness of sin not offered in Joshua's day. By the power of Christ's dying and rising, people can be separated from the satanic forces that may have afflicted them. Christ announced forgiveness in the present hour and a postponing of the hour of retribution so that people could be saved.

James and John were ready warriors but easily fooled into firing away across false battle lines. Jesus rebuked them soundly in order to redirect their warfare prayer away from enemies and patiently took them to the next village to continue the "seek and save" mission (Luke 19:10).

Implications for Today's Prayerwalkers

• **Discern your own spirit.** Prayerwalkers who set out to cleanse the land of "enemies," spiritual or otherwise, can possibly open themselves to be influenced by "another kind of spirit." We are told to confront sin with a "spirit of gentleness" and with a view to restore people trapped in it. This exhortation comes with the warning to examine yourself "lest you too be tempted" (Gal. 6:1). Apparently, when bringing healing to sin-afflicted lives, we're susceptible to the same disease. For example, when praying against heartfelt hatred, be sure that hatred finds no foothold in your prayers. Another example might be the Christ-imparted purity required to prayerwalk through red-light districts. Praying against sexual impurity can backlash in subtle ways.

• **Abandon any semblance of search-and-destroy missions.** Prayerwalkers at this time don't continue in Joshua's war assignment. You don't carry the burden of meting out God's punishment for sin; neither should you assume that you have the job of wiping out the paraphernalia of false worship.

Joshua was charged with demolishing idols and shrines. We now have a ministry of greater power. Our job is not to destroy idols but instead to convert idolaters. Following Paul's strategy, if we can help move people to turn to God from their idolatry, they will burn their idols without our help. (Compare 1 Thess. 1:9 with Acts 19:17-20:1, in which an entire system was shaken from the bottom up.)

• **Be wise in territorial war.** As a gateway city, Jericho often comes to mind when Christian workers seek to bring permanent entry for the gospel in a territory long given over to false worship. Remember that the show of force at Jericho was God's idea. Allow God to stage whatever showdown might be necessary, and even then be content to see little of the closed-curtain drama in the heavenlies.

Soften your celebration when forceful power encounters bring devastation to God's enemies. Celebration is the cleanest when focused on God's gain. Achan tried to profit personally from a triumph which God had designed as a display of his glory. Keep your motives clean from the start.

Occupying Our Inheritance

Joshua 1:3 ranks highest in popularity among prayerwalkers: "Every place on which the sole of your foot treads, I have given it to you, just as I spoke to Moses."

Let's lift our attention from the apparent power of falling feet to the heart of the promise: God's long-standing pledge to give the land to the people as an inheritance. God had summarized the goal of Joshua's warfare as bringing about inheritance. "He shall cause Israel to inherit [the land]" (Deut. 1:38).

Inheriting From God

Many present-day societies restrict the idea of inheritance to that of shuffling unspent assets after the death of a relative. We all realize that God was not passing on leftover portions of his estate because he was about to pass away.

Biblical inheritances were often apportioned while the senior figure of the family was still living (Luke 15:12). When a person was given responsibility over a portion of the family's land, immediate stewardship was realigned, but family honor and ownership continued. The land and its fruit were viewed as ultimately belonging to the fathers of the family, though these ancestors may have lived generations before (Num. 36:1-12; 1 Kin. 21:3-4).

When God gave inheritance to Israel, he was entrusting family wealth as if to his own sons. In fact, there are numerous references to the Lord's own inheritance or possession (Ex. 15:17; Deut. 14:2; 2 Sam. 14:16, 20:19; Ps. 79:1, among many others).

Possessing the Land

Possessing land meant taking charge of territory which had already been assigned to them as an inheritance. We could easily surmise that their feet were empowered to possess land just by stepping on it. But God did not say, "Every place on which the sole of your foot treads *is yours*." He said that every place they walked *"I have given it to you."* God was doing the giving.

Neither were they licensed to seize whatever they wanted. In the very next verse God gave clear boundaries to contain their conquest, according to an ancient promise (Josh. 1:4).

The process of receiving inheritance went through two stages under Joshua's advance: First, based on the authority of God granting the land as an inheritance, the entire nation of people was charged with possessing it as a united force (Josh. 1:11).

After they had subdued a major portion of the land together, they divided it into specific inheritances for the different tribes. "So Joshua took the whole land...and Joshua gave it for an inheritance to Israel according to their divisions by their tribes" (Josh. 11:23 and all of chapters 13-19).

At this point the second stage began, with each family or tribe pushing onto their allotted terrain and pursuing whatever warfare was necessary to subdue it. "Joshua...dismissed the people...each to his inheritance to possess the land" (Judg. 2:6; also Josh. 24:28).

Ousting Enemies Little by Little

Overcoming opposition and settling the different portions became a lengthy process. "I will drive them [Israel's enemies] out before you little by little, until you become fruitful and take possession of the land" (Ex. 23:30). God had slowed the conquering of enemy forces so that the Israelites would establish themselves as fruitful in every way. He did this so that one enemy wouldn't be replaced by another.

God designed the inheritance process to balance the confrontation of enemies with their displacement by his heirs. As God's people matured in their strength to bring forth the fruit of the land, God gradually expelled enemy forces.

Abraham's Family Inherits the World

Abraham and his descendants were promised that he would be "heir of the world" (Rom. 4:13). The entire earth! God ultimately intends to entrust the whole earth to his priestly people (Rev. 1:6, 5:10, 22:5).

There is one descendant of Abraham who opens inheritance of the world to all peoples: Jesus. By God's choosing, Jesus in effect became the sole heir of Abraham. He has been "appointed heir of all things" (Heb. 1:2). But Jesus opens his inheritance to any person who trusts in him.

The Open Inheritance of Jesus

The inheritance of Christ means more than reserved mansions in heaven. We can already see Jesus including members from every people in the family of God. Cities which languished for centuries without gaining or sustaining the blessings promised to Abraham are becoming places in which Christ is served. Membership in Abraham's family is open to "all who believe" from any nation (Rom. 4:11). Jesus grants this growing family of new heirs great measures of blessing and responsibility in the cities of the earth.

At this hour the matter of inheritance cannot be reduced to simple political domination or ownership of a few plots of land. As we see in the lives of Daniel, Joseph and Esther, God designs significant stewardships of responsibility for his people by which they can bring great blessing to their own families and all peoples (Dan. 2:48, 5:29; Gen. 41:39-41; Esth. 4:14).

Our Most Ancient Mandate

Our authority to possess the cities of earth as an inheritance has roots in our most ancient mandate: "Be fruitful and multiply, and fill the earth, and subdue it" (Gen. 1:28, 9:1,7).

God has never changed that purpose. Deuteronomy 32:8 says that "the Most High gave the nations their inheritance when He separated the sons of man." At the tower of Babel God assisted the human race in spreading out over the earth as distinct peoples (Gen. 11:2-9). Our race was not scattered just to wander, as Cain feared (Gen. 4:14). God dispersed the nations to enter lands where each people could ultimately be fruitful unto God. God intends inheritance for every people group.

Paul tells why God pressed the nations to cover the globe and to establish cities: "[God made] every nation of mankind to live on all the face of the earth, having determined their appointed times, and the boundaries of their habitation, that they should seek God" (Acts 17:26-27).

No people has governed a city or a country apart from God's assent. The migrations and conquests which have shaped the epochs and maps of mankind have all taken place by his sovereign oversight, with the constant purpose that people would seek him.

The Greater Joshua

Jesus is the greater Joshua who now leads God's people in a concerted effort to fill the earth. In Psalm 2:8 we read of Christ's conquest for inheritance: "Ask of Me, and I will surely give the nations as Your inheritance, and the very ends of the earth as Your possession" (NAS revised).

This promise is only directed to one person: Jesus. He is the one who would be called "His Anointed" (Ps. 2:2), to be installed by God as "My King upon Zion, My holy mountain" (Ps. 2:6). He is the only one who could truly be addressed as "My Son" by the Lord himself (Ps. 2:7).

We can be sure that the Son of God has asked the Father for the earth as an inheritance. And the Father has done what he promised. Jesus has been given governance over all. "The Father loves the Son, and has given all things into His hands" (John 3:35). In this time Jesus is breaking spiritual powers with force, as an iron scepter might shatter a piece of pottery. He breaks the conspiracy of spiritual rulers who try to escape the restraints God has established against evil. The Messiah crushes this rebellion so that the human kings of the earth might be given opportunity to worship with joy (Ps. 2:1-5, 9-11).

Jesus is even now ruling "in the midst of [God's] enemies" (Ps. 110:2). Only he can overwhelm the principalities and powers that hold sway over territories, taming and shaming them as "a footstool for [God's] feet" (Ps. 110:1). He possesses the cities for himself and then apportions inheritance to those who serve in his name.

He leads his little ones, the meek, as joint heirs to confront powers of evil in the weakest possible way: praying. When we request that the nations be given as an inheritance to the Son, we voice a little echo late in time to the mighty request Christ has already made (Ps. 2:8). But we are heard as we enact the possessing of cities by our praying presence. There is no place on earth where we can set foot that the Father has not already awarded to Christ as an inheritance.

Implications for Prayerwalkers

- **The meek inherit the earth.** Focus on inheriting from God more than on invading enemy camps. Your meekness might be reflected in some of the language you choose. Belligerence can backfire. Language of assault on God's enemies can sometimes generate a momentum of cocky supremacy which is powerless.

• **Aim your claims.** If you use the language of "taking" or "claiming" streets or territories, be sure to stipulate that you are "taking" this or "claiming" that for the Son of God. Steer clear of wording that might imply that you are claiming things for yourself. Instead of saying, "We claim this high school," try praying something like, "We lay claim to this high school for you, Lord Jesus. These students and this place are yours." What can go amiss by joining all of heaven and the Father himself in giving all things to the Son? Trust Jesus to distribute inheritance as he will among his people. You aren't so much wresting cities from the clutches of Satan as you are receiving cities from the hand of the Father for the Son.

• **More than conquerors.** From Joshua's experience we can expect that God will allow us to be as victorious as we intend to be fruitful. Prayerwalking works best when incorporated into plans to further Christ's kingdom.

Plan on the process of warfare to be slow and sure, paced by the emergence of fruit. God could easily vanquish spiritual enemies in a flash, but among other purposes, he delights in seeing wickedness displaced by spiritual fruitfulness.

Don't load your prayerwalking plans with hopes that evil will be suddenly eradicated. God has not unveiled prayerwalking as a secret weapon late in the game to force the devil to capitulate abruptly. The struggle has many dimensions, of which prayerwalking is only one. God works through his people in a thousand different ways to bring the full power of the gospel to every community of earth.

• **Take cities *for* them, not *from* them.** Stand with others in their struggle to receive their inheritance. Joshua rallied different tribes to fight as one, even though it was known that the target city would be inhabited by only one of the tribes (Num. 32:18; Josh. 22:3-4). In a similar way we have a responsibility to help residents of distant lands to contend for the inheritance God has for them in their own cities.

With Christ's open inheritance in view, we can pray with authority that the current inhabitants would inherit their own city. Ask God to restrain spiritual forces which have tried to thwart his will that the people would seek God and find him in Jesus. Pray for thousands to be added to the family as joint heirs with Jesus. Ask Jesus to grant worthy disciples the stewardship of cultivating the life of God in their city.

6

JESUS: PREPARING HIS WAY BY PRAYER

> The Lord...sent them ahead of Him to every city and place where He Himself was going to come.
>
> Luke 10:1

On one occasion Jesus sent seventy followers to specific cities so that they might bring about a welcome for him. Their task involved prayer of a sort that could not be done from a distance.

They were sent to win a citywide response to him. Jesus looked forward to being greeted in each city by people who had already received him. Households and entire cities could receive him by receiving those he sent (Luke 10:16; Matt. 10:40).

Jesus Received or Grieved by Whole Cities

Christ could transform the future of a receptive city. He mourned the Galilee towns which had tolerated a few miracles but had not turned to him in any firm communal repentance so that he could do more (Luke 10:12-15).

Jesus openly anguished over the chronic refusal of the city of Jerusalem. "O Jerusalem, Jerusalem, the city that kills the prophets and stones those sent to her!" (Luke 13:34).

Despite the record of rejection, his heart steadfastly longed for the future generations of the city: "How often I wanted to gather your children together, just as a hen gathers her brood under her wings, and you would not have it!" (Luke 13:34). Jesus did not seek to appeal against the verdict Jerusalem handed him. He left them with the emptiness they demanded. "Behold, your house is left to you desolate; and I say to you, you shall not see Me until the time comes when you say, 'Blessed is He who comes in the name of the Lord!' " (Luke 13:35). How many generations would pass until he would be welcomed with explicit blessing?

Approaching the city of Jerusalem just before his death, Jesus "saw the city and wept over it" like one bereaved. He saw devastating things in store because the city, as a responsible entity before God, had not recognized "the time of [its] visitation" (Luke 19:41-44).

Visitation: His Arrival, Our Revival

By using the term *visitation,* Jesus was not referring to a brief social visit or a series of supercharged religious meetings. What might have happened if Jesus had been welcomed? He implies that his visitation could have meant a huge manifestation of peace throughout the city for long times to come. "If you had known in this day, even you, the things which make for peace! But now they have been hidden from your eyes" (Luke 19:42). It's hard not to think that a fully welcomed Jesus would have brought a citywide infusion of God's nearness in a glory so vast that the word *revival* would barely apply.

Without question, the visitation intended for Jerusalem was unique among all cities Jesus yearned to touch. But Christ came to establish a healthy outbreak of his kingdom life among believers in every city and people.

Consider the welcome Jesus sought in Jericho. He encountered the receptive Zaccheus while walking. Jesus enjoyed friendship in that household, obviously declaring life-changing truth. Jesus said, "Salvation has come to this house" (Luke 19:9). But Jesus declared salvation as it became clear that the blessing of the gospel was going to ripple through the entire community, starting with the generosity of Zaccheus, who quadrupled his restitution to the people he had overtaxed (Luke 19:1-10).

Jesus announced to everyone at Zaccheus's party that he had come "to seek and to save" the lost, apparently household by household, toward a transformation of the life of the city.

In recent generations many have noted that the momentum of Christ's seeking and saving sometimes erupts into citywide movements we have called *revivals*. Perhaps we could more accurately call them *arrivals* because of the centrality of Jesus' word and manifest presence.

The Seventy: Forerunners to the Nations

A demonstration of Jesus' continuing purpose to visit cities with his saving presence is found in the sending of the seventy. "The Lord appointed seventy others, and sent them two and two ahead of Him to every city and place where He Himself was going to come" (Luke 10:1).

The seventy were to so completely embody Jesus' life that he could say, "The one who listens to you listens to Me, and the one who rejects you rejects Me" (Luke 10:16). Matthew records Jesus' words to a similar sending of the twelve. "He who receives you receives me" (Matt. 10:40). Their task was to prepare a welcome for Jesus in "every city and place where He Himself was going to come" (Luke 10:1).

Consider the purpose of this elaborate operation toward specific cities and regions. Could it be that Jesus needed each of the thirty-five pairs to arrange an overnight stop to cover what was at most a four-day journey? Hardly. Luke 13:22 suggests that many of the actual visits were brief. "And He was passing through from one city and village to another, teaching, and proceeding on His way to Jerusalem."

What then was the point of so carefully selecting cities, especially in conjunction with the number seventy? The number is significant. Seventy was the accepted figure in that society of the full number of nations.*

Jesus had selected twelve apostles with obvious reference to the tribes of Israel. Now he selected seventy, symbolically encompassing all nations.

If the seventy somehow correspond to the nations, we must also consider the prophetic significance of what they did at Jesus' instruction. Jesus was showing disciples of every generation his intentions to advance the gospel through every nation until the end of the age.

The sending of the seventy stands, by Christ's design, as a prophetic portrait of the completion of his kingdom purposes. There was an aspect of closure to their mission to initiate a movement in "every city and place."

Comparing the instructions given to the twelve and to the seventy shows slight differences. The seventy were not named apostles, as were the twelve (Luke 6:13), suggesting that Christ's task is entrusted to ordinary believers along with those ordained as apostolic servants. The seventy were not advised beforehand of every aspect of the spiritual power entrusted to them as the twelve had been (Luke 9:1). They discovered soon enough that vast spiritual authority had been given them (Luke 10:17-19). The twelve were sent to preach and heal (Luke 9:2,6). The assignment of the seventy was similar but simpler, focused almost entirely on prayer. Their preaching was to accompany their praying.

---

* Some translations use the number seventy-two. The meaning remains the same even when recognizing that variant manuscripts use the number seventy-two. In the Greek version of the Old Testament of Jesus' day, there were seventy-two nations listed in Genesis 12. In the Hebrew version, the count of nations is seventy. Seeing the sources of this apparent discrepancy lends credence to interpreting the number as referring to the nations or peoples of the earth.

Jesus repeated to the seventy what he had told the twelve about asking God to send out workers into his harvest. For the twelve, this admonition to pray for workers had come before their sending (Matt. 9:37-38). But for the seventy, prayer for workers was the foremost item of the instructions. Prayer was primary, not just preliminary, to their task. Whether it was blessing homes, praying for the sick or asking for laborers, every part of their instructions involved specific dimensions of prayer. The plan was bold and simple: Go to specific cities and pray for people.

We are not attempting to press the sending of the seventy into the mold of today's prayerwalkers. Our point is just the reverse: Today's prayer efforts in our cities and amidst far off nations have much to gain from the style and structure of the sending of the seventy. There is no place for rigid re-enactment of the details of Luke 10, but as Jesus now sends a contemporary counterpart to the seventy to every city and nation, his instructions will be found relevant. Perhaps they are even more pertinent at this moment in history. Serious plans are being formed as never before to see the gospel come to "every city and place" on earth.

A Vision for Harvest

Jesus' first directive established the basic purpose of their venture: harvest for God. "The harvest is plentiful, but the laborers are few; therefore beseech the Lord of the harvest to send out laborers into His harvest" (Luke 10:2).

Jesus knew that their praying eyes would see people differently. Their hearts would almost break at the spiritually magnified sight of wounded, wasted lives. Without a large hope of harvest, frustration over the immense need could have easily diverted them into a fervid activism.

Praying in this way, the disciples were established in hope as they lifted their attention toward the stupendous mastery of God over the affairs of the gospel. The Father's lordship is constant, governing the harvest with infinite wisdom. It is his harvest, planted from his hand and to be reaped unto him again.

Jesus taught them to prepare the way for harvest by prayer. They were not clearly commanded to sow or reap. Instead they were to intercede on-site for a huge harvest, larger than anything that they themselves could have ever brought about.

Implications for Today's Prayerwalkers

- **Envision ingathering.** Exalt God as Lord of the harvest, worthy of the fullest ingathering of life. We will pray most boldly if we keep God at the center of our prayers. Harvest means people gathered to God to live for him in the present and to live with him forever.

God said of one city what is true of every people group and most cities: "I have many people in this city" (Acts 18:10). Who has God been "growing" in your city for himself?

• **Lift the vision to God. Don't carry it.** As you pray, you will sense need so vast that the weight of it can easily crush the life and hope from you. More than a few short-term missionaries have returned home with faith flattened by their inability to reconcile the magnitude of needs with the scarcity of workers. Instead of questioning the love or faithfulness of God, boldly appeal that he would send many laborers. Press in to the fact that he is lovingly governing the harvest.

> I'm the last one to talk about perseverance in prayer. I think God gives us a special dose of enthusiasm and endurance if we're touching something that's on the Lord's heart. We were actually encouraged by our sense of burden for the city. It indicated to us that God was going to do something in his time. We kept praying over a period of years, systematically going through every subdivision of the city, trying to visit the schools, the mosques and the government offices. A day came when we were sitting up at one of the high places. We'd been praying for quite a while. We finished and looked at each other and both had the sense that the Lord said we had finished what we were to do for then. He would send others now to pray and work for that city. Sure enough, within six months I started hearing about Christians from different countries who have gone to that spiritually darkened city to pray and to launch long-range efforts.
>
> —*Rose Desman, telling of her work as an intercessory missionary in a nation hostile to the gospel. Rose and a partner spent three years in the country, primarily praying on-site, particularly in one city recognized as a stronghold of satanic worship. Rose recently sensed God's release to return permanently to that city to continue praying. Long-term, church-planting missionaries are laying plans to declare Christ in that city.*

• **Pray bigger than yourself.** Pray huge prayers, for which you are not the answer. Your vision will shrink if you pray or act as if you were the only available resource. Jesus wasn't using prayer as a ploy to assign some disciples their next job. You may be a candidate for God's sending, but keep your prayers enlarged far beyond your capabilities.

> We realized that with only two weeks we ourselves could not

meet all the needs of the city. That was not our job. God called us to pray for those whom he was sending, that they and those already present would meet the needs of the city. I think we had a real sense of what our calling was for that time.

—Lorrain Anderson, a homemaker and mother of two children from Tempe, Arizona, speaking of prayerwalking through a city in the Middle East which has been strongly Muslim for seven centuries. That two-week prayer journey strengthened the conviction of her home church that God was giving them a part to play in planting new churches in that Muslim city.

Confronting in the Opposite Spirit

Jesus mandated that they do the weakest thing imaginable: pray. To help them keep prayer as their mightiest action, he called them, for a season, to lay aside symbols of strength. "Go your ways; behold, I send you out as lambs in the midst of wolves. Carry no purse, no bag, no shoes" (Luke 10:3-4).

The seventy would face ferocious hatred. Consider the metaphor: Lambs, not even full-grown sheep, facing a pack of wolves. Was he referring to wicked people or spiritual forces? Probably both.

If this word had been a warning about the inherent dangers of spiritual war, we might have expected Jesus to stir them with pep talks about the superior spiritual firepower available to them. But Jesus said nothing at all to inspire them toward a mentality of having superior power or authority. Why a warning without a solution?

Jesus was not actually warning them about the risks ahead. Instead, Jesus trained them to step into kingdom victories with the greater potency of weakness. They were to pay careful attention — *behold* is his word — to the way Jesus had designed the encounter with the entrenched evil of sin-gripped cities. The uneven fight was Jesus' idea.

They were prohibited from blitzing cities with amassed manpower. Instead Jesus told them to "go your ways." In other words, "Split up!"

To be sure that they ventured in the meekest, weakest way they could, he gave them specific instructions about traveling without replacement supplies. They were to break the patterns of self-sufficiency for a special season. They were not to rearrange the encounter as a siege to be won by superior supply lines.

Implications for Today's Prayerwalkers

• **Keep the battle uneven.** Aspire to a mentality of divine weakness. The truth of the believer's authority can be talked about with much chest-thumping hype. But that authority is best expressed by humility in the face of arrogance, kindness in the face of hatred and blessing in the face of anger. In the drama of your daily encounters, be ready to demonstrate the power of a lamb-like posture.

> We didn't know when we booked the main plaza that the gay community usually launches a week of attention to their cause on that same day, so it really became a warfare. They didn't appreciate the fact that we had booked it first. And they were threatening to have big demonstrations, but the Lord helped us. We made sure it was communicated that we would not confront or respond in any form. A few gay protesters showed up, but because we didn't in any way take a defensive posture, there was nothing for them to speak against.
>
> —*Bob Gal, of Calgary, Canada, speaking of a citywide prayer event on Father's Day that involved many churches. Churches in the city of Calgary have continued to rally together for public prayer every year on Father's Day.*

• **Contest by contrast.** God delights to countermand enemy power with Christlike weakness. To demonstrate a spirit which is opposite to Christ's avowed enemies doesn't mean conceding supposed rights or forfeiting every open contest. You aren't called to lose, but to win in an unconventional way. As God guides you, be ready to demonstrate Christlike character in humble contrast to those hostile to the gospel. Opposite-spirit ministry is really a form of repentance, so avoid being cute or cocky; otherwise, everyone loses.

Establishing Entrance for Jesus

> Greet no one on the way. And whatever house you enter, first say, "Peace be to this house." And if a man of peace is there, your peace will rest upon him; but if not, it will return to you. And stay in that house, eating and drinking what they give you; for the laborer is worthy of his wages. Do not keep moving from house to house (Luke 10:5-7).

It might appear that the disciples were told to stride through the streets like zombies, speaking to no one. Just the opposite is true. They were to focus their friendship and prayer efforts with people of the city and not be distracted by people met en route. Jesus was pressing them to deepen their relationships by focusing them.

They were to search for people of proven worth and respect who already manifested some features of God at work in their lives. They weren't necessarily to contact the religious intelligentsia, but rather people "of peace."

Jesus told them to find men of peace by speaking blessings upon households. A blessing isn't a perfunctory politeness. It's a statement which articulates and endows homes with the promise of the gospel.

Jesus' instructions were not designed to find the most sociable contacts or locate the best host in town. Somehow the process of meeting people in their homes and speaking blessings would reveal the key persons of God's choice. A man of peace (literally a "son" of peace) was one with a special heritage who had a part to play in the ongoing work of God in the city long after the disciples had gone.

Jesus preferred to touch an entire city from one home. We can see this from the very start of Jesus' ministry with Peter's home in Capernaum (Mark 1:29-33). And perhaps again in that same city (if Matt. 4:13 reflects a permanent move to Capernaum) amidst another social strata, Jesus repeated the same pattern by blessing and befriending Matthew, whose house seemed like home to a wide circle of friends (Matt. 9:1, 9-10). In the same way, the disciples were not to try to spread their friendship evenly by overnighting in every house. Instead, they were to concentrate God's work in particular homes to leave an enduring entrance for the gospel into entire social networks.

Implications for Today's Prayerwalkers

• **Prayerwalking opens the way for church planting.** Many contemporary church planters begin their efforts with people respected by their community, often using the terminology *men of peace*. The homes of such people usually draw friends like magnets. Their households become places of easy interaction with people throughout town because of the history of help they have given to their social network.

People who have blessed or helped their communities seem to attract the blessing of God, much like Lydia or Cornelius (both of them hosted the embryonic church in their homes; see Acts 10 and 16:13-40). As you pray blessings of peace upon families, be alert to how God may establish certain households as lighthouses to their town.

• **Bless first.** Prayerwalkers are beginning to find creative ways to prayerfully announce God's intended peace. For example, some intercessors have directly approached civic leaders, asking how they might pray; then they speak words of blessing as they pray with them.

Receptivity flows from blessing, but don't force it like a formula. Blessing is perhaps the most powerful form of affirmation. Don't be surprised if you find people open or even attracted to you as you exercise the art of blessing.

While traveling with my family, I had the distinct impression that I was to turn off the freeway and visit Savannah, a city completely new to me. It's a long way to Richmond, and I really didn't want to go. We were there for about an hour. We drove around historic sights and gained some appreciation of the pains and pleasures of this beautiful place. Finally the family gathered over the river, and we began to pray. I felt that I was to pray a prayer of blessing. I spoke out all kinds of specific things about the redemptive purpose for the city. Then I felt ridiculous: a little family from California standing in a parking lot proclaiming such bold things? Maybe I imagined the whole thing. I don't care. I'd rather be childlike and risk embarrassment than miss God.

—John Dawson gives leadership to the urban ministries of Youth With A Mission. John prays regularly through the streets of his neighborhood in Los Angeles.

Pray, Then Proclaim

And heal those in it [the city] who are sick, and say to them, "The kingdom of God has come near to you" (Luke 10:9).

Their prayer was not only to be focused on the fine, reputable people of town. They were to touch the sick, the poor, the disabled, the outcast and the troubled. We know they touched some difficult cases because of their report that "even the demons are subject to us in Your name" (Luke 10:17). Apparently they dealt with the demonized by praying in the name of Jesus.

They were to address their testimony to the very ones for whom they prayed. But their proclamation was to come after they prayed. Their word was more of an explanation than a declaration. Few statements in Scripture are as dense with meaning as the announcement "The kingdom of God has come near to you" (Luke 10:9). But the last two words tilted the emphasis of their message toward being a personalized prophetic statement — that God's mighty purposes have touched you, and that there is more goodness to come, specifically "to you."

Implications for Today's Prayerwalkers

• **With "answered prayer preceding."** While God often authenticates his message "with signs following" (Mark 16:20, KJV), we need to recognize the pattern of answered prayer preceding testimony of the gospel. God delights in answering prayer on behalf of those who have yet to even hear the gospel. Perhaps we should try the sequence that was clear for the seventy: first pray, then proclaim. Truth is eagerly believed when taught after answered prayer. Jesus healed and evangelized people more than once in this way (the demonized man in Luke 8:35 and the blind man in John 9:35-41).

Although answered prayer becomes an inarguable apologetic, the community often fails to respond to the unbeatable evidence of God's kingdom. Jesus told the seventy about whole cities which saw miracles done by Jesus himself and still did not repent (Luke 10:13). In the cases of the demoniac and the blind man, Jesus was rejected by the whole community though he was sought out by the individual who was healed. Even when opposed, Jesus was still faithful to proclaim the Word of God.

> A man named Ralph Bethea was a Southern Baptist missionary to Mombasa, Kenya. He felt called to the Muslims in that city. He tried every evangelistic technique that he learned in seminary to win Muslims in Mombasa — but he didn't win anybody. So he said he'd better start trying some things that he'd never tried before. He started brainstorming in his own mind and among his friends, and he decided that he had to attract attention somehow. So he got on a bridge over a river and advertised that if any Muslim would allow him to tell them about Jesus Christ, he would jump off the bridge. After jumping off the bridge a few times and still seeing no Muslims come to Christ, he began looking to the Lord.
>
> God said to him, "I want you and your team to pray for three months." They organized into a team, and they had enough people so that they went into prayer twenty-four hours a day for three months. They obeyed the Lord. Part of their prayer was to go out into the community and bless people. They went down the streets of Mombasa — not to evangelize or pass out tracts or jump off bridges — but to bless the Muslims in the name of Jesus. They got the reputation of being people who had a heart for the Muslims and who blessed them in the name of Jesus. One day Ralph got a telephone call from the main leader of a mosque. He was about eighty years old, and he said, "I'd like to know if you'd come to our mosque and bless our people in the name of Jesus."
>
> *— C. Peter Wagner, of the School of World Mission, Fuller Theological Seminary in Pasadena, California, recounting the story of Ralph Bethea at a conference on spiritual warfare*

We didn't have freedom to go and speak or preach at that time, just to pray. We were led of the Spirit to go to places like a businessman's house or to hospitals, sometimes as specific as the third story and bed number 3G. We were amazed how the Holy Spirit supernaturally led us to people whose hearts were tender to the Lord. We had no idea who they were. But we would come and tell them we were there in the name of Jesus to bless them and that we would like to pray for them. We prayed for thousands of people over the last seven years, but I can't remember once when anyone refused for us to bless them in the name of Jesus. They sometimes refused to allow us to share the gospel or to pray in Jesus' name for their salvation. But never to simply receive a blessing of Jesus.

—Ralph Bethea, now residing in Oklahoma, turned over the work in Mombasa to national leaders in 1991.

• **Pray for people's needs as they understand them.** Open the prayer agenda beyond physical healing, though you should avoid honoring mere wish lists. Your purpose is to deal with matters in which something has been wounded, lost, violated or perverted.

If you present yourself as one who is willing to pray instead of one who merely wants to preach, you will find people coming your way with all sorts of serious life predicaments. Serve people without trying to solve their problems for them. Sincere prayer might open ways for you to offer practical help. But never restrict your intercession to those for whom you feel you can afford the time or money to help.

This kind of prayer is not restricted to the few who are specially gifted. You can begin even if you do not have a proven track record. Furthermore, heaven's attention is much more fixed on the little faith of the "pre-believers" than on your praying. Jesus made a point to clarify that what mattered was the faith of the person God was healing, rather than the power of the person praying for a miracle, even when the pray-er was himself (Matt. 9:22; Luke 17:19, 18:42).

The message is not that you have come to town, but that the kingdom of God is near. Jesus is coming, desiring to bring a visitation of God's kingdom — a piece of heaven lived out on the earth.

This Muslim leader had asked us to come and pray for his people in the mosque because he had heard there was such power in the name of Jesus. I told him, "Sir, do you know that I'm a Baptist missionary?" He said, "I don't care what's wrong with you. I just want to know if you will come in the mosque. I don't want you testifying or preaching or spreading any of that heresy in my mosque. I just want you to come in to pray in the name of

Jesus for the blessing of Jesus upon our people. We have heard there is such power in his name." I was amazed that the Holy Spirit would open up such an invitation.

We went and began to pray for various people gathered there for various things. The men were all sitting in their place. The women and children were all up in the balcony with their black robes. There was such an expectation there — you could sense it. My inner prayer was, "Lord, this would be a great time for you to do some miracle to show them that you are alive."

I'll never forget when a man in the back stood up, a very distinguished-looking man, in his long white robe. He left the main area and returned through the door with a black bundle in his arms. The bundle was a little girl. He brought her down to the front of the mosque, and in doing so was breaking the very strict rules of conduct in a mosque. Females aren't permitted there. But in respect for him, nobody stopped him. He told me, "This is my eight-year-old girl. Will you pray for her?"

She was a gorgeous little girl, with big brown eyes. He pulled back the covers from her legs. They were just withered limbs. "My little eight-year-old girl has never walked. We have heard there is such power in the name of Jesus."

I felt the leadership of the Holy Spirit to pray for her healing. I said, "I'll pray for her healing, but it has nothing to do with power that I have or any power, just the Lord Jesus himself. He loves you and he wants you to know his love. Whether he will heal your daughter's legs today or not, I don't know. That's up to his healing power. But I will pray for that because I know he wants his love to be shown to you and that he is the God of miracles and he is alive."

He said, "I have heard about you Christians believing that he rose from the dead; we don't believe that and teach that to our children. But will you pray for her?"

And I did. There was such an incredible air of expectation there in the mosque. People stood to their feet as we prayed, and, boy, my heart was just going. "Lord, if there was ever a time for even a small miracle, now would be the time." I remember being so disappointed when nothing happened. I remember even taking the little girl's legs and trying to pull them out, to move them some. The little girl hollered and screamed, and both the man and I were embarrassed. He was very disappointed. He thanked me in polite Muslim fashion, and he turned and started walking off.

The little girl was looking back over her daddy's arms. It just broke my heart. I remember my heart being burdened and yearning for her. If somehow she could have that chance to clearly hear the gospel. "Lord, surely you can break through in this situation."

The man turned and came back up, and he said simply, "I would like you to pray that the blessing of Jesus would be on me and my family." I was amazed because what had just happened seemed to confirm what they had said for years — that there is no real power in Jesus' name. But here he was turning around saying, "We want to know him and his blessing on us." We prayed for the blessing of Jesus on his family. He again thanked me and turned and walked down the aisle.

I watched them, weeping for them there at the front. As he walked back, all of a sudden this little girl shoved her daddy back. And she shoved him again. People started looking around, and she kept pushing him back. The long black robes hung down over the carpet, and she kept pushing him back and pushing him back until he had to lower her down. All of a sudden his eyes got as big as saucers. He felt the weight of that little girl taken off his arms. It was incredible to see as they realized this little girl was standing there on her own power, [though she] never stood before in her life. They all knew her. Somebody stood up and said, "Jesus is God! Praise be the name of Jesus! Jesus is alive!"

The man lost control. God brought a movement, people falling on their knees and calling out to the Lord. The love and power of God reverberated all across that Shiite Muslim mosque. Some of the Muslim leaders got real agitated and ushered me out. "Thank you for coming, but please leave." This old Muslim who walked me out to the car was awed by the glory and power of God. He said, "I've never seen the power of God like that before." I started telling him, "Neither have I."

—Ralph Bethea, from rural Oklahoma, now works with several interdenominational mission groups. At the time of this story he served with the Southern Baptist Foreign Mission Board.

Preparing the Welcome

Whatever city you enter, and they receive you, eat what is set before you; and heal those in it who are sick, and say to them, "The kingdom of God has come near to you."

But whatever city you enter and they do not receive you, go

> out into its streets and say, "Even the dust of your city which clings to our feet, we wipe off in protest against you; yet be sure of this, that the kingdom of God has come near."
>
> The one who listens to you listens to Me, and the one who rejects you rejects Me (Luke 10:8-11,16).

In Jesus' day someone was received by being offered some sort of special meal. Greater or lesser parties could be thrown to display the measure of honor extended to a visitor. Jesus commands them never to be offended by a meager reception. Any kind of greeting — even a cup of water from just one person — signals a worthy acceptance (Matt. 10:42).

We have already seen Jesus show his willingness to be received by Zaccheus in the city of Jericho. Jesus recognized the mixture of rejection and acceptance in the city — rejection on the part of the religious elite and eager openness among the "sinners." He routinely sought out the receptive and was not troubled at offending the high-minded by celebrating with circles of people considered sinful (Luke 19:1-10).

Jesus came to cities by invitation rather than by invasion. He did not give the seventy a fail-safe plan to conquer cities. In fact, he prepared them for possible rejection.

The public act of shaking the dust off their feet was to be done with all the grief that Jesus displayed in telling of the cities who had rejected him (Luke 10:12-15). It was a testimony against them which would have bearing on what Jesus referred to as "that day" or "the judgment" (Luke 10:12,14). Though this negative testimony would last forever, it did not have to be the only testimony of that city. God in his sovereignty could choose to allow more testifiers of his grace to visit the city.

The gesture was not a curse or a retaliating insult. It was a sober act to be done with mourning, documenting the incriminating truth that the kingdom had come near but was refused. Though they were prepared for rejection, few, if any, were rejected. In fact, they came back rejoicing.

Implications for Today's Prayerwalkers

• **Pray for a citywide welcome.** Ask God to turn so many to himself that the entire city becomes marked by the message of the kingdom of God.

Lift your prayers beyond the salvation of a few. In opening his famous conversation at a Samaritan well, Jesus was not aiming to lead one Samaritan woman to faith. He orchestrated an invitation into her city. Many believed initially at "the word of the woman." A citywide movement began, welcoming him to stay for days. As a result of this visit "many more believed because of His word" (John 4:39-42).

• **Be quick to eat and slow to shake your feet.** When Jesus said to "eat what is set before you," he meant something other than not quibbling about the menu. He meant that you should be willing to serve cities even though you may not be honored as a great messenger of God.

Your identity before God has nothing to do with the response you may get from people. You may only get a cup of water, but you are still one of Jesus' "little ones" (Matt. 10:42). Neither is your identity demonstrated by power over demons. Rather your name is forever inscribed in heaven (Luke 10:20). Because of your security in God, you can deal with citywide rejection in a sorrowful way. The foot-shaking gesture may falsely communicate an insult instead of a solemn testimony. Ask God to give you the best farewell prayer. Jesus broke down and wept during his farewell prayer over Jerusalem (Luke 19:41).

Joy in the Return

Jesus had made specific arrangements for a time and a place to regather and to report what had taken place during the disciples' ventures. Instead of returning under the weight of unrepentant cities, they came back with joy. There were three kinds of joy during that debriefing.

First, they tasted the joy of surprise. "The seventy returned with joy, saying, 'Lord, even the demons are subject to us in Your name' " (Luke 10:17). They were happily amazed to find their prayers answered.

Second, Jesus opened their eyes to a deeper joy, the joy of their identity in God. "Rejoice that your names are recorded in heaven," Jesus said (Luke 10:20). They were naturally exuberant about experiencing the supernatural power of God, but Jesus pointed to a greater joy of being honored by name before God.

Third, Jesus gave them a taste of the joy of God over their testimony.

> At that very time, He rejoiced greatly in the Holy Spirit and said, "I praise You, O Father, Lord of heaven and earth, that You have hidden these things from the wise and intelligent and have revealed them to babes. Yes, Father, for thus it was well-pleasing in Your sight" (Luke 10:21, NAS revised).

Something about that very hour thrilled Jesus in the greatest recorded outburst of joy of all his earthly days. Jesus knew that what had been stored up in the heart of God, hidden for generations, was now at last coming to pass. God was making himself known to whole cities through ordinary believers. When Jesus saw the seventy return, he knew he would eventually win a welcome in households of every people group and nation.

PART III

The Practice of Prayerwalking

7

AN INTERCESSION AGENDA

Jesus prayed so fluently and with such obvious power that his disciples pressed him to teach them to pray as he did. "And it came about that while He was praying in a certain place, after He had finished, one of His disciples said to Him, 'Lord, teach us to pray' " (Luke 11:1).

It is a familiar passage, but take note of the context. At the time the disciples asked Jesus for prayer lessons, they had already been sent out praying through whole villages and towns. They came back thrilled with what had happened. Now they sincerely wanted further training. Those who practice prayer always want to learn more. Jesus gave them a basic agenda of prayer which we have called *the Lord's prayer.*

He had taught them the same guidelines much earlier to strengthen them against the preposterous ritualism of prayer which was in vogue. At that time he had taught them to develop a life with God in secret (Matt. 6:5-15).

But at this much later time they were "traveling along," visiting different villages, staying in different homes (Luke 10:38, 13:22). They were being stretched in the process of maturing as productive coworkers with Jesus. They wanted to bear fruit as he did. The issue at this hour wasn't secrecy but direction and structure for their prayer for ministry.

Whether alone or praying with his companions, Jesus' preferred prayer closet was a mountain, sometimes with people or places in view (Mark 6:46; Luke 6:12, 22:39-41; John 18:1-2).

In Luke 11:1 it says that Jesus prayed "in a certain place." Is it far-fetched to suggest that Jesus focused his prayer upon the people or villages in view from that "certain place"? It could well be that he was practicing prayer in proximity to those for whom he prayed. Let's look at what we know as the Lord's prayer as a prayer agenda for our cities.

An Agenda for Prayer in Proximity

The top points of this prayer agenda are too long to be contained in private devotions. They are as deep and high as earth and heaven, and as wide as the cities and peoples of earth.

• **Pray for God's glory.** "Father, hallowed be Your name" (Luke 11:2, NAS revised).

Of uppermost concern is God's glory. A clear translation shows that the top item is a request, not a statement of praise. "Hallowed be Thy name" could be crisply translated, "Sanctify your name." We are to pray that God would work so that he would be honored, adored, lifted up, revealed and praised by name among the cities and peoples of earth.

This prayer for God's name aligns with the core theme of the Bible. God has worked throughout history to make himself known and worshipped by name among the nations (Gen. 12:8; Ex. 9:16; 1 Kin. 8:41-43, 10:1; Ezra 6:12; Neh. 9:9-10). The prophets and psalmists grew louder through the generations regarding God's purpose to bring explicit glory to himself by name from every people (Ps. 66:1-4, 86:9, 102:18-22; Is. 12:4, 56:6-7; Jer. 33:9; Ezek. 20:1-44; Zeph. 3:9; Mal. 1:11-14). Jesus summed up his ministry as manifesting the Father's name to his followers (John 17:6). John and Paul alike articulate the advance of God's purpose on earth as being for God's name (Rom. 1:5, 15:20; 3 John 7).

• **Pray for God's kingdom.** Next on the prayer agenda: "Your kingdom come" (Luke 11:2, NAS revised).

Of course, this cry has ultimate fulfillment at the culmination of history, but clearly we are to pray with expectancy for the coming of some measure of heaven's liberating dominion amidst the families and cities of earth. The Father in heaven is addressed, but the desired answer is to be visible on earth. Enormous outbreaks of heaven's life here are in view.

This eager cry for God's kingship stands as a dominant theme of all Scripture. God's steady desire has been to entrust the earth to a kingdom of devoted servants (Ex. 19:5-6; 2 Sam. 7:12-19; Rev. 1:6). Generations unfold with patient urgency to defeat his enemies and to establish his rightful reign as the Messiah (Ps. 2, 110, 145; Dan. 7:9-28; Matt. 12:15-29; Rev. 12:10-12).

• **Pray for reconciliation.** "Give us each day our daily bread" (Luke 11:3).

The rest of Jesus' prayer agenda continues to rise above our customary individualism. We are to call open windows of heaven's provision to provide "our" daily bread for "us."

Forgiveness cannot be experienced apart from being extended to others. Hence the line, "And forgive us our sins, for we ourselves also forgive everyone who is indebted to us" (Luke 11:4). Perhaps we unduly privatize the prayer, as if it said, "forgive me *my* sins." Jesus' instruction provides us a mandate to appeal for the forgiveness of others, at times the accumulated wrongdoing of whole families and generations. We need to stand ready to identify and forgive sin on this scale as well.

• **Pray for God to release and to lead.** "And lead us not into temptation" (Luke 11:4).

Spiritual war at its simplest is to pray that people be rescued from evil to follow God. We find this reflected in the final request, by Luke's account, that God would lead us. The term *us* can refer to a family, a church or perhaps a neighborhood or a city. It's a request that the process of testing (one way of rendering the word *temptation*) be curtailed and instead that we may find that God has rescued us from the ravaging forces of evil. ("But deliver us from evil" [Matt. 6:13].) This prayer is suitable to pray on behalf of believers as well as the pre-believers of your community.

Two Fundamentals of Prayer on the Streets

The key to effective prayer on the streets lies in the two fundamentals of praying Scripture and praying with the Spirit of God. The prayer agenda of Jesus evidences both these fundamentals: His prayer for God's glory and kingdom was centered in the mainstream of biblical promises, but the prayer is presented in condensed form. To pray authentically for God's name to be sanctified and for Christ's kingship to prevail requires dynamic help from the Spirit of God to flesh out your praying. How will God's glory shine? How will his kingdom be manifest? The Spirit of God helps us pray with specific clarity.

Pray With the Word

As you discipline your mind to follow the thoughts of Scripture, you will find your prayers gaining weight and coming to life.

• **Carry Scripture with you.** You'll find a small pocket Bible to be a valuable item to bring along. Of course, large study Bibles are cumbersome. Carry a smaller portion with you. Don't miss out on the wealth of Old Testament books because you lack an easily carried version. Instead, premeditate your prayers from books which may not be included in a small New Testament. Photocopy favorite Old Testament passages for one-day use. Many prayerwalkers write out beforehand on small cards or in notebooks passages which they feel will be useful during the walk.

> Praying from Bible memory verses keeps my mind on track. With my eyes open I'll sometimes get distracted in the midst of my prayer. Sometimes I end up praying only two or three verses. Other times I'll do a lot of verses if I'm having trouble keeping my mind on what I'm doing.
>
> —*Candy Spears, homemaker and homeschool teacher in Chandler, Arizona. She carries a "verse pack" with her when she prayerwalks her neighborhood in the mornings.*

• **Read Scripture aloud in God's hearing.** Scripture is powerful because God has breathed it and loves to bless it. He loves to hear his Word. Read it over and over again as if God were listening intently.

Some people can read fairly well while keeping a normal walking gait. A group can designate a reader for those who have trouble reading afoot. The pace of most prayerwalks allows many pauses to read the Bible together.

• **Restate the truths in your own words.** The place to begin with any passage is to recognize the glories of God's character and restate those same excellencies in your own vernacular. Try to do it in first person, directly to God's face. Paraphrasing is a skill which increases with the doing. Keep using the Bible, and you'll soon find your own best eloquence: voicing prayers with God's thoughts but in your words.

• **Base petitions and praise on select passages.** Stick with particular passages for a while. If you pray for one mile from one choice verse, you well might feel that you have delved a mile deep in biblical truth. As you discipline yourself or your prayer band to stay focused on preselected passages, you will soon grow accustomed to grounding your petitions and praises in Scripture. Soon you won't want to do it any other way. Prayer without roots in Scripture will seem feeble to you. Because the promises of God give basis for worship as well as intercession, you'll soon find yourself fluently passing from exultant praise to ardent petition.

> We prayed one week from Psalm 67. All of us agreed during the one- to two-hour prayerwalk that we would pray Psalm 67, especially the part that says, "Let the peoples praise You, O God; let all the peoples praise You" [v. 5, NKJV]. We would pray for houses that there would be Bible studies started there. We would pray for the people we'd see that God would raise up praise songs and worship from among them.
>
> —*George Parvis, a member of a short-term prayer and research team to the city of Samarkand in Central Asia*

Walk With the Spirit of God

The Spirit of Christ lovingly dwells in us always but seems to draw nearer to us when we pray. As quiet as light he probes our souls and divulges the Father's heart. He exposes the authentic cry of our hearts and thus helps us to pray.

Listen to the Spirit of God

Revere the Spirit rightly: He is a divine person rather than a disembodied force. His control is non-coercive. He does not commandeer bodies as our hands might fill gloves. We are his valued servants, not utilized as tools. He honors us by the gentleness of his leading. How sad to ever grieve him! Consciously submit to him by resolving to hear him in all that he might say.

You won't have to strain your ability to hear, but you will need to learn to listen. Sorting out spiritual or psychological signals is important but not difficult. Communication from the Spirit of God will at all times exalt Jesus and reiterate the written Word of God.

- **Practice silence.** Most accomplished prayerwalkers still consider themselves learners in the relational art of listening to the Spirit. Learn to pray with the Spirit by building disciplines of silence. Spend time walking or standing in hushed attention.
- **The Spirit gives through his gifts.** Listen to each other to hear the Spirit. Someone with a gift of discernment may describe an impression they have. Weigh their words with a receptive heart along with what others may say. Someone with a strength in teaching may offer scriptural grounds for a prayer offered by someone with a prophetic gift. No gift stands alone. God's life flows through the concerted voice of the body.

Follow the Spirit of God

Prayerwalking is simply walking with God. He comes alongside by his Spirit in order to help us pray.

- **The Spirit helps us pray together.** Use gifts wisely. Views differ on spiritual gifts, but nearly all agree that God gives spiritual gifts to build up the church. Each of the gifts that the Spirit gives can come into play while prayerwalking, yet no single gift is essential for prayerwalking. We are each uniquely equipped by the Spirit for prayer.

Those who do pray in tongues might find it suitable to do so while prayerwalking. Many consider praying in tongues indispensable during prayerwalks. As valuable as this mode of spiritual prayer may be, it is more essential that the body of Christ not be sundered, especially while putting our fellowship on display in the courts of heaven and on the streets of earth.

Paul gives instructions about practicing spiritual gifts in the presence of "unbelievers" and "ungifted" (1 Cor. 14:20-25). These guidelines may well apply to prayerwalkers since the walks usually take place before unbelievers and some walks involve many churches, resulting in a mixture of giftings. When many churches walk together, it is often God's wisdom to energize a diversity of gifts. Paul urged his readers to consider other people's impressions when speaking in tongues or prophesying. People are in charge of their giftings. This may be an appropriate time to curtail the most exuberant prayer in tongues. Christians are called to walk the higher way of love, building up the body toward peace rather than confusion.

Steward every gift, not just tongues, in wisdom. By using language everyone can understand we can aspire to exercise together the higher gift of prophecy in prayer (1 Cor. 14:39). And what faith-filled prayer is not in some way a prophetic statement if it expresses God's mind and heart?

• **The Spirit helps us to pray physically.** God's Spirit may prompt you with ideas about gestures with prophetic significance. Though you may at first feel self-conscious, it is always best to be obedient.

On the other hand, do not attempt to repeat a prophetic act that you or someone else may have done in the past. Some of God's finest children have obediently done some outlandish things which have been greatly honored by God. However, God may never want that faith-gesture to be repeated. The key is to seek fresh guidance from the Spirit.

While we were praying across Germany recently, our whole group paused at an overlook point over the city of Potsdam. As Graham Kendrick led in singing, I lifted my hand to bless the city. As I prayed for the German people to fulfill their destiny as a servant nation, I sensed God stirring me to turn my palm upward, with a lifting gesture. After doing this obediently for a few times, I realized that I was turning upside down the notorious "*heil* Hitler" salute. I felt my praying was reinforced because I was able to act out symbolically the answer to a specific prayer for exalted humility.

There seem to be at least two orders of prophetic symbol in prayer. First, there are the *basic prayer postures and gestures* found in Scripture, such as standing (Deut. 10:8; 2 Chron. 20:5,13, 29:11), lifting hands to heaven (Ps. 28:2, 63:4, 134:2; 1 Tim. 2:8), lifting eyes to heaven (John 11:41, 17:1), bowing (2 Chron. 20:18; Acts 20:36, 21:5) and, we would suggest, walking.

As you become comfortable with some of the standard physical dimensions of prayer, you will find yourself at ease with the other order of prophetic symbol, the *special prayer actions* that God prompts from time to time. God may use these prophetic symbols more than we may ever know. Even if they make little sense to us, obedience to the Spirit is what is required. A little bit of faith goes a long way when reinforced with the total concentration of spirit, mind and body.

• **The Spirit helps us pray intelligently.** Prayerwalkers often fortify their praying with researched information, but not every data point should be prayed. The difficulty in using researched insights lies in the sheer volume and diversity of facts that can be learned. Information does not equal agenda. Look to the Spirit of God to help sort out what needs to be emphasized in prayer. Bona fide intercession is always uneven. We do not otherwise need to pray uniformly through entire databases.

> I had that same week been reading a book on the history of London. I noted how greed often seemed to be a feature of the history of London. I shared this with the group, and we took it back to prayer. Prompted by this, I began to do some more systematic research. The whole project was a mixture of prayer and study.
>
> —*Peter Adams, from his book* Preparing for Battle: A Biblical Strategy for Spiritual Warfare *(Kingsway Publications, 1987). In the book Peter describes how he did research for intercession and prayerwalking in London sponsored by Youth With A Mission. He used reference and history books, newspaper clippings and memories of older residents of London. Eventually Peter's research helped inform citywide prayer efforts, which God used to break the spirit of unrighteous trade.*

> We need to re-pray the old prayers. We need to find out what God got men and women praying for and pray along with them. If they took the time to write them down, they probably had a sense that they were being heard for what they asked. Daniel prayed Jeremiah's words generations after him. Jonathan Edwards prayed that all of New England would become a powerhouse for the end-time revival.
>
> —*Mark Pritchard, a leader with the Boston Prayer Foundation which has introduced themes from some of the prayers of Jonathan Edwards at citywide prayer rallies in Boston.*

Widen the scope of information. Many prayerwalkers have emphasized historical research, targeting specific sites of past incidents. Open your research efforts to include sociological trends, demographic data or even a current newspaper.

Our investigation of the social structure helped us pray with a sure-footed compassion through the streets. We came to know which homes were Chinese and which were probably Thai. We knew that the sweatshop laborers in some of the dark one-room factories were from rural villages in the Northeast. We knew that many of the prostitutes put on display throughout Bangkok were from those same villages. It hurt to know that many had been virtually sold by their parents into this. A five-minute conversation could confirm our hunches and fuel prayer for half an hour. That kind of firsthand acquaintance with the community helped us pray with real urgent sorrow and hope.

—*Steve Chism, speaking of a prayer effort in Bangkok, Thailand*

8

Ways to Walk Together

God never intends prayer to be boring. Much of the fun of prayerwalking is discovering the thousands of ways to intercede for the same city with new prayers and new friends. You will enhance your growth as an intercessor by praying with others, observing and sampling the ways of your praying companions. As you gain experience in prayer, innovate and share useful approaches with others. The rest of the book is made up of proven ideas gleaned from many prayerwalkers.

Ways to Walk in Prayer Teams

The greatest joys and toughest challenges of prayerwalking are found in walking together in teams of every kind.

Team Idea #1: Prayerwalking Alone

Christians have long practiced solitary devotional walks to meditate and pray. Perhaps these private walks with God could be termed *Enoch walks*, after the biblical character Enoch, who "walked with God; and he was not, for God took him" (Gen. 5:22). As much as we encourage personal devotional prayer while walking, we think it's helpful to differentiate walks alone with God from walks which bring us interceding through our communities. It may appear to be an artificial distinction, but prayerwalking is a special challenge of intercession.

We encourage prayerwalking with at least one partner for two reasons. The main reason is that praying in groups is so much more powerful. God loves to hear concerted prayer (Matt. 18:20).

A second benefit of prayerwalking with friends is the increased freedom from distracting concerns for personal security than when going solo. There can be hazards, both spiritual and physical, in certain troubled neighborhoods and spiritual hot spots. Without the presence and combined wisdom of friends, such threats can divert attention from praying.

Although a word of caution is in order, we do not want to suggest a ban on unaccompanied prayerwalking. The Holy Spirit inspires a great deal of impromptu prayerwalking at times when comrades cannot be found. If you do prayerwalk alone, here are some points to consider.

• **Pray aloud.** When you are praying alone, you will find that your spoken prayers tend to be hushed or even fade into silence. Obedience in prayer sometimes requires silence, but pray out loud if at all possible. Your mind is the battlefront any time you pray. Without friends listening and agreeing, most people find it harder to keep their minds concentrated on prayer. Use your vocal cords to keep focused.

A single person praying audibly in public can appear odd to passersby not accustomed to on-site prayer. A word of explanation will generally earn deferential respect from onlookers. Be more concerned about what God thinks than anyone else.

> This huge man came up to me and asked me what I was doing. I told him I was praying over this landfill and that we were going to plant a church right here. He looked at me for a while and said, "If you will pray for a landfill, will you pray for me?"
>
> —*Erwin McManus, about the initial stage of starting a new church in south Dallas, Texas. He is now planting more churches in connection with The Church on Brady in Los Angeles.*

> I like to lay hands on the school buildings, praying for all the students while they're all in one place, that God would touch them and bring salvation to our high schools. One day I was leaning on the building praying for the school and the coach drove up for the pep rally and smiled at me. We didn't say anything, but he was aware of what I was doing. I just think it's a physical witness to the officials of the high school.
>
> —*Terry Teykl, pastor of Aldersgate United Methodist Church in College Station, Texas. Terry prays around high schools almost every day while jogging. His "prayer jogging" is purposeful intercession. Before setting out, he asks God to help him choose which school or region to cover in prayer.*

• **Re-walk routes.** Your solo prayerwalk may just be an opening round. Bring some friends back to re-pray the routes you have done solo. You will be able to recapitulate some of the same prayers with added faith.

• **Avoid engaging evil powers alone.** If you must prayerwalk alone, do it wisely with respect to spiritual forces. Some praying is openly antagonistic to evil powers. Other modes of prayer are exploratory, as were Paul's long, prayerful walks through the city of Athens. "Now while Paul was waiting for them at Athens, his spirit was being provoked within him as he was beholding the city full of idols" (Acts 17:16).

Paul was no stranger to confronting evil powers while walking the streets. He had recently come from Philippi, where he had prayed to free a woman from demonic oppression. That act lit a fuse which ignited a spiritual bomb that literally shook the entire spiritual, economic and military power structures of the city. Throughout that conflict Paul was accompanied by supporting friends (Acts 16:12-40).

But in Athens he was alone. Instead of provoking evil spirits, Paul allowed *his* spirit to be provoked. He observed the avalanche of idolatry engulfing the entire city. God used the anguish of Paul's insight to frame one of the most important messages of his life (Acts 17:16-34, especially v. 23).

> Most of our prayer is positive: "Save these people. Bring these folks to repentance. Give these ones a chance to be discipled." But there is a place for binding demonic powers so that you can get on with the job. If we ever pray specifically against demons, we make sure we have mature Christians in small groups. I know I would not have lasted by myself. They throw too many things at you.
>
> —*Tim Davis, program director of South Hills Community Church in Highlands Ranch, Colorado. Tim leads the spiritual warfare team of the church, which uses prayerwalking as one part of its outreach plan.*

Team Idea #2: Prayerwalking as Families

Prayerwalking is a big help for the challenge of praying as a family. Family prayerwalking takes a literal step toward involving kids in advancing the kingdom of God.

• **Choose routes with kids in mind.** Involve your children in planning short and varied routes. Driving or taking public transportation affords endless options for quickly walked routes. Strollers and wagons help little ones tag along on more extensive walks.

• **Talk about it.** Advance briefings will help kids understand the importance of prayer and help them enjoy the experience. Discussing prayer topics before you go can help kids verbalize their own prayers without rotely repeating the promptings of parents. Simple liturgies can be devised with readings shared by all. You might rehearse them ahead of time. Let the kids know they can suggest that prayers or blessings be spoken for whatever or whomever they might see along the way. At the close of a prayerwalk, affirm everyone for work well done for God's kingdom.

• **Pray and play.** Your children will not keep lockstep with you for every prayer that is offered, but they can be expected to participate fully for shorter portions. Keep the time very brief that the children are expected to give full attention to praying. During these moments, make it clear that the activity is prayer. Expect to mix fun with intercession. Become adept at widening conversational prayer to include necessary fun tangents.

• **Pray for kids' concerns.** What bothers or thrills them? Children experience incredible pain and exhilaration in matters that can appear petty to adults. Pray for what troubles them. Is it possible to take a short prayerwalk near homes of friends or those they consider to be enemies? After-hours you can prayerwalk their school grounds with them. There are so many ways to incorporate their interests into prayer. If fire trucks excite a young boy, prayerwalk past the fire station, praying for God's protection upon the neighborhood to be added to the services firemen provide.

Listen to what requests they come up with during family prayer times. When possible, use a prayerwalk to take kids closer to what they already pray for. Or you can lead them in prayer adventures by exposing them to people and neighborhoods much different from their own.

• **Vary the participants and places.** Freshness can come by welcoming extended family members or friends to join the family. At other times you may want to decrease the number of people participating to just mom and dad. The praying example of parents or grandparents can make a lasting impression. The value is not only in seeing God answer prayer, but also in the children observing the most important people in their lives in the act of prayer.

> It was a good testimony for my children because they wondered why we did that. The kids thought I was crazy when we prayed around the place. My husband opened the paper one morning and told us that Happy Church bought Beaumonde. Our kids were amazed. I said, "You didn't believe that God was faithful? We serve the God of miracles." It sure strengthened the faith of our children.
>
> —*Nikki Rossi, mother of two from Englewood, Colorado. In*

1986 the Rossis marched with their bewildered children seven times around Beaumonde, a shopping center that was struggling financially, though it had a prime location. It was an impromptu prayer that God would use the shopping center for his own purposes. A year later, to the surprise of all, their own church was able to buy the property at a low price.

Team Idea #3: Prayerwalking With Small Groups

Prayerwalkers tend to bunch up into small groups as they go along, usually two or three people side by side. There is no official terminology, but we are using the term *prayer team* in this book to refer to the unit of people who pray together.

- **Form prayer teams.** Prayer teams will materialize spontaneously, but there can be good reasons to arrange them deliberately. Give thought to matters of safety. Consider what kinds of team composition and gender mix might bother local sensitivities.

The smaller the prayer team, the greater the participation of the pray-ers. A larger group tends to invite longer and louder prayers which can dampen conversational interaction. Those lacking oratorial gifts or courage sometimes drop out of voicing their prayers and straggle behind.

- **Shuffle prayer team assignments.** Shifting prayer team assignments can help bring out the best from every pray-er. Some highly organized prayerwalking efforts make a point to plan short routes that converge at set points in order to rest and to reassign prayer partners.

Grouping experienced intercessors with those just learning may have far more advantages in the long run. Prayer is reportedly contagious. If so, then let's take advantage of the mentoring opportunity that prayerwalking offers.

- **Anticipate prayer team life span.** Prayer triplets can break up the back-and-forth conversational rhythms that eventually get tedious in groups of two. Triplets are a proven size for a prayer team with a life span of weeks or months.

> Tens of thousands of prayer triplets have been formed in our country alone, praying for specific friends who have yet to believe in Christ. Triplets as a prayer strategy was launched in this country as a "prayer-closet" activity with friends. Only now are we saying to the prayer triplets, "Get out and walk around the neighborhood. Pray on the streets of people for whom you are praying on a regular basis." We've found that prayer triplets have a working lifespan of twelve to eighteen months.
>
> —*Brian Mills, author of* Three Times Three Equals Twelve:

God's Strategy for Church Growth Through Prayer Triplets *(Kingsway Publications, 1986). Brian helps encourage prayer efforts in conjunction with the Evangelical Alliance of Britain.*

Team Idea #4: Prayerwalking in Larger Groups

Larger groups of seven to twenty-four can prove to be the ideal format in certain situations. For example, prayer rallies have been formed by large prayerwalking groups converging from several different outlying areas. Church buildings have been emptied onto the street for a quick, one-time sweep of the surrounding area. When walking with a large group, we have found the following guidelines to be helpful.

• **Plan routes well.** Think through how best to negotiate traffic and streetlights. At what points and how long will you stop along the way? Walk the route ahead of time with an eye on the clock to gauge how much time will be needed.

Consider asking the larger group to form smaller prayer teams for the longest stretches of the walk so that everyone can file along together without cumbersome clumping. You might try launching small prayer teams at one- or two-minute intervals to walk a set course.

• **Work within restrictions.** In some cities laws may require advance permission to walk if the group exceeds a certain size — however informal the group may be. In other places regulation pressure begins when public address systems are used. Consider other areas needing diligent, creative administrative attention, such as liabilities and interaction with the media.

> We found it was very important to find the bylaws that govern an event like that. For example, we had to have a liability insurance policy in place. And we found the easiest way to obtain it was to put it as a rider on an existing policy. We would ask if a church would be willing to do that, and then we would pay the premium for it.
>
> *—Bob Gal, a pastor in Calgary, Canada, speaking of preparations for a citywide prayerwalk*

• **Preparing the way.** It may be beneficial to ask some of your experienced prayerwalkers to precede the larger group by covering the route earlier on the same day. Consider the value of priestly feet first touching the water, opening a way for others to follow (as in the crossing of the Jordan River, Josh. 3:14-17).

• **Use liturgy and music.** Sometimes the dynamics of larger groups give rise to more overt expressions of prayer and praise. Enjoy public worship — whether spontaneous or well-planned. Printed programs are not much trouble to create. They can free leaders to select from a range of songs on the spur of the moment. In addition, printed programs can offer a way of praying in the power of unison, infusing prayer on the streets with the strength of our liturgical heritage.

If singing is intended, remember that it requires a higher level of organization. Choose appropriate music. Make sure that words to songs are well-known or make printed programs available. For accompaniment, most worshipping prayerwalks use something simple, such as a guitar. The competent use of horn instruments such as the trumpet or trombone can add an exciting sense of occasion and draws attention, if that is what seems desirable. Street acoustics severely limit the value of hand-carried tape players. Test them for yourself before launching a prayerwalk which depends on them.

There is obviously an overlap between a simple prayerwalk emphasizing worship and a full-blown praise march. Try to decide ahead of time which level you are aiming for, and prepare appropriately.

Prayerwalking on Special Occasions

Special Occasion Idea #1: Evangelistic Events

On-site prayer has long been a part of preparing for an evangelistic rally. Intercessors have often prayed around and through the place of assembly before meetings. There is an even longer history of special intercession on-site during the evangelistic meeting itself.

> Once we had [Christian apologist] Josh McDowell come and speak. We had been praying fervently for that time. Normally he speaks only three times on a campus. The third meeting was so crowded that we had to have two talks that night, which was very unusual for him. The campus had a total of about thirty-two thousand students, and we estimated a total of about twelve thousand came those three nights.
>
> —*Sherman Brand, speaking of the fruitful climate for drawing people to Christ at Penn State University in the late seventies, a period in which some found it difficult to find friends at Penn State who hadn't recently heard the gospel. Prayer was recognized as preparing the way for evangelism of every sort. Students gathered regularly for extended prayer, often walking across the campus two-by-two to blanket it in prayer. Sherman was campus director at Penn State for Campus Crusade for Christ at the time.*

Prayerwalkers are now more vigorously ranging throughout a city before evangelism events, directing their prayers upon the homes and workplaces of people in addition to the site of an evangelistic event. The subject of their prayers stretches beyond high attendance at the meetings and emphasizes the emergence of new discipleship groups and church plantings.

Special Occasion Idea #2: Protests and Demonstrations

Christians in some parts of the world have been emboldened to make known their convictions in the public square. While it is good to see such demonstrations for worthy causes increasingly attended by prayer, mixing prayer and protest must be done carefully.

> A girl got off the bus at the abortion clinic. She was very abusive to the sidewalk counselor who was trying to speak to her — swearing and cursing at her. The girl went in through the door. The sidewalk counselors all got together and prayed then and there for this girl who had gone in. Just a few minutes later she came out in tears. She said, "Will you really help me? Do you really have something you can do for me?" They took her to another place and offered her help, and they continued working with her all the way through her pregnancy and continued with her for years, helping her in different instances.
>
> —*Barbara Malek, codirector of the Crisis Pregnancy Center in Omaha, Nebraska. She encourages Christians to pray quietly while displaying small signs across from abortion clinics. Under her direction, most of the group prays continually while a sidewalk counselor approaches women entering the clinic to offer help in pursuing alternatives to abortion.*

- **Pray before and after public prayer.** Public prayers lay bare the soul of the church. Our life before God becomes evident. If our intercession on important matters is only done while on platforms before people, our prayers will be understandably feeble. Low-profile prayerwalking, along with every other kind of concerted prayer, is fitting before, during and after demonstrations.
- **Retain a jealousy for prayer.** Christians have sometimes sought to present their protest about complicated issues by asserting a right to pray about the issue in a public way. Be cautious about asserting rights to pray publicly as a ploy to pursue ulterior concerns or publicity. A helpful guideline may be to avoid initiating public prayer to provoke a test case on any issue, especially if the situation is loaded with other matters. The biblical example of Daniel suggests that we should quietly continue our habits of prayer. Public prayer became an issue for Daniel,

but others had provoked the controversy surrounding his ongoing disciplines. If open prayer itself becomes an issue, let it be because God's enemies initiate the complaint (Dan. 6, especially v. 10).

Special Occasion Idea #3: Special Festival Days

Under the guidance of the Holy Spirit, prayerwalks may have a special significance on religious holidays, anniversaries and national or civil festivals of every sort. Some traditions such as Christmas caroling seem ready-made for adaptation by creative prayerwalkers. If parades are planned by the community, the routes can be walked beforehand and following. Worshipping prayerwalkers have sometimes registered as official entries into public parades. Prayer rallies have brought a fitting Christian presence at the seats of government on days of dedication or commemoration.

> Let God's holy fire cleanse this nation, this very land on which this great new building stands, so that those who work in it may gather in righteousness and justice.
>
> *—Prayer by Joyce Jukes at the opening of a new Parliament House of Australia in 1988. When it was learned that official prayers at the opening ceremonies had been disallowed, Christian leaders organized what became the largest prayer meeting in the country's history. Fifty thousand Christians attended the prayer, forming a 3.5 kilometer circle around the new building. Joyce, a leader of a Catholic church in Canberra that ministers to aborigines, was one of hundreds of ministers who attended the event.*

> Let me share with you something you may not have known. Some sixty-five thousand Australians are also represented here tonight because they have taken the time to write out prayers that you would pray out on their behalf tonight. They couldn't be here, but they wanted to send their prayers and concerns and have them represented here.
>
> *—Tom Hallis, national director of Youth With A Mission in Australia, addressing the thousands who gathered to pray at the opening of the new Parliament buildings. Tom was in charge of organizing the on-site prayer event. Special teams traveled to nearly every city of Australia, inviting people to attend the event or to compose written prayers to be sent on to Canberra. Many of the thousands who did come prayed aloud through each prayer request, a task that took twenty-four hours.*

9

A Menu of Methods

Our cities are afflicted in complex ways. We dare not try to shrink our problems by reducing their cause to a single site or sin. God is not granting sudden solutions regardless of how close we get to the scene of our woes. But he is giving us prayers to pray. Part of God's slow work of healing is to bring our praying presence on-location to places of significance.

Prayer at Special Places

Sometimes you don't have to go very far to go a long way toward transforming a city. Here is a list of ten of the most prayerworthy places. Some of the most significant are usually considered quite commonplace. Others call for special wisdom.

Place for Prayer #1: Workplaces

God often inspires Christians to prayerwalk through their place of employment. For many the best time for job-site prayer is after hours.

> Usually when I walk around down here I'm thinking of this deal and that deal, and I'm thinking about business. It's crowded, and I'm in a hurry. Seeing the same place on a weekend with a bunch of other praying Christians moved me to see how this particular area really does need a lot of prayer.
>
> —*Guy Wickwire, vice president of Fidelity Investments in Boston, speaking of the downtown business district which he first prayerwalked with others on a Saturday morning during a citywide day of prayer. He and a dozen other Christians con-*

tinue to prayerwalk their downtown workplaces occasionally on weekends.

I had already begun to pray for every school in the Denver system, for their principals and teachers. Then I began to actually go to various schools and just walk around the sidewalk areas, praying for blessings to come forth.

—*Richard Smith, an assistant superintendent in the Denver school system*

Place for Prayer #2: Sites for Consecrated Use

God often releases to churches, missions or praying families real estate that has been diligently prayerwalked. Testimonies about property miracles abound in cases where prayer was offered around the outermost boundaries of the property.

Lynn Green called one day, excited about a property he felt God wanted to give them. "It's incredible, Loren," he told me over the phone. "A great big old English mansion...big enough to hold one hundred staff and students. It's called Holmsted Manor. I would have never picked something so big, but [we] have prayed, and we feel this is from God."

We drove to Crawley and then to Holmsted Manor, thirty-seven miles from the center of London. I wasn't prepared for the old elegance of the three-story mansion with other buildings surrounding on the thirteen acres of land. The asking price was around £60,000 [U.S. $144,000 at the time], which included £5,000 for the furnishings in the main house. The owner had divided up the original estate; three acres with a swimming pool and football field on one side of the driveway, plus three acres on the other side of the drive, were being sold separately. What was left was a guitar-shaped piece of land with the guitar's neck being a long, tree-lined driveway leading to the stately manor house and main buildings. Something inside me said, This is what I want to give you for a missionary training center for Britain.

After inspecting the main buildings, several of us decided to march around the perimeter of the property, praying for God to give it to us. We slogged through the muddy, plowed land in great excitement, praising God that he would release the money needed. (At the time, YWAM U.K. had only £200 in the bank — just enough to pay for having the place surveyed.)

As we concluded our "faith walk," rather than going back

down the tree-lined driveway to the highway, we decided also to troop around the parcels adjacent to the "neck of the guitar" — land which wasn't included in the proposal: the three acres with the football field and swimming pool, plus three acres on the other side.

After our prayer march that day, Lynn and Marti began telling other Christians in England of our plans to buy Holmsted Manor as a missions training center. Within four months, £6,000 came in — enough for the deposit. It seemed like it was going to be an...easy faith conquest. Unexpectedly, to our confusion and dismay, the Holmsted Manor property quickly sold to someone else!

We went back to the Lord and asked, "Why is this happening? We thought you said it was for us, for a missions training center." There was no answer...only the quiet assurance that he *had* spoken. Holmsted Manor was to be ours.

He confirmed this by inspiring Christian friends to give toward the purchase of Holmsted Manor, even though they knew the property had already sold. The balance of the £60,000 came in, and we carefully salted it away in a separate bank account.

Months passed, but God never let us give up. Holmsted Manor passed from the first owner to another...for three times the price we had originally offered! But, still, as months lengthened into years, it was hard to explain the delay to donors who had believed with us for Holmsted Manor and given sacrificially toward its purchase.

Finally, in the summer of 1975 — four years after we had taken our muddy prayer walk around Holmsted and the adjoining acres, word came from the owners. They would accept our original offer of £60,000!

Also, during those intervening years, the bits of land on either side of the guitar-shaped property had been added. Now for £60,000 we could get the property we originally tried to buy *plus* the three acres with the football field and swimming pool, *and* the other three acres of farm land — the parts we had included in our prayer march four years earlier.

After we moved into Holmsted Manor, we had another march — this time a march of praise with 175 YWAMers tromping over the land. We had gained so much more than a valuable property to use in the training of young missionaries. We had learned much about God's ways.

— Loren Cunningham, founder of Youth With A Mission, from his book Daring to Live on the Edge *(YWAM Publishing, 1991).*

For many, a march to claim real estate is their introduction to prayer-walking. Most prayerwalks for property use the Jericho theme and actions. There is a simple strength in the drama of Jericho, and people seem to grasp intuitively the prophetic act of walking a perimeter.

Beginning prayerwalkers can extend their walks to the surrounding area with a little encouragement. Such gentle nudges into the community will necessarily widen the scope of their prayers away from merely acquiring land from God toward the joy of blessing the community for God's glory.

> There were three loud blasts of the trumpets, immediately followed by "Hallelujah! Praise the Lord!" shouted by the hundred marchers who followed them. Farther back a second group of a hundred took up the refrain, "For he has done great and mighty things." Back and around the corner, the third group echoed, "We will praise his name for ever and ever." And the first of two interspersed choirs began to sing.
>
> It was the seventh and last of our Jericho marches. Six Sundays before we had been a band of about fifty who gathered to pray in silence as we marched the one and a half miles around the campus we were claiming for God. Today we numbered 350, including three trumpeters, two banner bearers, ten ministers, two choirs and the three praise groups of over one hundred each. Because we had to march two-by-two on the sidewalk, the group stretched for blocks, never in a straight line, as it wound its way around the campus.
>
> The six previous Sundays had been without incident. Only a few people noticed us, and in cosmopolitan Southern California, those few had not bothered to find out what was going on. When Ralph [D. Winter] first suggested that we march around the campus, there was almost no one on the staff who wanted to do it with him — it was too bizarre. "This isn't Jericho, after all. God hasn't commanded *us* to do that," they reminded him. Some were quite adamant. "Do we really want to seem like kooks? Is that the message we want to give the community?"
>
> It was true. God had not commanded us, and Ralph didn't really know why we should do it. He just felt that by this means we would announce to the world that we were claiming this campus for God and for his cause. "There is something about a public witness that is good for us as well as for the community," he said.
>
> *—Roberta Winter, telling part of the story of the beginning of the United States Center for World Mission in Pasadena, Cali-*

fornia (excerpted from her book Once More Around Jericho, *Wm. Carey Library, 1979). The campus was eventually purchased and used extensively as a place of study and strategy to complete the evangelization of every people group.*

Prayerwalks regarding real estate often call for many to be involved in a public way. Be sure that these prophetic actions are done faithfully by direct obedience to God's specific leadings. Without caution, this kind of prayerwalking can degenerate into a presumptuous device to acquire needed acreage or, worse yet, a dramatic fundraiser.

Prayer for properties does not have to be restricted to the real estate needs of churches and missions. Why not consecrate any properties for sale to God's glory?

> When places are for sale, they don't mind you walking around them and looking them over. We've done that with major properties here in the city. A "For Sale" sign means this is an opportunity for the Holy Spirit to demonstrate his perfect will. We walk around properties and say, "God, this is your property. Give the person of your choice the authority to buy this property. And, Father, we pray that you will prevent anybody else from being able to buy it."
>
> —*Ted Haggard, pastor of New Life Church in Colorado Springs, Colorado, a city which has recently become home to a large number of evangelical ministry headquarters*

Place for Prayer #3: Overlook Points

Prayerwalkers often gather at elevated sites to pray.

> As we worshipped and exalted the Lord, there was a break in the solid cloud cover, and a big rainbow formed over the Bering Sea. The worship team was pretty excited about it. We went back into the village of Uelena and found the people of the village all startled by the rare sight of a rainbow. A good majority of them had never seen one before. All of them were asking, "What is this?" This opened wide the door for them to share about God's promise never to judge the earth through flooding. It gave them wide-open opportunity to witness to the people of the love of God.
>
> —*Bob Fitts, a worship leader residing in Hawaii, telling of a Youth With A Mission team that worshipped atop a high point at the eastern edge of the former Soviet Union. Armed Soviet troops escorted the team to various lookout points throughout*

the northeastern Siberian area in late 1991, when the Soviet Union was still under Communist control.

Prayers from elevations tend to be too broad. To make these large-proportioned prayers more effective, discuss what you are beholding. Few people have a good geographical grasp of their city. Do more than identify the big buildings or sites of outstanding spiritual significance. Use a map to trace the historical development of the city and the design of its growth or decline. Explore the character of different neighborhoods and the needs of the residents.

In the mid-eighties many of us were going up regularly to Council Crest, the highest point in the city of Portland, Oregon, to pray for the whole city. Sometimes just fifteen and other times over fifty people from at least a dozen churches would gather. After worshipping for a while we would ask people to turn and face outward to the 360-degree panorama and pray with their eyes open for what they saw. We could see the financial district, an industrial area, the west hills residential neighborhoods and more. I remember one foggy morning we could hardly see anything, and we were moved to pray about the tremendous indifference and independence of people in the Northwest. Our people were in a blinding fog of apathy. Another time the river which passes through the city stimulated prayer for a river of God's life to flow through our city.

—Randy Roth, now the pastor of First Covenant Church in Oakland, California

Place for Prayer #4: Sites of Harm or Tragedy

Some prayerwalkers make a point to pray at the site of a tragic event as soon as possible after it has happened.

In 1990 some of us went to every murder site in greater Boston over the preceding six months. We wore red arm bands. We asked God to heal the land on each of those eighty-six murder sites. When we told the people on the street what we were doing, some of the people who lived in those places said, "That's right. The only thing that's going to change this city is prayer." The murder rate was cut in half the next year.

—Niel Wilder, as told to Mark Pritchard, speaking at Boston prayerwalks involving many churches during the 1990 National Day of Prayer

> The Youth With A Mission base in Los Angeles is only a mile away from the Rodney King beating location. After the riots raged, actually from the same spot, we felt we should go down to the lot and just worship. We stood there with our arms raised before God and sang the song "Let It Rain." Our prayer was that as violence had come down like rain over this city, "Now, Lord, let your love rain." We started walking all over the area, and the prayer that God gave us was that missiles of hate and violence had come from that lot and spread all over this nation, especially in Los Angeles. So we started praying that missiles of love would come from that very location as we stood there and worshipped and prayed. As we were doing that, a Hispanic man, a big guy in a small car, drove in; and he kept sticking his head out as far as he could trying to listen to what was going on. As we began our prayerwalk, two of our group approached him and led him to the Lord in about ten minutes.
>
> —*Dave Gustaveson, of the Los Angeles base of Youth With A Mission and the developer of the Global Opportunity Network helping local churches become strong mission forces.*

Place for Prayer #5: Sites Wrongly Named or Cursed

Prayerwalkers take geographical names seriously enough to pray that they be renamed. For example, some intersections or highways have been foolishly tagged with names that are virtual curses, such as Dead Man's Curve. On the other hand, take care not to add weight to the superstition by enlarging the issue beyond its merit.

There are other places which are named after false gods, criminals or Satan himself. Prayerwalkers often find fruitful prayer in seeking to rename a place for God's intended purpose.

> The original water source of Pasadena and Los Angles is a dam bearing the name of Devil's Gate. We sensed strongly that such a name literally brought a curse on the city. A 1947 *Pasadena Star-News* article said, "It's true [that] Devil's Gate is named because of the resemblance of the rocks to his Satanic Majesty." Prior to coming to Pasadena, the Lord gave me a word from the passage where Elisha poured salt into the water source of Jericho and healed the contaminated waters [2 Kin. 2:19-22]. Then it struck me with much force to go pour salt as an act of prophetic intercession into the stream at Devil's Gate, to ask forgiveness on behalf of our forefathers for naming it such, to break the curse and ask for revival to be poured out on Pasadena.

> We took our intercession team to the place and did precisely that. We asked God to release rivers of life and fruitfulness into the parched lives of thousands. At that time the drought in Southern California had been going on for five years. Thousands of Californians were praying for rain. We took courage that God was answering our prayers about the Devil's Gate Dam when, eight days later, the rains began to pour so much that the newspapers called the month "Miracle March."
>
> —*Lou Engle, speaking of an on-site prayer effort in early 1991. Lou is director of Pasadena for Christ, a ministry focused on seeking God for spiritual awakening in the greater Pasadena area.*

> *Hahamongna* — That's the name the Gabrielinos [early Pasadena Indians] gave to what now is known as Devil's Gate, the 250-acre area at the north end of the Arroyo Seco...The English-language translation is "Flowing Waters: Fruitful Valley." Nearly everyone agrees that *Hahamongna* will be a more appropriate name for this long-neglected community asset after it is restored to its natural state.
>
> —*Statement found in a civic publication "Pasadena in Focus" as reported in "Body Life," November 1992. Soon after the prayers of Pasadena Christians, but without their direct involvement, the city of Pasadena began the process of officially restoring the original name to the site while revitalizing some of the natural terrain.*

Place for Prayer #6: Sites of Past Sin

Prayerwalkers often target select sites, praying about things that happened there long ago. One could point out that they are at the right spot but too late. Why pray at places where things happened long ago?

In the same way that the sins of parents have ongoing consequences for their children and grandchildren, the cumulative sin of one generation can reverberate throughout an entire society for generations. The rampant sin of today may be yesterday's sin multiplied.

Sins committed at these sites are thought to give entrance to demonic powers. Repeated transgression may give these powers opportunity to magnify the lingering effects of sins long past. Their power bases may have remained unchallenged until this day.

> John Dawson has asked Native Americans all over the United States, "What is the greatest offense of prejudice, wounding and bitterness to the Native Americans?" Many have replied, "The

greatest offense to us is the Sand Creek Massacre." In 1864 an ordained Methodist minister organized the atrocity with the co-operation of the governor of Colorado for petty political gain. Over 150 non-hostile Indians, mostly old men, women and children, were slaughtered and defiled in perverted ways. These people had been told they were safe under the protection of the government. They were flying the American flag, believing that peace with the white man was possible.

A stronghold is a place of wounds and unresolved guilt, giving a place for the infestation of the enemy. Because of the tragedy, demonic influences and spirits were released at that place. We went there from Denver in January 1992 as a pilgrimage. We acknowledged the sins and injustices that were committed on the land through that atrocity. We humbled ourselves in repentance before God and before the Native Americans who were present. The Native Americans stood in the gap for their people and spoke forgiveness.

—Jean Steffenson, of Castle Rock, Colorado. Jean serves as president of the Native American chapter of the Reconciliation Coalition, which seeks to bring about the healing of peoples, cities and lands in Christ. Jean plans other pilgrimages to other sites of Native American tragedy, such as Wounded Knee in South Dakota and the Trail of Tears that ended in the state of Oklahoma.

- **Locate sites as a place of identification.** How can we get near the sins of our fathers? One of the best ways to touch past events which still live is to visit the sites of significant events physically and pray. Demonic powers may or may not actually reside nearby. The issue of demonic residence is much less important than our readiness to acknowledge the significance before God of what happened in our territorial past.

We had a lynching in our city square in 1906 on Easter weekend. A white woman claimed to have been raped, and an angry mob of five thousand turned their vengeance on three innocent black men. Two of the men were dragged to the tower in the square — ironically topped by the statue of the Goddess of Liberty, blindfolded, holding scales of justice — where they were hanged and their bodies burned. Not satisfied, the mob broke into the jail and grabbed a third black man, also totally innocent, who met the same fate. Within two days, thousands of blacks fled our city, leaving food on the table, thriving businesses,

> homes and property, never to return. To this day blacks only comprise 2 percent of the population of Springfield, where it had grown to approximately 25 percent at the turn of the century.
>
> Black people in Springfield speak of that evil event as if it happened yesterday. Many refuse to go to the city square, believing it to be cursed to this day. At the March for Jesus we had a public repentance for this tragedy. There were hugs and embraces afterward and a positive response from the black community. We didn't expect that one prayer would break all the hostility that has happened between black and white people in the eighty years since the tragedy. I think we need to be gradually hitting the stronghold until we really see the breakthrough God wants.
>
> —*Kurt Beerline, a sociologist at Evangel College in Springfield, Missouri, has been involved in research and prayer efforts in American and Middle Eastern cities.*

You'll uncover more sins and sites than can be wisely prayerwalked. Don't attempt to rewind the tape and entirely sanctify the soil of your city from every foul deed or spiritual force. The Spirit of God is masterful in bringing conviction for sin in a measure that can be carried, and at a fitting time for repentance. Trust God to give guidance for the timing and the urgency of ancient sins.

> The important point isn't digging through a city's history until every stone is unturned. The balance is [in] keeping the focus on the future in the present. Ask the question, Is there anything in the past which is prohibiting God's work in the present?
>
> —*Kurt Beerline also serves as director of CityWide Research, a research and consulting group which assists churches in sharpening their focus for their city.*

- **Deprive the demonic.** We can't be sure how evil powers come and go. But the healing of ancient sorrows deprives them of an easy base of operation. Exorcisms alone don't mend cities. As we repent of past sin and renounce the recurring patterns of iniquity by Christ's power, we deny Satan's intentions to hold people in bondage to their own sin. In dealing with demonic powers, Chuck Kraft, of Fuller Theological Seminary's School of World Mission, says, "To get rid of the rats, clean out the garbage."

It is not enough to snipe at demons. They have no access to human affairs except through the sins, hurts and debased worship of people.

God's solution has always been repentance that avails of his cleansing from sin by Christ's work on the cross.

Place for Prayer #7: Sites of Ongoing Sin

Treat places of sin as choice sites for repentance rather than for pompous recrimination. Carefully follow the Spirit's instructions regarding the institutions. Never fail to pray for the people involved, including those on-location and those elsewhere who may be affected by the sanctioned sin.

> We saw a sex shop near the leader's house. On our way home the next day we stood and prayed, and the word the Lord gave us was to curse the sex shop. We don't often get that [directive], but we felt God gave the word for us to do this. We weren't cursing the people. We prayed for the people, but we cursed the shop. About four weeks later a local leader sent us a copy of the newspaper. The front page showed that the sex shop had burned down. We found out soon after that the owner of the shop had even more recently become a Christian.
>
> —*Chris Leage, of Brighton, England, serves as the coordinator of Lydia Fellowship in the United Kingdom.*

> We have had city prayer in Zurich every month for about two years. Around seventy to ninety Christians from all denominations were gathering and praying for the coming together of the body of Christ in Zurich. Sometimes after the city prayer meeting, a smaller group would pray on a specific site: Platzspitz, the world-famous drug addict scene called "Needle Park," where up to two thousand people every day were dealing and consuming drugs. The smaller group would sometimes pray all night right at or around that park. Now that park is closed shut with huge iron gates! One day [after the closure] about fifty Christians were able to get permission to enter this park. We claimed the ground for God so that an empty park would now be filled with God's kingdom.
>
> —*Peter Hohn, of Campus Crusade for Christ in Switzerland*

Place for Prayer #8: Sites of Strongholds

Praying people have often identified select sites as strongholds of the enemy from which spiritual havoc is exported to an outlying region. If evil powers are suspected of functioning from a particular site, it may be a good setting to pray. But what should be prayed at a fortress of the enemy? As intriguing as it may be to lay siege on bastions of evil powers, Scripture emphasizes breaking down the operative hideouts of evil in human minds.

Paul described strongholds as being established in the minds of people, constructed from building blocks of speculative thoughts, cemented by arrogance.

> ...the destruction of fortresses. We are destroying speculations and every lofty thing raised up against the knowledge of God, and we are taking every thought captive to the obedience of Christ (2 Cor. 10:4b-5).

For Paul the significant feature of strongholds was not that they provided housing *for* evil beings but that they were built "*against* the knowledge of God." In this light Paul's spiritual war did not aim at ousting evil beings from fortresses so much as it was taking disobedient people captive as prisoners "to the obedience of Christ." The imagery of taking captives once again describes the basic goal of spiritual war: to rescue people to live in the joy of obeying and knowing God, built up as churches.

Many cities are notorious for fatalistic mindsets which leave people despairing that they are locked into a never-changing grind of slow-motion sorrow. Religious philosophies reinforce the hopeless thoughts, driving people to search for small reliefs from a battery of false gods and fortune-tellers. Astoundingly, the gospel of hope in Jesus doesn't make sense to people who would seem to be most likely to follow Jesus. The truth of Jesus doesn't hold interest. Why won't they see and believe? Because spiritual strongholds are holding people from hope.

> A stronghold is a mindset impregnated with hopelessness that causes us to accept as unchangeable something that we know is contrary to the will of God.
>
> —*Ed Silvoso, of Harvest Evangelism. Ed has organized several citywide prayerwalking efforts as part of comprehensive strategies to bring the gospel to entire cities of his native Argentina.*

Each of us knows what it is like to be duped by the devil into opposing God with our own arrogant thoughts. Consider the power of "groupthink" when thousands of people struggle under the same deceptive delusions. When such thoughts grip people throughout a discernible geographical area, then prayerwalking becomes a valuable part of the necessary spiritual war to bring light to darkened communities.

For areas held under deceptive strongholds, make requests for the people along the lines of Acts 26:18, that God would "open their eyes so that they may turn from darkness to light and from the dominion of Satan to God." Make wise use of the complete spiritual authority God gives to deal with strongholds. Paul longed to build up the church far more than he wanted to demolish structured evil "in accordance with the authority which the Lord gave me, for building up and not for tearing down" (2 Cor. 13:10, also 10:8).

Place for Prayer #9: The Gates of the City

Few cities today are walled. Fewer yet have gates. What does it mean to pray at the gates of the city? Some have pursued invisible gates as if they were sinkholes to hell which must be dammed up. The phrase *gates of hell* should not be confused with city gates.

In biblical times gates acted more like filters, restraining evil and welcoming that which was worthy of honor. Gates were places where respected elders governed. The seats at the gates were not thrones of imperial dominion, but they were the communal institutions of honor and appreciation, something like our present-day town halls, courtrooms and conference centers.

Cities are intended by God to be the gathered greatness of a multiplicity of tribes and peoples. Well-functioning gates open relationships between peoples so that honor flows and wickedness is repudiated.

Today's cities are filled with peoples from distant places, many of them unwelcomed and dishonored. Even long-time citizens reside as aliens in their own cities. Satan is the one who clogs up the gates of our cities with the accumulating garbage of generations, so that we reject each other and readily tolerate corruption.

How much like the final and greatest city can our cities be today? That final city will have gates ever open so that the glory and the honor of the nations will continually be brought in while all that is wicked will be shunned (Rev. 21:24-27).

Finding places which function like gates of ancient times does not require vast gifts of discernment. You can look to the history of how your city was formed and governed. Often the early walls and entry points continue to have significance.

> The old city walls of Istanbul have seven gates. The Belgrade Gate opens toward the direction of Belgrade in what is now the war-torn remnants of Yugoslavia. It was built centuries ago as a gateway for the Serbian people from Belgrade to the Muslim people of Turkey. Our approach in praying on top of this gate was to pray for the openly hostile relationship between the Turks and the Serbs. We decided to let one Turkish brother

represent the Turks and a Croatian brother in the group represent the Serbs; we prayed over them as they linked arms on top of the city gate. During that prayer there were loud rumblings of thunder and lightning flashes. After we sensed a breakthrough in prayer, the sun again appeared. Moments later a young Turkish brother noticed a rainbow in the sky. He and the others claimed not to have seen a rainbow for years in Istanbul. The Turkish believers were quite excited about the way God was confirming our prayers through signs in the heavens.

—*Geni Brewer, a missionary to Turkey, describing a prayerwalk around the old walls of Istanbul. At each gateway of the wall, her team stopped to discern God's desires and then prayed accordingly. While praying at the Belgrade Gate, they felt God wanted to redeem the gate as a gateway of forgiveness for wrongs committed by and against the Serbs.*

The easiest way to pray for the gates is to intercede at places of governance, transaction, communication, judgment and restraint. There may be such places of governance at which leaders long ago capitulated to evil by some kind of covenant with evil powers. There is a possibility that evil powers remain entrenched at sites where they have been invited by such power transactions. Just how evil powers wield influence we don't know and probably don't need to know. By bringing a praying presence to the site, the corruptive cycles of spiritual evil can be interrupted.

Prayer can't nullify every rotten decision of the past, but repentance can help reverse the process of corruption. Pray for the ones who are in positions of authority. Ask God to exalt wholesome elder figures as upholders of righteousness.

Place for Prayer #10: High Places

The biblical term *high place* refers to a site marked by a function different from the city gates, where we find governance by counsel. The sole function of high places in Scripture is worship. Quite often high places described in Scripture, or as they are found today, are places of high altitude. But geography isn't the prime factor. Places of established, continued worship of any entity other than God himself can constitute a high place.

Unlike city gates, which are to be redeemed, God wants the high places dismantled. Because of his jealousy for the worship of his people and because of the curse false worship brings on the land, God early and continually mandated his people to dismantle places of counterfeit worship. He spoke of them as if they were a standing offense to him (Num.

33:52; 2 Kin. 17:11, 18:4; Ps. 78:58; Jer. 19:5, 32:35). Joshua's assignment was to entirely demolish them. As Christ works with us today, he often guides believers to cleanse such places by asking God to disempower them, and even better, to bring about the conversion of their clientele.

> I took a prayer team to a New Age center here in Sweden that we discerned had Lucifer as the force behind the center. They had a coffeehouse, and we ordered coffee and were sitting there praying. We prayed against Lucifer. We proclaimed Jesus as King. It looked like just a discussion between us. Two months later there was an evangelist there who had a campaign in that area, and the whole New Age community came to that campaign. Four of them got saved.
>
> *— Kjell Sjoberg, a Swedish pastor now serving prayer efforts in many countries. He has led prayerwalking teams in more than twelve countries.*

There is no standard technique for Christians to deal with high places. It's not to be entered into lightly. By Christ's leading, some prayerwalkers have stood or encircled such places to pray that they be annulled or even annihilated by God. It's usually not your place to deface or disrupt objects and affairs of false worship. Accomplish all that can be done through prayer.

> We were at a high place overlooking the valley across from a mountain which has been identified as the home of the gods, the only mountain in the Himalayas illegal to climb. We were just doing worship, seeing what God would say for that area. One of the things that happened was the Lord gave us an insight about a fifteen-year-old Nepali youth who walked along with us. The word of knowledge was that his name was [to be] Christopher, that he would bear the light of Christ to that entire area — he would become a leader. We simply prayed it out because he couldn't understand our English language. When it was all over, the translator found out his Nepali name was Krishna. We discovered that only a week earlier the Jesus film had made its way to his village. He had just accepted the Lord and was reading the literature. That was an affirming word of his calling, his leadership, [and] that God would call him. We sensed that as a blessing and a proclamation over his life.
>
> *— Wes Tullis, a leader of the School of Strategic Missions sponsored by Youth With A Mission*

Presumptuous performance of ceremonies is what high places are all about, so be careful not to play into the hands of evil powers by repeating your own Christian prayer rituals as if they were more powerful magic. Defy the momentum of empty religious traditions by worshipping on-site in childlike simplicity. Emphasize truth encounter by declaring Christ's lordship.

Segments of the City

Some of the most heart-stretching prayers are prolonged, searching prayers that reach toward specific social segments of your city. Examples of city segments might include factory workers, elderly people, the unemployed, school teachers, Japanese students at the university, civic leaders and many more.

You will find most urban areas filled with people belonging to more than one identifiable group. The same urban population can be prayed for in different ways. Allow the Spirit of God to alert you to a class or sector of your city, and then find a way to get near them geographically. For instance, as you pray for the children of a city, get close to their schools and play areas. Walk neighborhoods emphasizing prayer for the children. Look children in the eyes and greet them with blessing. When praying for a group which may number in the thousands, it helps to have one or two representative people in your view. Pray for those persons as if they symbolize the whole group.

The most common subset to receive prayerful attention is the group sometimes called non-Christians. As you pray past homes and offices, pray for people who have yet to hear of Christ or follow him. Do not overlook many other groups who deserve special prayer. Here is a sampling of some of the groups most commonly sought in prayer.

Different Age Sets

Pray for children, the elderly, teenagers and others. Age-defined groups can be prayed for as a generation, such as the baby boomers. Give yourself adequate time to prayerwalk for a particular age set. Let your prayer representatively alight on individuals you encounter from the targeted age set.

Leaders

We are commanded to pray for kings and all those who are in positions of authority (1 Tim. 2:1-2). You can include parents, teachers, pastors and even the media in this kind of prayer. Pray on-site for civic leaders of your city by traveling near their homes or workplaces. Pray for teachers by name as you pass by the schools they serve.

> The Lord gave us this desire to pray over our state — seven communities in the state of Kansas, including our capital. We asked permission to get into the governor's palace and prayed for her in her office area. We prayed in the senate and the representatives' chambers too. Why? We wanted to pray in the place of decisions that affect our state. We prayed that God's will would be done, for His purposes to be accomplished that decisions would be right and just in God's sight.
>
> —*Earl Pickard, of Wichita, Kansas, who serves as the national prayer director of Campus Crusade for Christ*

People Groups

Missionaries use the term *people group* in a technical sense referring to any group that has common affinities and generational depth so that a church could eventually start among it.

There are yet thousands of people groups with no strong church movement in their own cultural setting. A widely used term for these groups is *unreached peoples*. In this case, the gospel has yet to extend across distinctives of language, race and culture to initiate fresh movements to Christ. Many Christians have already committed themselves to pray for specific unreached people groups in distant lands. God may lead you to pray for families who reside in your city from such a people group.

To leave no one untouched by prayer will bring out the shepherd in you. Prayerwalking becomes a search, probing for those whom God seeks for his family. Though not technically falling into the definition of unreached peoples, some marginalized subsets of our cities are especially prayerworthy. Some groups, such as gays and radical feminists, are defined by unbiblical life-styles and philosophies. As militant movements which usually rally against God's kingdom, they may rebuff our prayer. Pray for them as the people they are in the places they live and work. Adherents to non-Christian religions should attract your prayers. Look for the people left shattered from tragedies and social pressures, such as widows and the homeless.

10

THREE-DIMENSIONAL PRAYER

Praying in the streets throws open so many possibilities. In this chapter we have gathered some practical ideas into three categories — priestly prayer, warfare prayer and contact prayer. These three dimensions correspond roughly to the triple dynamic of worship, warfare and welcome mentioned earlier.

1. The Worship Dimension: Priestly Prayer

Martin Luther was right. The priesthood of God includes all believers. Each Christian has a place to stand before God, offering him the service truly pleasing to him. Often that place before God is right in the neighborhood. Here are three ways to pray as a priest.

1. Stand *before* God offering gifts of praise. The primary service a biblical priest performs is unto God himself (Ex. 19:6, 28:3-4, 29:44; 2 Chron. 29:11; Ezek. 44:15-16). As God's priests we are to "offer up spiritual sacrifices acceptable to God through Jesus Christ" (1 Pet. 2:5). God has ordained that the richest gifts of worship would come from ordinary people who are priests: "that you may proclaim the excellencies of Him who has called you" (1 Pet. 2:9). Consider your articulated praise to be a special present, made in the hearing of God, which brings pleasure to his heart. God not only deserves your expressions of worship, but he genuinely desires such heartfelt gifts.

The simplest gifts of praise are *thank offerings*. We are to offer thanksgivings on behalf of all people (1 Tim. 2:1). Think of the steady rivers of goodness that God continually bestows on millions of people, yet most fail completely to give him thanks. This is not a light issue. It's a major responsibility of every prayerwalker to articulate gratitude on behalf of those who refuse to acknowledge God or give him thanks (Rom. 1:21). As you walk past homes, hospitals, churches and schools, you can never exhaust the un-given wealth of thanksgivings of which God is worthy.

Another way to extend praise gifts to God is by speaking *gifts of future glory*. Thanksgiving looks back. Gifts of future glory look forward to prophetically give God praise in advance. This kind of transaction may seem intangible since it involves acting as a priestly broker, offering yet undone obedience of unknown individuals to an invisible God. But it is a valuable privilege of priests to offer God an early installment of the glory that will come to him from people of every nation.

Two simple steps will help you offer gifts of future glory. First, vigorously pray some of the richest promises of Scripture for a particular neighborhood or family. You can't help but sense, with sanctified imagination, what life might be like in the city when just a few of your requests come to pass. Dare to envision Christ's purposes accomplished in your city. What unique treasures of godliness lie in potential behind the closed doors and shuttered windows? Consider the joy of God's heart as individuals turn to him and love him from every people.

Second, with the sights and sounds of the city all around you, tell God of his worthiness to receive that city's glory. Describe to God the redeemed brilliance of the thousands that you expect to turn to him. You can be sure that Christ will eventually be followed, loved and worshipped by some from every people and city. Anticipate the sanctified power, riches, wisdom, might, honor, glory and blessing that will come from your city to God (as in Rev. 4:11, 5:12, 7:12 and especially 21:24-26). You are not out of line to allow your emotions to meet the supreme joy of heaven: that the Lamb would receive the reward of his suffering.

The issue of highest contention when Satan directly challenged Jesus was custody of "the kingdoms of the world, and their glory" (Matt. 4:8-10). The high stakes offer was entirely exposed as a matter of worship. Jesus sternly rejected the bogus deal offered to him. "Begone, Satan! For it is written, 'You shall worship the Lord your God, and serve Him only' " (Matt. 4:10). He later taught his followers how to preempt such satanic offers in the last phrase of what is called the Lord's prayer. The prayer crescendos with a priestly acclamation, extolling God in his worthiness to receive the kingdom, the power and the glory of all humankind (Matt. 6:13 in view of Rev. 11:15). Your act of hopeful worship does not substitute for men, women and children who will someday actually give their allegiant devotion to God. But by acclaiming his worthiness to receive such love, your priestly work calls forth the glory you anticipate.

> We were praying through the streets of Alexandria, Egypt. It's pretty squalid in some areas, but we came to the realization that he wasn't going to save these people by pulling them out of these majority Muslim neighborhoods. It's going to happen here. Salvation wouldn't be escape from Egypt as it had been in Moses' day. We prayed for God to do another exodus but to keep the people in their families and streets, to establish them in these communities. We prayed, "Let my people go, that they may worship me!" We knew that it might be some time until Jesus got a huge following there. But the more we told God what kind of love he deserved from this place, the more we felt sure it was going to happen. We knew how hard it would be for those future believers, so we couldn't help feeling proud of them for loving God at such cost, even though most of them hadn't done it yet.
> —*Steve Chism, speaking of a recent prayer journey in a poor Muslim area of urban Egypt*

> You are worthy of the true worship of everyone who squanders their devotion in this place. Come near. Come now and gain their worship for yourself, Lord Jesus!
> —*A prayer of Lynn Woodring while walking near the hundreds of Hindus going in and out of the huge Minakshipuram temple in Madurai, India*

2. Stand *with* your city in repentance. As you take a priestly stance before God, you can also stand *with* your neighbors in profound identity to cry for mercy. As you stretch your vision to glimpse God's future for a city, prepare yourself for prophetic empathy. You might get a glimpse of catastrophes of judgment soon to come. Jesus experienced the impending sorrow of a city. He described with profound regret the forfeited future of peace, the woe to come and still a postponed hope that he would someday be received with blessing.

> He saw the city and wept over it, saying, "For the days shall come upon you when your enemies will...level you to the ground and your children within you" (Luke 19:41-44).

Jesus so suddenly burst into advanced grief in an event that was otherwise filled with joy (Luke 19:37) that we must surmise he had often gazed upon the city in prayer with deepening sorrow. Not surprisingly, his preferred place of prayer was in the Garden of Gethsemane, which overlooks the entire city of Jerusalem from near the top of the Mount of Olives (Luke 22:39-41; John 18:1-2). However, he could have found other places to hide away. A comfortable house was open to him in adjacent Bethany at the home of Mary, Martha and Lazarus (John 11:18, 12:1-3). But the place he chose for frequent prayer gave him, by way of physical eyesight, a nearness to the whole city. It was the place he chose to spend a night of even greater grief, to taste the cup of sorrows of all humankind.

As we look upon our own cities, we are tempted to respond inappropriately in one of two ways: either to condemn the city or to carry its sorrows. Neither way is God's way.

Do not try to *carry* the sins of others so as to atone for their wrongdoing. You are a priest, not the sacrifice. Only one person is able to carry our sorrows. The Father has given this cup to Jesus alone.

The opposite error is to see the doom of the city and to *condemn* it. Jonah displayed this kind of abusive prayerwalking. Did his compassion run short? Nineveh was a "great city, a three days' walk." Jonah only "began to go through the city one day's walk" (Jon. 3:3-4). Perhaps Jonah's suicidal despair was a backlash of his condemnatory attitude.

What then is our priestly responsibility? There is only one way we can care for the city without carrying its sin. It is also the only one way we can confront the city without condemning it. That way is to identify with the city in order to express repentance and cry for mercy. Here's how to step into priestly prayers of identification.

First, *identify with sinners.* Begin to speak in first person for the aggregate sins of generations or neighborhoods. Somehow find an honest way to say, "We have sinned," rather than, "They have sinned."

An example of this kind of praying can be found in the biblical character of Daniel. Though separated by generations from the primary perpetrators of rebellion against God, he numbered himself among them as he prayed for mercy. "Open shame belongs to us, O Lord, to our kings, our princes, and our fathers, because we have sinned against You" (Dan. 9:8, NAS revised).

Second, *cry out for mercy.* Use the cry Jesus commended to us: "Be merciful to me, the sinner!" (Luke 18:13). Without trying to excuse, explain or solve the sin, simply appeal that God extend his kindness and grant favor undeserved.

Third, *seek repentance.* You can repent on your own behalf, though you cannot repent on behalf of others. Each person must turn to God by choice. But perhaps your act of repentance will be one of the first of many. According to Jesus, cities can somehow repent as collective entities. "He began to reproach the cities in which most of His miracles were done, because they did not repent" (Matt. 11:20). Who will initiate the repentance your city needs?

> When I stood up to address a group of Native Americans, I unexpectedly began to cry and weep. I told them, "I can't stand before you without asking you to forgive us [the white race] for the sins and atrocities that our ancestors have committed against your [ancestors]." There wasn't a dry eye in the place. Many of them came to me and said how meaningful it was to them that I asked for their forgiveness. They had never experienced anything like that. They knew it was bringing healing to their hearts.
>
> National sins that are retained generation after generation will become corporate strongholds. Repentance is one way — whether individual or corporate — to break these strongholds and undermine the enemy. I haven't met a Native American that didn't have some bitterness in their hearts toward whites because of all the injustices committed against their people for nearly five hundred years. They cover it up and try not to think about it. After establishing relationships with some Native Americans, I've had them approach me and tell me they didn't realize the hatred they had in their hearts toward white people and [many] have asked me to forgive them. We have seen many times where repentance has brought miraculous healing.
>
> *—Jean Steffenson, referring to a recent gathering of Native Americans and white believers. Jean is president of the Native American chapter of the Reconciliation Coalition, a network of believers seeking God's healing in whole communities.*

3. Stand *amidst* your city, extending blessings. Blessings are word gifts from God's heart. This form of priestly prayer enunciates a portion of his intended goodness. God creates by speaking words. When people bless, they align themselves with the creative force of God's Word and release measures of God's promise.

God speaks blessings himself, but he authorizes parents and priests, among others, to vocalize blessings. The Bible records instances of Isaac and Jacob each exerting fatherly faith by stating blessings (Gen. 27:1-33, 48:8-20, 49:1-28). God accords to us significant responsibility to give definition to his promises for families, generations, cities and nations. Blessing is a prophetic way of praying. It's like interceding in reverse: Without stating the requests, answers to prayer are declared in faith. By such blessings, futures are bestowed. Destinies are altered and opened.

God consecrated priests to "stand before the Lord to serve Him and to bless in His name until this day" (Deut. 10:8). Another classic passage about priests giving blessings shows that while priests pronounce

God's goodness upon people, it is God himself who bestows the substance of blessing: "Thus you [the priests] shall bless the sons of Israel...and I then will bless them" (Num. 6:23-27). Let's practice this high privilege, learning how to do it boldly and carefully. Here's how to speak blessings.

Discern the heart of God. Look to him as the magnificent Father of every one of the households for which you are praying. If the yearning of God's heart could speak, what would be said? You are not left to your own supposition. Scripture is loaded with the generosity of the Father. Let the promises of Scripture ruminate in your heart as you walk near households. Let your words give voice to God's highest intentions.

Blessings naturally arise from petitions. If you first spend time concentrating on a matter by making explicit request, you may then find it easier to package your prayer as a blessing for people. One of the best examples of priests giving blessings occurred in King Hezekiah's day. "Then the Levitical priests arose and blessed the people; and their voice was heard and their prayer came to His holy dwelling place, to heaven" (2 Chron. 30:27). God heard their blessings as prayers.

Get physically near to those you are blessing. Blessings are prayers, but they are almost always stated by the "blessor" in the presence of the "blessee." In many instances, blessings are stated directly to the ones who are to receive them. The biblical record of blessings suggests that blessings cannot really be offered well in absence from those being blessed. God brought creatures close to Adam for their naming, which is a form of blessing (Gen. 2:19). Isaac blessed his sons with physical touch, as did Jacob (Gen. 27:1-28:4, 49:1-28). Balaam took care to come within sight of the people he was blessing (Num. 22:41, 24:2).

God often reinforces the word gift by physical touch. Jesus was an intimate blessor. At one point he welcomed children into "His arms and began blessing them, laying His hands upon them" (Mark 10:16). As his final gesture on earth, Jesus "lifted up His hands and blessed" his followers (Luke 24:50).

> We bless each house. We do it very quietly. People might see us going door to door, but they wouldn't notice us doing anything other than leaving a packet on the door knob. We don't knock on the door. Communicating with people is not the primary purpose. That may happen, and that would be fine. But that's not the point. The purpose is to bless the household with specific prayer. We want to physically touch the house, even for just a moment, as a point of contact for prayer.
>
> —*Ted Haggard, pastor of New Life Church in Colorado Springs, Colorado*

> When we first came to the island [in Indonesia] we didn't do any loud worship. Instead we maintained a "prayer-closet" attitude in our hearts as we walked around the whole island, tracing every pathway for a week. We went into the different Buddhist temples. We stopped at the mosques. We shook hands with as many Muslim leaders as possible. We tried to make eye contact and shake hands with as many as possible. We believe that if we can just shake hands with them, then somehow God's anointing begins to loose them.
>
> —*Mark Geppert, director of the Southeast Asian Prayer Center. As a result of the team's prayers and subsequent ministry, many of the villagers gave their lives to Christ, including one of the Buddhist temple leaders.*

Speak out loud. Lest your blessings turn to soggy sentiment in your mind, say your blessings out loud. The priests of Hezekiah's day blessed the people in their hearing, but God was the most important listener. Give your blessings the declarative volume they deserve.

Giving blessings is a matter of great power and urgency. Proverbs 11:11 portrays the struggle for cities as a war of powerful words: "By the blessing of the upright a city is exalted, but by the mouth of the wicked it is torn down." God desires a continual stream of blessing by righteous people giving voice to what he longs to do.

2. The Warfare Dimension: Warfare Prayer

Praying Within Your Authority

Heaven's assignments do not work by the volunteer system. No one can appoint themselves to a place of great prayer authority. It may not even be accurate to say that we "take authority." God alone gives authority.

Authority is a relational reality. Let's not make an elitist mistake of thinking that authority is merited by hours logged on bended knee. Authority is not earned. It is entered. Intercessory authority is a growing relational reality in two directions: intimate cleanness before God and a love for the people for whom God has assigned us to pray.

Spiritual warriors in Scripture were granted authority to pray. Their authority did not stem from what they knew but from who had come to know them because of their growing life of prayer. They were known before God and the angelic entities of heaven. It's not who you know but who knows you.

Daniel was told by heavenly visitation that his prolonged prayer had shaped the war raging in the heavenlies. Take note of how he was addressed by the heavenly visitor: "O Daniel, man of high esteem..." (Dan. 10:11, also v. 19). Daniel was a respected name and voice in the councils of heaven. He prayed with powerful impact, but from what we know, he never addressed or even knew that principalities were being thwarted by God while he was praying (Dan. 10:1-21).

Recall the story of the seven sons of Sceva who tried to use Jesus' name as a talisman of authority. They had challenged a man possessed by an evil spirit with the words, "I adjure you by Jesus whom Paul preaches." The spirit's response keyed on the well-known name of Paul among heavenly demonic beings. "I recognize Jesus, and I know about Paul, but who are you?" There were violent repercussions for these men for dealing with demons without any position before God's throne (Acts 19:13-17). (In light of the demon's recognition of Paul, it is significant that Paul had lived more than two years in this city, coming to know it well, accomplishing much by prayer [Acts 19:10-17].)

Jesus sent seventy followers on prayer journeys without giving specific word about their authority over demonic powers (Luke 10:1-16, as he had done before with the twelve in Matt. 10:1). They returned amazed at the power they had exerted when they prayed in the name of Jesus. "Even the demons are subject to us in Your name" (Luke 10:17).

Jesus told them there were arenas of authority in war that they would probably never see or enter. "I was watching Satan fall from heaven like lightning" (Luke 10:18). He then told them that the authority they had wielded was even greater than what he had yet told them or what they had even guessed.

The crux of the matter was that the authority had been added to them by divine grant. They were not intrinsically powerful. "Behold, I have given you authority to tread upon serpents and scorpions, and over all the power of the enemy, and nothing shall injure you" (Luke 10:19; note the footwork involved in triumphing over evil).

Jesus calmly urged them to direct their joy away from triumph over evil to the matter of surpassing significance: that they were known before the courts of heaven by name. "Do not rejoice in this, that the spirits are subject to you, but rejoice that your names are recorded in heaven" (Luke 10:20).

Having their names recorded in heaven probably does not refer to their being duly registered for eternal salvation (though no doubt this also was true of them). In the society of Jesus' day, honor and reputation were matters of highest value. Jesus directs their joy to what they would have been nurtured in their society to prize most: a permanent honor granted by God. This renown was theirs quite apart from their exploits of trampling demons. They were esteemed before God as beloved children.

The core of their authority was not that they were wise and mighty men of war. Authority in prayer never stems from being knowledgeable. They were the "babes" through whom the Father was pleased to accomplish his purposes (Luke 10:21-24).

Push Past Your Comfort Zone

Our point is to encourage you to pursue your maximal authority in prayer. Be on the stretch, praying beyond a comfort zone. You probably are using authority beyond what you know, as Daniel and the seventy discovered. At the same time, let's be wise not to overstep our authority in spiritual war but instead resolve to continue praying as Christ gives us specific assignment.

We all face different kinds of struggles in spiritual war. God grants appropriate power for each distinctive battle. For example, every believer endures a constant defensive struggle with sin, the flesh and the devil in order to follow God. The Lord is continually with us as well, giving us sufficient spiritual fortitude to resist and stand. But there are different battles that take place in the domain of one's personal life.

Some battles take place on what some are calling a "strategic level." Strategic-level warfare involves contending for the redemption of large numbers of people in specific geographic areas by integrating evangelism, prayer and service. Under some understandings of spiritual war, hierarchies of angelic beings hold sway over territories. As mighty as these principalities may be, it is a grave error to suppose that God deploys against them a corresponding hierarchy of human prayer warriors, with higher and lesser echelons of intercessory power. The simplest of God's children can pray effectively according to God's assignment.

We will only be able to renounce elitism on the one hand and cowardice on the other if we keep focused on Christ. He himself is our power and the fullness of our authority. He is with us in his might every day. He alone is worthy forever to retain and use what the Father has granted to him: all authority in heaven and in every locale of the earth (Matt. 28:18).

> Spiritual warfare is hard work. It requires us to roll up our sleeves and slog it out. No magic wands. I'm distressed when I hear people talking as if there were some sort of magic wand, as if you could go into one of these areas where for century after century, thousands upon millions of people have used their own free-will choice to welcome demonic powers and principalities to live amongst them and rule over them. Don't tell me we're going to send in a little prayerwalk team to set aside the logical consequences of their free-will choices, pulling up centuries of

demonic entrenchment just because we quote a verse or sing a good worship chorus. I'm sorry. It just doesn't work that way. There are no magic wands. But the effectual fervent prayer of righteous men and women avails much. If that verse (James 5:16) were not in Scripture, you and I would be in a bad way today. Fear might have a place in our midst. The next verse makes a point to say that wonder-working Elijah had no magic wand at all. He had "a nature like ours." He simply prayed "earnestly" (James 5:17).

—*George Otis Jr. has led many intercessory prayer teams to investigate and pray at the spiritual hot spots of earth from whence it is thought that evil powers hold sway over large territories. As president of The Sentinel Group, George serves as a leading authority in the newly developing field of missions research called "spiritual mapping."*

We went through a phase where some of our people were trying to speak to this or that principality or power over a neighborhood, and they found out that their lives were really getting trashed. I don't believe the Lord had given them authority to do that.

—*Bob Branch, pastor of the Vineyard Christian Fellowship in Framingham, Massachusetts. He continues to prayerwalk regularly with teams, including people from his church.*

Stages of Warfare Prayer

There is no doubt that in some way prayerwalkers step into the spiritual battle for their cities. Without attempting to assemble a complete map of spiritual war, we offer this primer of basic stages of warfare prayer. It has been distilled from the experience of many prayerwalkers. Keep in mind that these points pertain to the struggle for spiritual influence over specific territories and cities.

The main value of this short list of prayer topics is the strategic sequence in which they are given. Pursue stage one as a beginning point and a platform for all subsequent warfare prayer. Then push on to the later stages as God gives clear guidance to do so. You will not need to go further than the first or second stage in most cases.

Stage One War: Appeal Directly* to *God

Get right to the core of the war. Before you come *against* anything or anyone, come reverently *to* the Most High. Come before God in his throne room. His courts are in session. His throne presides over all spiritual war. If angelic forces are to be sent to engage in battle, they will take their assignments from God's throne. Stand at attention before him with joyful fear. The dreadful and beautiful King of creation has named you to be his child. You have bold, confident access through faith in Jesus. Come near and make your appeal.

When Paul mentioned the weapons of spiritual warfare, he described them as being "not of the flesh, but divinely powerful" (2 Cor. 10:4). But the weapons were not innately powerful, as if anyone could pick them up and utilize them. A literal translation of the full phrase would be: "The weapons...are...mighty *before God*" (2 Cor. 10:4). The royal courtroom language "before God" shows that Paul regarded the entire war as happening under God's immediate oversight and direct authorization, as if it were all taking place within a few feet of God's throne. It is almost as if these weapons have a power cord that is only so long.

Psalm 18 is one of many places where David, the great warrior, says the primary act of spiritual warfare is in taking refuge. David chose to "take refuge" by appealing to God in "His temple" (Ps. 18:2,6). The result: God himself "sent from on high....He delivered me from my strong enemy" (Ps. 18:16-17). David understood that spiritual war was essentially God's rescue operation. As a result he knew the experience of God training his "hands for battle" to pursue enemies (Ps. 18:34). But the entire affair began by taking refuge and remained a matter of "great salvations" (Ps. 18:50, literal translation).

David's songs continually show the same pattern: David approaches God so that the Lord himself would step into the battle. David initiates warfare by taking refuge, which is not at all a matter of retreat, but tremendous victory. "I will cry to God Most High, to God who accomplishes all things for me. He will send from heaven and save me" (Ps. 57:2-3). In Psalm 144 David mentions that *his hands* were trained for war (v. 1). But his greater hope is for *God's hand*. "Bow Your heavens, O Lord, and come down...Stretch forth Your hand from on high; rescue me and deliver me" (Ps. 144:5-7, NAS revised).

The heavenly courts of God on high are consistently regarded as the decisive theater of war (Ps. 76, 82). David knew that he had access to the King of all to make appeal. How much more do believers in Christ have sure access to the throne of God to appeal for his triumph? (Heb. 4:16 in light of 2:8-16, and Eph. 3:10 as activated by the standing privilege of 3:12).

How do believers wage this kind of war? It is not a matter of methodology but relationship. Come as a worshipper. Speak humbly as if you were actually standing before God's glorious throne and he had interrupted all other business in heaven and earth to give you full attention. Be careful about gratuitous mental images, though such scenes given in Scripture are not imaginary. Although Christ remains veiled from your sight, he is indeed exalted to the right hand of the throne of God (Mark 16:19; Eph. 1:18-23). We are called to set our minds on "things above where Christ is, seated at the right hand of God" (Col. 3:1-2). Resolve to speak to no angelic power whatever as you register your complaint in the courts of heaven. Make a straightforward plea to God.

Boldly request that God would arise and send forth from heaven to execute judgment on his enemies. God's judgment is his central act of spiritual war. In acts of judgment God brings punishment on those who have opposed him as enemies, and in the same stroke he brings salvation for those he favors. Request the salvation God has promised. You do not need to directly accuse angelic beings that you may or may not know. (Psalms 7, 17, 20 and 94 show truths underneath the familiar prayers of Jehoshaphat in 2 Chronicles 20:5-23, of Hezekiah in 2 Kings 19:14-37 and especially of the church in Acts 4:23-31.)

> God, how could you leave 850 million people under the thumbprint of this thing? Surely you are going to rise up and deliver them. Come on, God, let's see your stuff here.
>
> —*Mark Geppert, praying in front of a Hindu temple in Nepal*

> During the Jericho marches around the cities of our adopted country, we learned something about dealing with demonic principalities. The book of Jude (especially vv. 8-10) teaches that addressing spiritual principalities directly is not something we should do lightly. It's more appropriate in most situations to say, "The Lord rebuke you," rather than to shout directly at these demonic forces. So in most circumstances we will focus on the Lord and pray only to him. We praise him for his power, his authority and for what he accomplished in binding Satan by the work of the cross. And then we ask God himself to rebuke and bind these demons.
>
> —*Joshua Brinkley, a missionary to a country in North Africa which is hostile to Christianity. No local believers were known in the entire country when Joshua arrived. Now a small church is growing for the first time.*

Stage Two War: Truth Encounter About *God*

Another basic part of spiritual war is what could be called "truth encounter" in which believers proclaim truth about Christ and his kingdom. Relatively few engagements of spiritual war erupt into full-blown "power encounters" in which God's prevailing might is put on open display. But almost every battle of spiritual war involves some kind of truth encounter.

Speak the truth about Jesus right out into the atmosphere of the street you are walking. You won't need to address your declaration directly to demonic powers for them to take notice. It's probably just as well that you don't. You have not been assigned to be a prosecutor of evil powers. You have merely answered the subpoena of heaven to give testimony to Christ in a specific setting on earth. Resist the urge to accuse demonic powers. Don't be baited into angry, sarcastic comments about the devil. Such invective merely coarsens your own thinking. Speak straightforward gospel truth as if you were under oath in heavenly courts.

All of heaven loves to hear testimony about Jesus. Describe what the Father has done for the Son he loves. Declare the love and obedience that Jesus offers to the Father. Announce the wonders of the Spirit. Read Scripture in a proclamatory way. You may be prompted to recount a particular story of Scripture.

Recount your own story of redemption as you pray. Your spoken testimony is an overcoming weapon of astounding power (Rev. 12:11). The weapons Paul refers to in 2 Corinthians 10:3-6 were designed to bring down fortresses that suppressed the knowing of God. Satan masquerades behind speculations and grips people in their own high-minded blindness. Your statement of truth could be part of a mighty event taking place before God in heavenly dimensions, dismantling schemes of deception.

What particular deception has bewildered the people of your city? Whatever the lies may be, declare corresponding truth. You may spare evangelizers hundreds of hours of quarreling with nonbelievers later on.

Restate the biblical declarations that every false god and angelic being will eventually bow in worship to God (Ps. 29:1-2, 97:7; Phil. 2:10-11; Heb. 1:6). Without ridicule or any supposition that you are evangelizing angelic beings, call for their worship and subjugation to the Lord Jesus Christ.

> We had been meditating on 1 Corinthians 15 in light of the Easter season while on a prayer journey in Egypt. On Easter morning it dawned on me that Islam denied just about every gospel truth in 1 Corinthians 15:3-11. Islam denies that Jesus died, that Scripture is faithful to speak of Jesus, that there was sin to die for, that he was buried or that he rose from the dead. We went out that day and for many weeks afterward declaring these elementary gospel facts — not to people, but right out into the atmosphere in different neighborhoods.
>
> — *Steve Chism, leader of a prayer journey to Egypt*

Stage Three War: Character Encounter* for *God

Prayerwalkers often gravitate to praying *for* Christ and his kingdom rather than *against* Satan and the evil he incites. The aim of spiritual war is the glorification of Christ. God's primary way of defeating the bragging might of evil is to manifest Christ's character, even in the weakness of those who follow him.

God's basic strategy for spiritual war is not to eradicate evil in order that good might have a chance. Instead God reveals and empowers his own goodness in people so that evil is overwhelmed. This is why he mandates the risen Messiah to "rule in the midst of Your enemies" (Ps. 110:2, NAS revised). God has planned a unique invasion of every community with the resplendent goodness of his Son. Prayerwalkers can diligently pray that Christ's character will eventually expose, weaken and displace evil.

This way of triumph over entrenched wickedness is succinctly stated by Paul. "Do not be overcome by evil, but overcome evil with good" (Rom. 12:21). The Christian community is to resist the ever-escalating forces of evil that bait us to fight fire with fire (or perhaps "ire with ire"). By seeking peace with all people, Christians can patiently endure ugly hatred and wage war in the mightiest way of all, by leaving "room for the wrath of God" himself (Rom. 12:19).

Later in the same letter, Paul calls believers to become wise in what is good and to become innocent in what is evil (Rom. 16:19). Christians emerge triumphant not because of their encyclopedic knowledge of evil beings and their names. God himself does the crushing of Satan — but under the innocent feet of believers. "The God of peace will soon crush Satan under your feet" (Rom. 16:20). Prayerwalkers easily recall such imagery as they walk their towns. As you walk, fix your heart on what good things God is bringing forth. God will align your steps to defeat sinister schemes of evil.

Engage in character encounter by praying that God would bring forth the fruit of the Spirit which may correspond with the outworkings of the flesh. It won't be hard to see the corruption described in Galatians 5:19-21 in your town. "The deeds of the flesh are evident, which are: immorality, impurity, sensuality, idolatry, sorcery, enmities, strife, jealousy, outbursts of anger, disputes, dissensions, factions, envying, drunkenness, carousing, and things like these."

In the same places you see these things, pray for the corresponding fruits of Galatians 5:22-23 to grow. "The fruit of the Spirit is love, joy, peace, patience, kindness, goodness, faithfulness, gentleness, self-control." Pray for the fruit of the Spirit as if you were planting its seed in the ground, patting down the soil and watering it with your prayer. Where there is immorality, pray for the fruits of faithfulness and self-control. Where there is strife, pray for the fruits of kindness and gentleness. Where there is the depression of drunkenness, pray for the fruits of joy and patience.

Cultivate the spiritual soil of your city by praying for healing of relationships of every kind. Reconciliation suspends Satan's efforts to stir up septic sin which may lie below the surface of everyday life in your city. Restoration amidst families and friendships provides an environment of clean potency for God's character to mature and multiply.

Stage Four War: Prayer Encounter* Against *God's Enemies

Spiritual combat according to the first three stages may be sufficient for most prayerwalking encounters. Sometimes, however, God gives believers a specific duty of voicing direct challenge to heavenly powers. Opinions vary at this point. There are strong feelings by some that demons need a good verbal drubbing to take their eviction notices seriously. Others feel that a Christian who speaks a single unprovoked word to a demon is dangerously reviling high angelic majesties (2 Pet. 2:10-12). There is obviously middle ground, and it is likely that the issue boils down to timing and authority.

Many people's discernment outstrips their authorization from God. You might indeed accurately sense strongholds or demonic assignments or even names of principalities. Your perception does not necessarily constitute a commission for action. Knowing the mind of God is more important than discerning the schemes of evil. Has God authorized the ousting of demons from a territory or household? It may take but a moment or it might take days to be confident of understanding the Lord's will. No matter how long it takes, seek God first for guidance before directly engaging the enemy in spiritual combat, especially when contesting spiritual influence over specific terrain. Be ready to sense that God may have plans other than direct confrontation.

Timing may be a significant issue in connection with restraining the enemy. Jesus never spoke of binding the enemy without mentioning the loosing, or rescue, of people (Matt. 12:29, 16:19, 18:18; Luke 11:20-26). God may indicate that you wait so that your insight regarding evil can serve the work of many. Perhaps by waiting for God's timing several churches might band together to be not only more effective in suppressing evil but to follow through with a solid plan to free people and establish righteousness. Envisage your prayer as having an incapacitating effect on powers of darkness, long enough to fruitfully proclaim the gospel. You may want to precede your prayer with fasting. Anticipating the results of your prayer, you may want to prepare for the harvest. Either way, urgency does not always mean haste.

Compared with the huge backlog of experience Christians have gained in delivering individuals from demonic oppression, most Christian leaders admit that we know relatively little about dealing with territorial spirits, whatever they may be. Exorcism routines that are suitable for dealing with demonized individuals are not necessarily appropriate when dealing with neighborhoods or territories.

We can safely assume that each case will be unique, requiring express authorization as well as clear instructions as to what to say and what to do. Those who feel that they have contended successfully with territorial forces rarely resort to what we have called "stage four" war of direct encounter. Other more indirect avenues of confrontation usually suffice. Those who claim to have been effective in speaking against angelic majesties residing in assigned territories rarely boast about it. If they tell of the encounter, they usually report of giving a simple word of restraint. The actual statement is usually quite brief and authoritative, often with some kind of symbolic gesture.

Some have suggested that the wind and the waves that were blocking Jesus' entry into a new region were energized by territorial powers assigned to the area. Jesus' word to the weather — and the forces presumably behind it — displays the brevity and faith required in this kind of spiritual war: "Hush, be still" (Mark 4:35-41).

Having waged and won this struggle, he went on to a further encounter with a throng of embodied spirits more determined to stay in the country than they were in the oppressed man (Mark 4:1-20, especially v. 10). Still Jesus did not invade the area with unassailable power. He left rejected by most, received by few and yet praised among all (Mark 5:17-20).

> I believe our task in spiritual war is to neutralize the "tractor beam" hold these territorial strong men have had over the minds and spirits of the people who have welcomed them to dominate them. We are asking here for the grace of God to be shed abroad. These people [in the least-evangelized areas of the world] are deceived because they chose to be deceived. Romans 1 [vv. 18-23] tells us this clearly. It's not that they didn't have truth; they elected to suppress truth in unrighteousness; they chose to believe a lie. And the enemy met them at this point of contact, animating religious systems which came to life, supernaturally glued together. And [these religious systems] became a powerful, deceiving shell.
>
> We're not asking God to make them Christians. God doesn't force anybody to be a Christian. We're asking God to give these people something they don't deserve — a second chance to process truth. We're asking God through intercessory prayer to

break the enchantment over these people — to level the playing field so that when evangelists come in behind the intercessors, there will inevitably be a harvest of some magnitude.

—George Otis Jr., among the first in recent times to enter Mongolia at a time when there were no known Christians. Many others joined in the effort before and after George, but there are now thousands of Mongolian believers in churches which are growing at a brisk pace. George has done on-site prayer in some of the least-evangelized countries in Asia and the Middle East.

When we first went to [a country in North Africa], there was not a single believer in the entire country. We were the only Protestant missionaries. When I first stepped into the country, I felt as if I had walked into a brick wall. During the first year, we didn't see a single Muslim person come to Christ. We thought, Even if we keep this up for twenty years, this will not plant a church.

A year after we entered the country we began to do what we call "Jericho marches." We would fast all day, sometimes two or three days. Then at night, for security reasons, we would walk the entire circumference of the city, praising the Lord, praying over the city, claiming the city for Christ, trying to bind the demons over that city and over the country as a whole. We did this around every major city in the whole country.

On our third Jericho march in a certain city, I remember around 1:00 A.M. I felt clearly led by the Holy Spirit to pray about the evil powers over the city. In fact I sensed he was giving us the specific authority to address the prince of this country. I said, "Prince of this country, I rebuke you. I bind you. I cast you out." I said all of those things you've probably heard said before. When I did, my wife and I both sensed that something cracked and broke in the heavenly realms. Actually it was a vision of Satan's power stretched over the country like a geodesic dome. This dome cracked and was shaken, and there was room for light to come pouring in. It was during the week following that we saw the first local person come to Christ. And we have seen people come to Christ fairly steadily ever since at the rate of about one every two months.

Does this mean I have eradicated the principalities over the country? A month later we sensed demonic resistance building up again. The way I put it together is that we should be sure that we are being led by the Holy Spirit to speak against evil. I've come to the conclusion that it was naive on my part to think that

> if I just say, "I bind you and cast you into the abyss," then there won't be dark powers over the territory anymore. Not so. The struggle goes on. I think we have made substantial progress, but they [evil spiritual powers] aren't going to be obliterated until Jesus comes back.
>
> —*Joshua Brinkley, a missionary to a country in North Africa*

3. The Welcome Dimension: Contact Prayer

By *contact prayer* we mean occasions of praying directly for people in their presence. This dimension of on-site prayer is most often connected with engendering a welcome for Christ in a community.

Jesus prayed for people directly. He often prayed for people who approached him (Luke 5:12-15, 7:2-10, 17:12-19). At times he initiated conversations which turned to prayer (Luke 7:11-15, 13:12-13).

1. Open relationships. Of course, follow the leading of God in knowing who to pray for and when. Spontaneous hunches move most prayerwalkers, although some churches have attempted to pray with someone from every household in a neighborhood in a systematic way.

> We felt that the leading of the Lord was to do the entire area and not to leave anyone out. I just feel that everyone needs an equal opportunity to receive a Bible and to be prayed for. By walking the land literally, the entire area has been covered by praying Christians, and we believe that there's a work done in preparation for the further work of God.
>
> —*Caroline Erickson, member of Church on the Way in Van Nuys, California. She and her husband, Larry, help organize the church's citywide prayerwalking program called Operation Saturation.*

When you encounter someone you would like to pray for, start with a simple introduction. Explain something of who you are and what you are doing. You'll get trapped into preaching small sermons if you attempt long explanations of your motives. Be content to be somewhat misunderstood. Don't ever imply that your motives spring from observing the troubled condition of the neighborhood.

Be unapologetic about your willingness to pray. If you obey standard social sensitivities, you will not intrude at inappropriate times. Converse with easy, authentic graciousness.

You don't need to ascertain whether someone is a Christian or not in order to pray for them. Christians usually speak up about their faith. Make only light inquiries about their needs.

2. Get permission to pray. By asking something such as, "Is there any concern about which we can pray for you in Jesus' name?", you can gain permission and discover one or two topics of prayer. It's quite rare that people refuse such gentle offers to pray.

> We walk up to people and say, "We're Christians, and we're walking through the neighborhood and asking God to bless you. We wanted to know if there was anything specific we could pray for you today." Generally nine times out of ten they'll say they want us to pray for a certain situation. One guy's father died, and he knew his mother was suffering. So he asked us to pray for his mother. We prayed for his mother, but we also prayed for him that he would know how to minister to his mother, how to say the right things to his mother, show her love and support.
>
> Then we ask them if we can lay hands on them. We might say, "Do you mind if we touch you while we pray for you, because if Jesus were here, he would be touching you. In fact, he is here. He sent us here today to assure you he's for you and not against you. He's reaching out to you now." Then we pray simple prayers. They love it. We have never had anybody say, "Get your hands off me. Don't touch me. Who are you?" Never.
>
> —*Maury Millican, associate pastor at Mission Hills Church in Austin, Texas. He sometimes walks through apartment complexes with a partner, asking people if he can pray for them.*

3. Pray to the point. In particular, remember that you are providing a prayer model for some who may have no other contact with believers. Use a style that's easily understood and imitated after you are gone. Stifle the habit of preaching rambling messages within prayers. Don't give sermons before or after your prayer. Surprise people by simply praying.

4. Stay available. Find ways to follow the results of your prayer. For example, offer to pray again or further. Writing down what you prayed and for whom is a way of demonstrating that you really believe God heard your prayer. Your prayer can become a topic of conversation for years to come.

> You don't need to be reminded of who this is [referring to a picture of Jesus accompanying this message], but it is in his name that we are praying for you this week. Please feel free to display this picture in a prominent place in your home to remind you of our prayers.
>
> —*Message left at houses in Wigan, England, by St.*

> *Nathaniel's Anglican Church. The notes come attached to a picture of Jesus dying on the cross and are brought to houses that have been prayed for during prayerwalks and in other prayer gatherings. Members of his congregation later distribute another leaflet inviting the people to submit prayer requests or to request prayer inside their own homes. After doing this for four years, Brian Gregory, the parish minister, reports that prayerwalking has become as much a characteristic of community life as the beat policeman. Many people have joined the church, in part because of friendships begun by receiving prayer from prayerwalking parishioners.*

Contact prayer is best done as a component of the service a church offers to its own community. This leaves you free from the pressure to turn the simple prayer event into an evangelism episode or a counseling session. Other times of interaction will follow. Contact prayer can either seize God's timing or sow seeds for later harvesting. Learn how to know God's timing. It is not necessary to load contact prayer events with involved testimony or standard evangelism techniques. As God answers prayer you will find abundant opportunity to explain the gospel.

Ed Silvoso of Harvest Evangelism in Argentina trains people to pray for their neighbors by writing their requests in a book, leaving a space to record answers. The person receiving prayer is asked to report any answer to prayer to the intercessor so that the request can be registered as being answered. Any unanswered requests on the list serve as an ongoing reminder for prayer. Reporting back to the intercessor becomes a wonderful occasion to celebrate God's goodness and to tell more about his love.

PART IV

STRATEGIC PRAYERWALKING

11

CITYWIDE PRAYERWALKS

Citywide prayerwalks tend to be fluid, evolving affairs, involving many churches and grass-roots leadership. Every city calls for a unique prayer strategy.

Ideals for Citywide Walks

When believers prayerwalk their communities, their plans usually press toward four ideals.

• **By local believers.** God grants residents a unique compassion and persistence in praying for their own city. At the same time, Christians from anywhere in the world should be welcomed to pray for your city as they visit. But the real work is done by hometown saints.

• **Multichurch.** It is great when individual churches or families set out to blanket their community in prayer. Often such initiatives lead to several churches joining together to cover the entire city. Every church should not be expected to immediately join in the prayerwalking. However, you can still include every church by praying for them!

> Walking prayer and celebration is a mechanism that rises above ethnic and denominational barriers. To be the church in the streets simplified things. There is common ground with Jesus as the focus.
>
> *—David MacAdam, music director of "Pray For Boston '92," a citywide prayerwalk and prayer rally in June 1992 that drew approximately one thousand Christians from dozens of churches. As believers prayed at City Hall Plaza, hundreds of balloons flew overhead stating, "One in Christ Jesus."*

• **Focus on prayer.** Intercessory prayer dominates the agenda without ever standing alone. Other essential ministry activities, such as evangelism or church planting, come to be integrated with prayerwalking, but prolonged, concerted prayer is given its own distinctive place.

• **Every part of the city.** Coverage can be one-time or continual. Prayers are sometimes directed widely for streets or whole neighborhoods. Other times prayer narrows to every dwelling on every street. Industrial and business sectors call for yet a different prayer agenda than homes.

The Value of Citywide Prayerwalks

• **Churches agree together.** Just as two or three believers can enhance their praying by agreeing, so churches find that they can magnify their intercession by joining together to pray for areas inhabited or touched by the respective congregations.

• **A vision lift.** People naturally focus on their neighborhoods. When citywide prayer takes off, forays into the most troubled parts of town become balanced by systematic coverage of areas not typically perceived as needy — for example, wealthy neighborhoods or middle-class suburbs. The entire city comes to be understood as needy before God. This kind of leveling turns us to him for more than a superficial shuffling of resources.

• **Involvement in ministry.** Nothing seems more futile than trying to pressure busy Christians into serving their community. Christians will have the desire to pursue the ministry that they feel God is authentically giving to them. Most believers genuinely love God and want to do his will. But many lack a sense of assignment and authority from God. As churches come in contact with their communities, without pressure or hype, people find their initial concerns mature into authentic biblical compassion.

When the scope of prayer encompasses the entire city, the focus for everyone can shift from a pure neighborhood watch idea. Prayers have less chance of degenerating into a watchdog defense against minor intrusions on the status quo.

• **Fruitful friendships.** Side-by-side prayerwalking opens relationships between ordinary believers of different churches. As believing neighbors meet each other, a simple and valuable point of contact is made. Friendships are formed with a sense of local mission, in effect weaving nets for ingathering to the church. As tides of revival sweep through cities, such networks can become a basic infrastructure of evangelism and service.

At 4:00 A.M. Pacific Time on September 11, a few of us met to

> pray for each group as they started at 7:00 A.M. in their time zone. As we prayed over a map, I had a sense of God's hand sweeping across the nation — maybe just an inkling of his perspective. I realized how unique this was to have so many from so many denominations and organizations uniting to call upon the Lord for the youth of this nation — and without any big super-structure or budget to pull it off! I saw how students would get the vision for themselves as they prayed about the urgency of reaching their campuses. As they met together, they became aware that other Christians are present that they may not have known about. By praying together at the pole, they saw that they aren't standing alone.
>
> —*Chuck Flowers, one of the founders of the "See You at the Pole" movement, an international, student-led prayer gathering that takes place once a year around campus flagpoles before school hours. On September 16, 1992, between 1.5 and 2 million students participated in the event in more than nine countries. The movement started in 1990 when students across the state of Texas decided to gather at their school flagpoles to intercede for their campuses. Chuck is director of youth evangelism for the Southern Baptist General Convention of Texas.*

- **Help activate revival.** Many feel that God is ousting the church from its reclusive obscurity in its buildings. We hope that he is doing this to prepare the church for a season of awakening that will bring us into close redemptive contact with our community.

> Revival will come when we get the walls down between the church and the community.
>
> —*Jack Graham, pastor of Prestonwood Baptist Church in Dallas, Texas*

In light of all the values we have listed, you may need to take care that you do not oversell the benefits when you are calling others to join you in systematic prayerwalking. Limit the objectives at the beginning so that you can allow God to enlarge the vision. Articulate hope in terms of what God surely wants to do in your city instead of how specific prayer programs are sure to usher in the end-time revival. Christians are weary of the pendulum swing between apathy and intensity. Commend prayerwalking by the report of others who are serving their cities in prayer rather than theories and projections. Trumped-up guarantees of outbreaks of revival may backfire instead, causing some to feel let down to the point of stubborn complacency.

Three Kinds of Citywide Prayerwalks

Citywide walks tend to fall into three rough categories.

- **Neighborhood walks,** often done on a continuing basis, usually by nearby residents.
- **Preparation walks,** anticipating a special citywide event of worship, evangelism or concerted prayer.
- **Saturation walks,** systematic praying directly connected with plans to accomplish evangelization in the entire area, usually by planting new churches.

1. Neighborhood Walks

Neighborhood walks target areas close to the home or business of the prayerwalkers. Many neighborhood walks continue for months or years, concentrating on places within a few hundred paces of home.

> I think their most effective time was when they were prayerwalking on an estate [a housing project]. It was a place with considerable satanic opposition; a coven was meeting there. A drug ring was operating. The prayerwalkers went out for an hour or so every Sunday evening in that particular estate for some time. The result was that the coven closed down and moved out. The police busted the drug ring, and we now have home Bible studies [taking] place there.
>
> —*John Houghton, speaking of a prayerwalking team from Hailsham Christian Fellowship in East Sussex, England, where John serves as pastor. He coauthored the book* Prayerwalking: A New Approach to Spiritual Warfare *(Kingsway Publications, 1990).*

Organization can be as simple as two neighbors agreeing on a time to meet. Many families diligently walk through their own community almost daily. Students occasionally pray on campus. Fellow employees walk through their workplace.

Although the Spirit of God spontaneously inspires most neighborhood walks, be ready to structure your neighborhood prayer in a way that would help you toward ongoing effectiveness. Here are some ideas.

- **Go with a blessing.** Advise your pastor or other significant leaders of what you hope to do, even if you aren't sure of detailed plans. Ask them to pray for and bless you in the endeavor.
- **Recruit some partner prayerwalkers.** One friend will do. Build a nucleus of friends by adding new companions rather than trying to get a commitment from every person in an already-existing large group. Seek out Christians from other churches who share your neighborhood.

Some of the best prayerwalking efforts get started amidst home fellowship groups. Leaders of standard prayer meetings have introduced prayerwalking as a fresh format.

• **Limit length of commitment.** Announce or agree from the very start that the prayerwalking effort will continue for a limited number of weeks or months. You can always evaluate the experience and decide to continue for another term. People are less likely to plunge into something labeled "Walking our city till Jesus comes."

• **Train prayerwalkers.** Set up a short training time for new prayerwalkers. Simply review some of the basic ideas found in chapters 1, 2 and 3 of this book and deal with questions. Perhaps twenty minutes of this kind of presentation is enough to get started. Appendix A should prove useful as a written introduction.

Be sure to put feet on the street. Do a prayerwalk, however briefly, as part of the training experience, even if the group proceeds around just one block. For best results, however, allow two hours for an initial prayerwalk. The key element of learning to prayerwalk well is to link a newcoming prayerwalker along with an experienced partner.

As mentioned earlier, there is value in experiencing the first few hundred steps of prayerwalking in a setting that is not familiar. A quarter mile from home may be far enough off beaten paths to allow the joy of exploring with fresh eyes.

• **Schedule prayerwalking times.** As in any kind of prayer, it will only take place when blocks of time are set aside. It's common to establish weekly times, such as Saturday morning or Sunday evening, when prayer teams launch out together. More ambitious neighborhood walks have organized daily times assigned to rotating parties. Whatever method you choose, allow prayer teams some measure of freedom to adjust their schedules.

• **Form prayer teams.** If a larger group is to be divided into teams on a particular day, think first of an arrangement which will stimulate effective praying. On the other hand, if teams are expected to keep appointed times on their own throughout the week, think through what composition will provide the best reminder and motivation. Triplets have proven to be the sturdiest size for self-starting prayer teams.

• **Choose routes rather than following routines.** Some intercessors find it tiresome to keep passing by the same places. Master maps can help open new ways around the terrain. Some carry small hand-drawn maps with the names of the people who live in specific homes as a prayer reminder.

• **Debrief and report after each prayerwalk.** Even if there are only two or three of you, discuss what you prayed and learned while walking. Keep a simple record of what was prayed, what biblical promises seemed to come alive, which people and places received prayer, and who actually prayerwalked. You may receive handwritten remarks, which should be filed. Reports aren't hard to do compared with their long-standing value. Just doing a report lifts the whole affair from being a happenstance matter. Faith is crystallized, and vision can be shared. Vital prayers can more easily be pursued again. Progress can be marked, and God can be praised for answering prayer.

In one American city, several Christian couples decided to prayer-walk their huge apartment complex every weekday. They laid out a calendar with different married couples taking different nights of the week. They were surprised to find that initial enthusiasm faded after a few weeks. Upon reflection they realized that by making married couples the prayer teams, they had also made it difficult to circulate reports of each day's prayer to other prayer units so that the entire group could sense themselves praying in concert. Without debriefing gatherings they missed out on much encouragement and accountability, because they had not planned any way to check with each other. They are going to try again with another format. One of the lessons they learned from the flop: Find simple ways to report your prayer.

2. Preparation Walks

Preparation walks build toward special events or anticipate even greater seasons of spiritual breakthrough throughout a community. They tend not to continue on an ongoing basis, rather becoming an event in themselves. Multiple churches are almost always involved. The walk can prepare for a special evangelistic event, special festivals of worship or even another citywide event of united prayer.

> We usually have a prayer committee praying right through the times of the meetings. They pray for the Spirit to be at work, convicting and convincing of Jesus and sin. Wherever possible, we encourage those committees to go through the stands of the stadium long before the crusade and pray that God would make it a special place.
>
> —*Fred Durston, manager, Field Ministries Department, Billy Graham Evangelistic Association*

Preparation walks work best if God's people sense their community stands at a historic juncture. The prayerwalk can take on a healthy glow of historic significance. This makes it all the more important that wise leadership guide the expectations and guard the relationships between participating churches. The wisdom doesn't need to be expensive or elaborate. Here are some ideas others have found useful.

• **Invite friends from many churches.** General announcements and printed notices for prayer gatherings usually fail to rally believers. The call to pray for the city needs to come from two directions: from pastoral leadership and from the grassroots, within friendship circles to other trusted friends. Hopefully your pastor is one of your trusted friends. Invite your pastor to join you and some other friends for a prayerwalk around the church or in a place you have prayed before.

A pastor needs to be the one to invite other pastors to pray together for their city. Once several pastors can endorse prayerwalking from their own experience, it becomes easy to grow a movement of prayer by inviting the few most likely intercessors from one church to join in a prayerwalking experience with pray-ers from another church. After a core group of practicing prayerwalkers is developed in many churches, no hype is needed to launch prayerwalking attempts on a larger scale as God leads.

If pastors show no immediate interest in endorsing prayerwalking, you are better off not attempting a large-scale prayerwalk of the city. Instead, patiently pursue a quiet "grow from below" plan. Keep on practicing neighborhood walks and other efforts of concerted prayer until God's timing appears.

• **Set dates and places wisely.** The concept underlying most preparation walks is to cover key parts or all of a city within a limited time. Of course, seek God's guidance first. But also consult with pastors, elders, businessmen, weathermen and the civic calendars about the best dates and the places to be covered.

Pray over a master map of the city, if possible. Look for good beginning points. It's much better to cover less area with more people than to scatter pray-ers thinly throughout the city limits. Pre-set routes should be short and significant, emphasizing residential and governmental sites.

> We wanted to come together for prayer, praise and proclamation, but we also wanted to march beforehand. So we subdivided downtown Boston into ten sections. Then we broke each of the ten sections down into ten prayerwalks. So we had one hundred distinct areas near city hall. We prepared a map for every route and called the maps "Prayer Triptiks." Each of them had a map with the suggested route, Scripture verses, historical events in those areas and a sample prayer. Each route took less than an hour to do.
>
> *—David Murphy, member of the Boston Prayer Rally Committee. About a thousand people gathered at City Hall Plaza on June 27, 1992. Many remained at city hall to pray while hun-*

> *dreds fanned out in groups of six to twelve to pray with "Prayer Triptiks" in hand.*

Often prayerwalkers take responsibility to pray through an area within a period of days or weeks. Prepare maps which will allow prayerwalkers to clearly understand their assigned area and the expected completion date. The city of Austin, Texas, was systematically covered twice using a master map to keep track of which sectors had been assigned to volunteering prayerwalkers. Each person requesting a specific area was given an enlarged map of that area along with simple instructions as to how to prayerwalk.

Look for themes that God is giving to inspire his people. As mentioned before, you will find an understandable concern to put up a spiritual guard around your own neighborhood. Many citywide prayerwalks have been organized by taking advantage of this concern and challenging believers to each pray for their own neighborhoods. The vision is easy to communicate but can fall short of covering the entire city for the obvious reason that praying Christians are rarely found evenly distributed through all areas of population. Without some cross-town assignments, many areas will lack prayer. Why not break the community into smaller areas and encourage people to take on responsibility for two areas, one close to home and another in a different area of town?

- **Special sites.** Another geographic way of covering the entire city is to call for prayer at select sites. Give special attention to the site of upcoming events.

> We're calling it "Operation Overlord" to declare the lordship of Jesus Christ over the city of Los Angeles. The purpose is to lift up a mantle of prayer, the prayer of blessing. We encourage men to partner in groups of three to five guys, and on that particular Saturday morning we'll go to one of twelve select places, which basically encompass the city of Los Angeles, to pray from those points. If you could, imagine [that you're] a mile tall, standing with one foot in the Coliseum and the other in the Hollywood Park Racetrack, and your hands are extended over the city of L.A., reaching out and blessing, because God has ordained the blessing through the extension of [the] prayers of his people. Pray blessing on the city: "Now, Lord, we are the seed of Abraham, and we speak blessing upon the people of Los Angeles, the different nations of Los Angeles. Let your salvation, healing, deliverance and reconciliation settle over this city."
>
> —*Jack Hayford, pastor of Church on the Way in Van Nuys, California, presenting a plan that beckoned hundreds from dif-*

ferent churches to walk and pray over most of Los Angeles before the Olympics in 1986

> During a time of worship, I got the idea to pray at some specific places in the weeks just before the March for Jesus in 1992. There were five places; one of them was Mount Bonnel, the highest place in the city. Another was the University of Texas, at the tower right below where it says, "You shall know the truth and the truth shall set you free." We invited friends from different churches who knew each other and had prayed together before. It prepared us for the march by preparing our hearts to magnify Jesus as Lord of the whole city.
> —*Joann Davis, Austin, Texas*

• **Special gatherings for leaders.** Pastors often find it easier to invite fellow pastors of their town to pray together if they are meeting at a neutral site. With a small measure of extra care or cost, such prayer gatherings can happen in places which beckon large prayers for the entire community. Pastors have gathered for such open-eyed prayer on bridges, mountains, riverbanks and the top floor of tall buildings.

A house with a panoramic view of much of Los Angeles was donated to Church on the Way in Van Nuys, California. For some time a handful of pastors in the Los Angeles area used it as a place of prayer because of its strategic location. That prayer meeting eventually grew into a large gathering of pastors from all over the metropolis called "Love L.A." The prayer meeting has since moved to another place to accommodate more than eight hundred pastors who gather every three months to pray for the city.

3. Saturation Walks

Saturation walks are becoming a standard part of efforts to systematically evangelize neighborhoods. They often play a part in planting new churches. The term *saturation church planting* refers to ministry efforts which aim to have a sufficient number of churches geographically and culturally near every inhabitant of a region.

• **Integrate prayerwalking in an overall plan.** Several proven church-planting ministries have found that the best way to link prayer and church planting is to let prayerwalking stand as a distinct stage or step in an overall plan. In this way, prayer is stressed, but not as an end in itself. The key is to leave no church-planting effort prayerless and no prayerwalk fruitless.

> In our efforts there are roughly four stages. The first stage is

intercession, which continues throughout the time we are pursuing all the rest of the stages. Next comes proclamation, keying on the places we have prayed for. We find the Holy Spirit has readied them. The third stage is innovation. By that we mean that something new comes about, usually a new congregation. Finally, there is the stage of multiplication.

—*Carol Davis, director of ministries, The Church on Brady, Los Angeles, California*

The overall strategy we use in church planting has four parts: walking, warfaring, speaking the word and then winning people. Walking is a matter of trying to get the heart of God for the heart of the city. Walking is done in part by physically walking through, but it's a matter of getting the spiritual temperature of the city, hearing its outcry. Once we discern the pain at the heart of the city and sense the compassion in the cry of the heart of God, then we step into warfaring as God directs. After these we are ready for the third and fourth parts, which amount to evangelism and discipling.

—*Simon Thomas, of Ichthus Christian Fellowship in London, England. Simon travels widely encouraging churches in spiritual warfare and church planting.*

Prayerwalking is only one piece of nine things we do in spiritual warfare. It's impossible to isolate the effectiveness of prayerwalking all by itself. We have never done it by itself. But I can tell you about a neighborhood where people [first] prayed for two weeks, walking around it, praying over maps all night, offering to pray for people on the spot, setting up lighthouse prayer meetings so we could continue to pray for people's healing. We [then] did all kinds of work bringing the church in contact with the neighborhood for months and saw God's intervention. At year's end we had twenty thousand new people in the church. We don't know how much of this was directly due to prayerwalking. It is just a part of what needs to be done. But it's a creative, vital piece of the whole effort.

—*John Huffman, of Latin America Mission, who gives leadership to the visionary program called "Christ for the City" from his home in Costa Rica*

- **Systematic prayerwalking.** One vision may call for methodical prayer for every dwelling. Other groups may plan for contact prayer after covering the streets.

Systematic prayer doesn't mean pronouncing prolonged prayers on the doorstep of every dwelling. Some places need more prayer than can be discreetly uttered while walking past at a normal gait. John Huffman helps his prayer teams to pour themselves out in prayer for select homes by a good use of maps. Huffman trains prayerwalkers to prepare maps depicting every dwelling. Intercessors learn how to use the maps in prayer rooms away from the neighborhood after they have first done extensive prayerwalking in the neighborhood.

It's good to cover a city thoroughly, but geographic coverage isn't the primary goal. Persistence and sustained creativity stimulate enjoyable variations which go further in the long run than a one-time meticulous coverage.

For instance, Church on the Way in Van Nuys, California, set out to prayerwalk every street of the entire San Fernando Valley, home to 1.3 million people. They weren't afraid of aiming high and adjusting their plans based on their experience. Barry Lagemann, one of the pastors of the church, describes their approach.

> Our first attempt was to cover the whole San Fernando Valley. It was such a massive project. We found that we were just doing bits and pieces of that huge area. So we ended up finally specializing and zeroing in on the Van Nuys area at the heart of the whole valley. We have been repeatedly covering that area about every four months. We call it Operation Saturation. We've taken Van Nuys, and using a map we've broken it up into 492 segments which are adjusted for the number of homes rather than square miles. If we have as many as a thousand people come out, we can cover much of Van Nuys, two-by-two, in about two and half hours on a Saturday morning.
>
> It took a lot of volunteer work by concerned intercessors to prepare all the maps and instructions. We've appointed captains for each area who are asked to survey their areas before the big day. They do some prayer in the area to bind the strong man of the area beforehand as they survey the sector for languages and special needs. We ended up dealing with over a dozen different languages. We trained our people to introduce themselves and say something [such as], "We are here in the area to pray for you and to offer you a free Bible if you don't have one in your home."

As successful as Operation Saturation has been, leaders are considering making more adjustments. For example, they've noticed a decreasing number of participants from a high of one thousand to a few hundred. Instead of pressuring more churchgoers to be prayerwalkers, the leaders feel that they have found scores of people with a calling to pray for their community. They are looking for ways to engage those people with proven callings in ongoing prayerwalks while continuing to invite the larger congregation to be involved.

• **Exploratory prayerwalking.** Prayerwalkers come to know their area. Carol Davis, director of ministries for The Church on Brady in Los Angeles, observed a difference in the teams who have pursued prayerwalking as part of their training for saturation church planting. "The ones who have actually done prayerwalking develop an unusual bonding with the area and with their streets and with the houses. They know it in a way that the other teams don't. I believe that there is something almost supernatural that happens in terms of their spirits being in tune with God's Spirit because of intercession. It changes them. It's almost like you can't take it out of them."

Most prayerwalkers find they are able to explore a long-range vision for their community. Prayerwalking is an excellent way to seek God's guidance for opening steps in ministry.

Some church planters seek the households in which they can meet divinely prepared people "of peace" such as Cornelius (see Luke 10:6; Acts 10:1-4). Or the plan may actually amount to a prayer process of elimination, focusing on a narrowing group of key homes.

> On day eight of the "faithwalks," the team went to a mobile home park. While they were praying in pairs, people came up to them and asked them what they were doing. When they told them, the people offered their homes for Bible studies. They were astonished to find twelve people who were interested in hosting Bible studies.
>
> —*W. D. (Doc) Lindsey, a Southern Baptist missions director in Detroit. Two cell churches now meet at that mobile home park. Doc trains leaders in a cell church-planting strategy which begins with fourteen days of on-site prayer. They pray that God would reveal "people of peace" who might be able to invite their extended network of friends and families into their homes to study Scripture.*

John Huffman, of Latin America Mission, has distilled many tested approaches for praying and evangelizing neighborhoods in many Latin cities. One highlight of his fourteen-day plan for prayerwalking neighborhoods is the day set aside for what he calls prayer of confirmation. According to Huffman's plan, different prayerwalking teams cover the same homes and communities at different times. They are trained to record their prayers and impressions of need or opportunity which emerge during prayer. These reports are turned over to a coordinator who compares and sorts through the reports of different teams. That coordinator examines "the specific prayer burdens which God placed upon us...the insights received through visions, dreams, the words of knowledge, wisdom or discernment [which] have been noted down on the report forms."

The reports are examined by the coordinator to see whether there is some confirmation to the burdens that God has been placing on the hearts of various intercessors. These relatively few homes are then held up for further prayer. Quite often, different prayer groups have sensed the same thing. Huffman calls this coinciding of prayer burden a confirmation that God is inspiring and answering prayer for specific homes.

About confirming prayer burdens by comparing reports, he says:

> Our experience has taught us that where a prayer campaign involves just one congregation, 31 percent of the prayer reports receive at least one or more confirmations. When the campaign involves a number of congregations, the confirmations increase to over 50 percent. This ought to remind us that the united prayer of the people of God has great power. When we have visited the homes where there have been at least two confirmations, the vast majority, if not all, have responded positively to the ministry and witness in each case.
>
> —*From the* Manual of Participatory Missionary Prayer, *edited by John C. Huffman, published by Latin America Mission, P.O. Box 52-7900, Miami, Florida, 33152-7900, 1992*

> Every single street of Huntington Park was prayed for. We walked through every street of that city, and it took eight solid months. Since then, we started the proclamation, or evangelism, phase. The first Saturday we started proclamation efforts in the homes we had prayed for, every single home had at least one adult conversion.
>
> —*Erwin McManus, The Church on Brady, Los Angeles, describing how a strategy to plant new fellowships is working in Huntington Park, California, a part of eastern Los Angeles*

12

Prayer Journeys: Inside Distant Cities

Prayerwalkers often launch out far beyond the horizons of their hometowns to distant cities and places.

> Our team spent one hundred days in the city of three million people, most of them Muslim, learning about the culture and envisioning how Christ's body could become a reality among people who are effectively churchless. We often prayed for the whole city from the rooftop of the eleven-story building we stayed in. But the best part of the whole effort was covering every sector of the city with what we called "Joshua walks." We somehow got a wall-sized map to chart our progress week by week. We'd head out two-by-two with a rough idea of our route. I think the prayerwalking gave us the freedom to allow ourselves to make friends and get emotionally attached to the city. After a while no neighborhood seemed really intimidating or beyond the reach of Jesus, which, for that city, is really saying something.
>
> —*Steve Chism, who at the time of his first prayer journey was a student in Pasadena, California*

Prayer journeys provide a way for many believers from local churches to make significant contributions among some of the least evangelized peoples.

One businessman said:

> I had been a bit skeptical, thinking that surely I could pray any of the same prayers from home. But I was amazed to find my-

self looking in the faces of kids and praying for them in ways I know I never would have done in the routines of my household and business at home. Especially when I realized that some of these kids hadn't been prayed for by a Christian in their lives, and may not get prayed for again for years. It was definitely worthwhile for them. But I think I got the most out of it.

A United Methodist church in the Midwest felt God was giving them responsibility to plant churches among one of the unreached people groups of Asia. But which people group? What city? And how would they begin? How would they form a partnership with an effective mission structure or church in a foreign city? Because of the major commitment of resources they hoped to make, they decided to send some of the lay leaders and staff of the church along with their senior pastor to prayerwalk through some select Asian cities. They visited and prayed through Bangkok and Bombay. In these cities there was no sense from God that he was giving them an assignment there. In fact, they felt confirmed that they should not initiate work in those places. But months later they received a report from some of their prayerwalkers who had traveled again to Asia, this time to one of the Central Asian republics. The church felt God giving them clear guidance to pursue long-range efforts to plant new churches in Central Asia.

We came to a mosque on a Friday while the people were doing their Muslim prayer rituals. I was expecting to have a sense of oppression, as I had while visiting other mosques. To the contrary, I sensed a beautiful desire to worship the true God. I don't understand that, but I began to worship God through Christ. I felt then that God was opening the door for us in Central Asia. It was as if he had challenged me, "Ask of me and I will surely give you this place." Our prayerwalk there confirmed for me and my church that God was opening works for us to do here.

—*Bill Jameson, a missionary from Indiana who had prayerwalked in several places in Asia before sensing God's assignment.*

Prayer journeys don't always head to overseas destinations. Capital cities are often the destination of a prayer journey. In October 1981 over 260 women from Lydia Fellowship, a network of intercessors in England, converged on London for a well-planned prayerwalk. Many of them were from London, but many came from other parts of the country. They set out at 6:00 A.M. on a Saturday morning. The first wave of more than two hundred accomplished the three-hundred-mile boundary of greater London in groups of twos and threes, each starting from a prearranged spot and prayerwalking no more than three miles. Another wave of walkers covered the central Westminster district. The intercessors gathered at a central church where many others had been fasting and praying and preparing for a time of celebration which included everyone. One highlight at the concluding celebration was a foot-washing for those who had walked. (Some had walked barefoot as a prophetic gesture.) This prayerwalk helped open the way for several other events of on-site worship and prayer which flourished later, among them the March for Jesus.

Barbara Boggs of Sacramento, California, leads intercessory prayer teams to do extensive on-site prayer at American state capitol grounds. She puts out a call to known intercessors to travel to the capital to do prayer and fasting at a special place of prayer. The team uses a special tent which imitates some features of the ancient tabernacle of Israel. Prayerwalks around the capitol and environs are conducted daily by the prayer journey team, but most of their effort is to continue a twenty-four-hour prayer vigil on the capitol grounds.

> Because our permit was denied and then reissued, the authorities ended up designating a place for us to place our prayer tent out of view. But it was within earshot of many key leaders since it was right next to the building. The legislators got to enjoy our constant worship and prayer.
>
> —*Barbara Boggs, telling of a recent prayer journey to Santa Fe, the capital of New Mexico. She serves statewide prayer movements through Rhema Vista Ministries.*

Prayer Journeys and Prayer Expeditions

There are two broad categories of long-distance prayerwalks. The *prayer journey* is the most common type. On prayer journeys intercessors travel to cities other than their own in order to prayerwalk within, throughout or around them. Prayer is directed to the concerns surrounding specific urban areas, special sites or people groups.

For a *prayer expedition*, the other basic type of long-range prayerwalking, pray-ers walk along strategically developed routes, often for long distances, across large territories. Prayers are aimed at the needs of entire regions, countries or even continents.

In both prayer journeys and prayer expeditions, prayers and blessings are lifted on behalf of God's glory among the people who live in the area. Intercessors may deal with spiritual strongholds as needed. Because most prayer journeys take Christians to destination cities in foreign countries, there is a cross-cultural flavor to what follows.

Prayer journeys and prayer expeditions are both specialized prayerwalks involving a few matters of basic preparation. It's not complicated, but the great needs of the cities of today's world, not to mention the large investments of time and money, behoove us to prepare for these efforts with excellence.

Building on material presented in all of the preceding chapters, this chapter will guide you in preparing for prayer journeys. With minor adjustments, most of what pertains to prayer journeys applies as well to prayer expeditions. The next chapter covers additional details about prayer expeditions by building on virtually everything in this chapter. We've organized practical ideas under three time frames: before, during and after the prayer journey.

Before the Journey: Preparing

- **Seek God's sending.** Most prayerwalkers agree on the most important part of the prayer journey: Be sent by God. The entire venture should come from God's heart, and he is eager to send. However, awareness of desperate needs in distant lands is not enough reason to launch a prayer journey. Before anyone initiates complex plans, specifically petition God to activate his highest design and timing.
- **Seek pastoral blessing.** It is ideal to be sent by a local church. Seek the blessing and wisdom of your pastoral leadership at the very dawning of the idea of a prayer journey. Some churches are unprepared to officially sponsor a prayer journey but may eagerly endorse and support it alongside other churches.

> A team like this has to be sent out by the leadership of the local church. There has to be pastoral covering because it's a warfare activity, and God's authority is vested in the local church. I wouldn't attempt to take a team out apart from the pastoral covering of our church. I meet regularly with my pastors. I want my pastors to see my blind spots, and if they were to say stop doing it, I would in a heartbeat.
>
> —*Jan Lenington, of Skyline Wesleyan Church in San Diego, California. Last year Jan ventured on a prayer journey to Croatia.*

- **Seek wise counsel.** Seek the continuing counsel of a group of wise, older leaders who are people of prayer. You may even want to form a temporary guiding structure to oversee the process.
- **Set goals and ministry limits.** Involve the senior leadership team mentioned above — in concert with missionaries and national leaders if

possible — in articulating goals. Clarity of purpose is essential. Are you expected to accomplish mission goals in the areas of evangelism, relief or other services? Senior leaders can give you the necessary authority and release that you will need.

Do as God leads, but consider emphasizing prayer as your primary ministry during the prayer journey. The key for engaging in direct ministry, such as evangelism, is to serve what God is already doing in the country. For example, in many parts of the "10/40 window"* or among "unreached" peoples, there is virtually no church. In such settings quick evangelism can yield even more complex issues surrounding the resulting new spiritual babes, who might effectively be left behind as orphans.

If your team considers itself to be the primary harvesting force, you are probably not praying for as great a harvest as Christ is hoping to give. Remember the first charge Jesus gave the seventy — to pray for more laborers to be sent. You express faith for more laborers by not trying to leave the city completely evangelized after your short stay.

On the other hand, teams have been led to do open worship evangelism and have enjoyed giving testimony to their faith and praying with people.

> We were in a tight Muslim land with reprisals against open evangelism, so for the purposes of our short time in the country, we agreed among our team not to initiate gospel conversations. But Muslims would seek us out about Jesus anyway. So we agreed to sleep on it before answering questions about Christ in any detail. If God was in it, there would be another day. So we kept at our work, but at the end of the time, everybody had gotten a chance to share the gospel, even though we had come for the express purpose of exploring the land for later efforts. We called it "grape picking" after Joshua's first experience in Canaan where he didn't go on a conquest but just sampled some of the fruit.
>
> —*Daniel Wombley of Los Angeles, telling of a prayer and research effort in the Middle East*

Prayer journeys are always contributory: They always add to what has been accomplished before and help prepare the way for other ministry. Seek God to grasp what contribution your prayer journey might be able to make.

---

* The least evangelized part of the world between the tenth and the fortieth latitude.

• **Seek God's choice of team members.** The most effective teams are sent by Christ as confirmed by their churches. The sending power is stronger when team members are selected or invited instead of being recruited by open appeal.

Who should be invited to join the team? The overriding concern should be the maturity and sincerity of the prayerwalkers. If they can be described as persons who walk with God intimately, they will likely do well when literally walking in prayer. Prayerwalking is new to most, so many prime candidates may not yet have experience in prayerwalking. But everyone on the team should have already demonstrated a heart for prayer.

Some have tried to rank different prayerwalks as to their difficulty, and choose team members accordingly. Some ventures are obviously not a good idea for baby Christians, but since it's really impossible to accurately quantify the unique challenge of every prayerwalk, weigh the matter before God.

Describe the unique challenges of your prayerwalk before considering people for the team. It will help you to develop some basic criteria beyond the essential spiritual and emotional maturity.

Before you even begin recruiting people, consider the overall size and composition of the team. Anticipate public reaction in your host culture to the kind of prayer bands which can be formed. Male and female mix can be an important consideration. For example, some cultures frown on unmarried couples. In other cities, women walking certain streets can be easily misunderstood. Look to enrich each team with a diversity of gifts, ages and skills.

Prayer journeys have been accomplished well ranging from just two people to twenty or more. With any group larger than twelve, however, certain dynamics will change, calling for more experienced leadership. Teams work best with clearly defined leadership. Strengthen team fabric by anticipating the best way to resolve minor conflicts.

• **Develop a team covenant.** Write a team agreement or covenant for everyone who will join the prayer journey team. Covenants help everyone sense a common vision and commitment. Be sure to draft a covenant which states highest team ideals rather than rules for minimally acceptable behavior. Possible areas to cover in a covenant include the following: commitment to love team members, readiness to perform rigorous prayer, pursuit of daily spiritual disciplines, submission to leaders, and commitment to honor fellow team members and local people. Keep covenant points simple and brief. The fewer items the better.

A team covenant opens the door just wide enough for earnest volunteers to join you during the prayer journey yet preserves the integrity of the team. The camaraderie of the team has valuable power in prayer agreement. New friends can stimulate, guide and enrich prayer. Prepare a sheet of information that describes your team, its covenant and the costs involved. This document can serve as a conditional invitation to join the team temporarily by sharing its disciplines and ideals.

• **Seek the wider team.** Explore what relationships your church may already have in the destination city. If you lack connections, seek out local leaders and missionaries in the host country, but be sensitive to any threats to their security that your actions may cause. Your prayer team can be immeasurably strengthened with local leaders giving you wisdom and companionship. Be ready to offer appropriate submissive respect to local leaders.

When you arrive in the destination city, it is often fitting to invite local believers to join you in prayer. However, it may often not be feasible for them to join you at the times and pace you need to keep. At first you may find it hard to believe that such new friendships could be distracting. Yet relationships with local believers can flourish so rapidly that you might find it wise to set aside times for team members to meet and pray as a core team.

Inquire ahead of time about the best approach to hospitality so that you wisely balance the values of deepening cross-cultural friendships with fulfilling the work of prayer. Providing housing for you may be very costly to poor local believers. If you stay in local homes, your hosts may express concerns for your safety and expect you to follow protocols which may unduly complicate your prayer mission.

> After getting settled for an anticipated stay in a Muslim home, only then did Joanie find out that her new friend, Sanaa, was the second wife of Hassan. Sanaa's home where Joanie stayed was Hassan's second home. The situation became really complicated when Hassan's first wife insisted that Joanie spend time in both homes. The unforeseen tension took a lot out of her. She couldn't easily back out from her desire to stay in an Arab home, and Joanie felt stuck for four long days.
>
> —*Katie Watson, describing the plight of her teammate while on a prayer and research journey in Damascus, Syria*

Part of your wider team may be *intercessory missionaries,* who reside in foreign cities for months or even years at a time doing almost nothing but praying. If you go to a place blessed with one of these rare intercessors, be sure to learn from them and inform them regarding what you discover in prayer.

Prayerwalks are most effective if they are part of a bigger, ongoing thrust. The desire for a fast fix is the most common error. A sincere desire to see the Lord Jesus extend his kingdom over the area should prompt the short-term team to join with the local brothers and sisters in their deep and ongoing commitment. We come to serve them, not to create a triumphalistic environment that the Lord will not honor.

Outside groups sometimes don't see the complicated social problems that have been there for centuries. Sometimes they do sense spiritual forces accurately but don't fight spiritual battles wisely. Properly executed spiritual war fights battles to the end. We do not bless the local churches when we stir up a territorial spirit unless we're willing to make a commitment to whip it. These things are real, and you don't mess with a territorial spirit if you're not willing to fight the battle through and defeat it.

Fighting through is not necessarily an easy thing to do sometimes, particularly if it has systemic implications on political structures. We take care working in neighborhoods where drugs are rampant, such as Medellin, Colombia; or in areas where murders are common; or in Mexico City, where Aztec gods managed to extort about eighty thousand human sacrifices for the dedication of their pyramids. That's a bunch of spiritual power built up over centuries of unbroken service to these gods. It can be like putting a stick in a hornet's nest. That's part of why we are not favorable to outside prayer groups who have no local base to continue the ministry.

—John Huffman, a missionary residing in Costa Rica who serves local churches in Latin America with the Latin America Mission. John has given guidance to many prayer journey teams working in partnership with local Christian leaders.

• **Build a financial support team.** You will need funds to do a prayer journey, and to handle those funds well you'll need flexible, clear budgets. The best approach is to work with a willing church program or mission structure that has the administrative manpower needed to receive finances and handle them well.

The best budgets include items commonly found on most short-term mission trips, such as communication with home, gifts for hosts and insurance. Liability and health insurance is a matter to consider in prayer and with professional counsel.

Build a clear, itemized budget so that you can easily let others know what each person needs. Good budgets become useful prayer tools to let others know just how much you are asking God to provide. You are launching into strategically valuable work, well worth the loving gifts of interested Christians. Don't be timid about asking people to help you with prayer or to support the effort financially.

• **Build a prayer support team.** This is a "don't-leave-home-without-it" item. Prayer support is your most valuable asset. Arrange for the team to be covered in prayer daily. Form prayer support in two ways. First, enlist personal intercessors to pray for you regularly. Approach individuals who already are inclined to pray for you. Second, recruit prayer support from church-wide prayer meetings. Find creative ways to direct their prayer for the team. Help your prayer partners do more than just pray *for* you. Help them pray *with* you by directing their prayers toward the needs of the city you are visiting.

> We organized a prayer team at home to be interceding with the prayerwalking team at the exact same hours [that] our team was going through the streets of the Middle Eastern city we have targeted. We were encouraged to no end knowing that they were sometimes tracing our very paths through the streets. It made for some interesting hours for some of them at home with the time zone difference. But they told us how meaningful it was for them to pray right along with us. It was definitely worth it to coordinate the daily routes in whatever way we could to keep the home prayer team connected. They never knew how interesting it could be to pray in front of a map. The whole church felt like we had done the prayer together.
>
> —*Wade Simpson, a pastor who joined the prayerwalking team for a week as part of the preparation for one church's further ministry in the Middle East*

Don't miss the joyous experience of a well-planned commissioning or send-off service. You can help sustain the zeal for sending you by scheduling phone calls or faxing the latest developments.

• **Get briefed.** Almost everything you can learn beforehand about your destination city will be useful in prayer. However, don't go overboard on assigning readings or lectures. Most of what you need to know will be learned on-site. The right amount of briefing information usually leaves prayerwalkers humbly confident of their first steps. Points of data become surprisingly prayerworthy once you finally arrive in the city. Ransack written resources for summaries of history, economy, demographics or social structure. Take special note of the spiritual history before and since the advent of Christianity to the city.

Much of the spiritual history should be confirmed from leaders in your host city. It's too easy to make wild conjectures from a distance.

> I was visiting the African country of Zimbabwe, doing some teaching on aspects of prayer. I had heard that child sacrifice had been practiced long ago at a site known as the Zimbabwe ruins. Before focusing on the site as a place to bind evil powers, I checked with some local pastors. To my surprise, although the local leaders recognized some kind of spiritual evil at the Zimbabwe ruins, they did not see the ruins as a big deal. The greater matters of spiritual war to them were the witch doctors and the worship of ancestral spirits in just about every village. These pastors had seen a few different groups of Americans come and do some elaborate prayer at the ruins and then leave, proclaiming that the big spiritual problems had been cared for. It seemed to them that we were coming over with spiritual warfare talk, but we didn't really know what was going on. They were happy for us to help them in what really afflicted them.
>
> —*Cathy Schaller, of Temple City, California, who has helped train leaders in intercession and spiritual warfare in several countries*

Cross-cultural stress is a major issue. Equip the team with practical sensitivity to cross-cultural differences and how to cope with them. Brief times of classroom lecture and a few simulation exercises will do the job. Search the churches of your city for resource people who can offer seasoned wisdom from their experience in your destination city.

• **Establish security guidelines.** Special challenges arise when working in the so-called "closed" countries (countries which restrict the entrance and activities of missionaries). Most government structures which officially restrain the advance of the gospel do so because of political volatility rather than naked religious hostility. Religious opposition usually gains its leverage from unstable environments.

Because security matters usually amount to dealing well with fragile political situations, avoid giving the appearance that you oppose regimes in power, or that you have an interest in military operations, sensitive minorities or disputed territories. Treat the government honorably, avoiding adversarial attitudes.

> When we were questioned by the police and they read through our journals, I was glad that I had not used terminology like "taking the country for Christ" or "prayer assaults" or "spying out the land" or "invasion of the gospel." The government of our host country has a real problem with terrorist groups coming from outside the country posing as innocent tourists. The police naturally connect that kind of language with terrorism.

—Geni Brewer, a participant in a prayer journey in the Middle East. Secret police couldn't make sense of the routes and random contacts the prayer journey team was making, and so they called the intercessors aside to verify the team's purpose. Geni now serves in the same country in which she prayed.

Think of the different parties that may benefit from precautions. Take care not to bring attention to your venture or, worse yet, complicate the testimony and survival of Christians in the country. Your aspirations to return to the host country could also be complicated by foolishly inviting official scrutiny.

Precautions should be defined in two areas: communications while at home and communications while in the country. Seek advice from experienced missionaries about how to best communicate while homeside. Are limits in order for needed publicity and fund raising, such as leaving out the name of the country and specifying it by its region instead (for example, saying *North Africa* instead of *Libya*)? What precautions may be wise for reports and publications after the venture?

While in-country, avoid reckless or explicit statements about government and religion in outbound mail, received letters from home, journals of prayers and daily activities, or even when speaking to each other in public.

During a prayer journey in Iraq in 1990, a sixteen-member team felt the scrutiny of the secret police. While they were on a guided tour of archaeological sites, they used code words during times of prayer. Israel was called "Michael's land"; Saddam Hussein was "Hey man"; Moslems became "musicians"; missions organizations were called "companies"; and shouts of Hallelujah were heard as "Honolulu."

Brace yourself for limited contact with those who are doing gospel work. Many missionaries in security-sensitive places try to keep from being stereotyped as traditional missionaries by serving in standard employment patterns. (They are sometimes called tentmakers after the trade that Paul worked during his missionary efforts). Too much interaction with visiting teams could complicate their long-range plans. Under even more severe scrutiny, first-generation converts to Christ often face serious persecution for their faith. As much as you would like to be in touch with them, and as much as they would love to honor you, often you are best advised to have no contact at all.

We know of no country where tourists are prohibited from quietly praying. God may give you guidance to pray and worship openly. Or you may find it wise to keep a low-profile presence. In either case, take care not to raise suspicions.

Depending on the region, some prayer journey plans should be kept very quiet while others should be broadcast in great detail. Those people experienced in the region can help you balance the potential prayer generated by open reports against the potential damage to vulnerable church movements.

The whole point of forming security guidelines is to agree on standards of operating that will best express your trust in God. Having agreed on guidelines, lean on God and relax. Your undistracted innocence is your best security.

- **Find the best time.** Most prayer journeys aim at a week or two of prayer. Try to arrange for at least ten days in the city. Any less than a week can amount to no more than an expensive case of jet lag. Deep identification with the people builds on hundreds of small impressions and a few enduring friendships. Authority in God for prayer may be formed in a cumulative way: The longer you spend, the more informed and heartfelt your prayers will be. Fulfill what God sends you to do. Some prayer journeys last for months, but much can be accomplished in a short time.

Can prayerwalking be added to an already planned trip? Concentrated times of prayerwalking can be added to trips planned for other purposes, such as vacations and business trips. Conventional short-term mission trips have also proven to be perfect occasions for prayerwalking.

The basic guideline in blending prayerwalking with other activities is to seek God so that your prayer arises from his heart and guidance. Be sure to make the prayer vigorous. Set aside large blocks of time for prayerwalking, preferably an entire day at a time. For the best results, try to dedicate at least a full morning or afternoon to prayerwalking.

- **Develop strength.** A prayer journey requires a season of spiritual disciplines that begins long before arriving at the host city. In addition, physical strength is a must, so choose a suitable training regimen. The best training — both spiritual and physical — is extensive prayerwalking.

Build prayer stamina. Intense intercession for more than two hours exhausts some who are new to long periods of prayer. You need to be at ease with praying for six or eight hours a day, sometimes more. There is no other way to learn the rhythms of extended prayer times than by doing it with others. Nothing will condition the team for prayerwalking better than prayerwalking. Consider it absolutely essential for every team member to log hours or miles in prayerwalking in their own community before going overseas.

Fasting can also be a part of developing your strength. Some prayerwalkers mix prayerwalking and fasting. Others dedicate themselves to a time of physical weakness in fasting for days or even weeks before the actual prayer journey. After breaking the fast, they are ready with a revived body and a stretched inner person for the prayerwalk itself.

During the Journey: Praying

Good prayer journeys require a blend of foresight and flexibility. Plan your praying, and pray continually to know the best plans. A basic dictum should be to have a plan in place that the Holy Spirit can guide you to change if need be.

• **Strategic first steps.** First impressions can be daunting. Cityscapes stretch out endlessly, filled with throngs of people who move, speak, act and dress differently. If some of their customs continue from ancient times, it's easy to get a sinking feeling that the city and its people are unalterable. Spiritual awakening can seem centuries away.

Don't be fooled by such faith-sapping impressions. Urban ministry has a redeeming paradox: The more intimately you come to know a small portion of the city, the smaller the entire metropolis usually seems.

Make your first day of prayer simple but significant. If you are not sure where to start, try gathering the entire team to a recognized landmark or tourist site. Quietly pray through the spot. Launch prayer teams from there on short, timed routes of thirty to sixty minutes and meet back at an appointed time.

Another initial idea is to find an elevated place, preferably not one complicated with false worship, and pray around the points of the compass. Access can be surprisingly easy to the top floors and rooftops of tall buildings.

• **Covering the city.** Discern God's design for prayer. A systematic coverage may call for encircling neighborhoods or tracing large zigzag patterns through them. Instead of attempting an even coverage of every sector, you may aim at certain neighborhoods or distinct populations.

Another option is walking the city's outer perimeter, though this can be difficult. Metropolitan areas are often the growth areas, making the outermost edges of cities quite ragged. Roads run toward the center of the city rather than tracing a perimeter.

If you are attempting to cover the entire city part by part, use a large map to trace out reasonable portions. Try to learn all you can about public transportation so prayerwalkers can get to and from their assignments quickly. If you try to cover the entire city from the center, you will find transportation eventually reducing what is possible to accomplish in a day.

The zones actually visited by tourists are usually quite small, making tourists themselves the points of attraction in most other parts of the city. Be ready to answer the inevitable questions about who you are, where you are going and what you are doing.

Many tightly knit communities view interlopers with extreme suspicion. Befriending longtime residents can be one of the few ways to legitimize your continued presence to others who live in poor or troubled neighborhoods off the beaten track. In such areas, friendships enrich prayer but can complicate freewheeling intercession.

> In our neighborhood it's customary for people to inquire about where we are going and what we are doing or even to walk along with us. We normally welcome such friendship since we came here to introduce new friends to Jesus. But we also feel it's important to intercede without interruption around our area every week. The only way we've found to prayerwalk without making a big scene is to go out before dawn. Even so our neighbors still notice us and ask what we were doing out so early. We tell them the truth, of course, in a sensitive way. But it's been an important part of ministry, well worth the early wake-up call.
>
> —*Bill and Delores Jameson, missionaries in a poor section of one of the world's largest cities*

Be very careful about coming near anything having to do with the police, government or military. You may not know you have breached a security area until it is too late.

> We wanted to pray for the television station. There's only one for the country, but I guess that means it's kind of like a military target because they had sandbagged machine guns installed on street level all around it. We made a couple of passes, but the better part of wisdom was to bless it all from a distance.
>
> —*Tim Johnson, a pastor in Ohio, speaking of the challenges he faced praying in a country with a fragile government*

• **Establish a daily schedule.** Set a basic daily schedule with at least two or three items which remain standard throughout the journey. A basic rhythm will help you recognize when God's Spirit is calling you to divert from your plan.

One suggested day plan has a Mediterranean siesta rhythm with a prolonged rest in the afternoon.

before 8:00 A.M.	eat and private time
8:00-8:30 A.M.	worship
8:30-8:45 A.M.	briefing

8:45-10:30 A.M.	prayerwalk
10:30-11:00 A.M.	break
11:00 A.M.-1:00 P.M.	prayerwalk
1:00-2:00 P.M.	eat and break
2:00-4:30 P.M.	rest
4:30-6:30 P.M.	prayerwalk
6:30-7:30 P.M.	eat and break
7:30-8:00 P.M.	debrief or worship
after 8:00 P.M.	personal time

A more full schedule is workable. This early-riser plan has advantages of some cooler times of day on the streets.

before 7:00 A.M.	eat and personal time
7:00-7:30 A.M.	worship and briefing
7:30-10:00 A.M.	prayerwalk the streets
10:00-10:30 A.M.	break
10:30 A.M.-12:00 P.M.	prayerwalk the streets
12:00-1:00 P.M.	eat and break
1:00-3:00 P.M.	prayerwalk at overlook points
3:00-7:00 P.M.	rest and personal time
7:00-9:00 P.M.	prayerwalk at special sites
after 9:00 P.M.	personal time

Using daylight hours enhances the largest factor of prayerwalking: vision. Be aware that there are different facets of the community only visible during night hours. Local customs or even curfews might inhibit prayerwalking after dark.

Be wise in scheduling head-to-head prayer according to the spiritual clock of the culture. Islamic calls to prayer have long been favorite times for prayerwalkers to begin and end prayerwalks. Nevertheless, get heaven's clearance before you attempt a showdown of prayer during hours of idolatrous worship or intense spiritual activity.

• **Persevere by keeping a balanced schedule.** The hardest thing about praying is to keep pressing on. It's at this point that many eager intercessors make a crucial mistake when on prayer journeys: They keep pressing on for days on end without adequate rest and renewal. The result is often a dangerously worn state of mind, body and spirit. Recognize that you have entered a long-range event. You are only adequate in Christ, so give Christ a chance to replenish your emotional and spiritual reserves.

Four items tend to get pushed off the day's schedule to everyone's detriment. Build these into the regular program so that other daily urgencies don't encroach on your effectiveness.

Worship. Be sure to spend time enjoying God together and individually. Direct your hearts, as Jesus did the hearts of his followers, to the joy of being named and known as a child of God. You'll do warfare all day. Enjoying your times with God in the holy place will help you pray at full strength when in the streets. Many songs are designed to generate a lot of fervor against the enemy. These songs have their place, but be sure to use your entire repertoire of songs in order to balance the worship times.

Rest. Adequate rest means more than time off from group responsibilities. Frenetic sight-seeing does not restore the soul. Many recreation activities do not re-create at all. Of course, allow ample time for nightly sleep. But we recommend some disciplined "down time" every day during daylight hours.

Journaling and reflecting in solitude. Prayer runs out if there is no time at all to take in fresh truth. Structure time for people to write or reflect in their own styles. Meditation on Scripture is essential for quality prayer.

Communication. It's not a daily item, but allow time to communicate with friends and family. Postcards, faxes and phone calls may take a bit of prearrangement in some cities, but they shouldn't take too long to do. It's well worth the effort to keep key supporters thanked and updated as to how they can pray with you.

- **Reporting.** Schedule daily briefing and start-up meetings. If occasional detailed debriefing (or "de-griefing" regarding relational issues) sessions are planned in evening hours, it can lighten stress and help bring about necessary adjustments.

Reports from the day's prayerwalking can be a highlight of your meetings, especially when some general guidelines are followed. Avoid speculative or presumptuous reports. Tell what actually happened and freely relate how you felt. In fact, it can help if you explain that some of what you are describing may have been just your view. Whenever possible, speak of what you expect God to do rather than what you think your prayer has already done. For example, instead of saying, "We broke the spirit of deceit over the city," you might say, "We prayed about the spirit of deceit over the city and asked God to do something to manifest truth."

A designated coordinator can occasionally collect reports or specially prepared prayer journals to strengthen accountability.

> One thing that works really well is to buy a team prayer journal and use it to record something from every prayer time. We made journaling part of the task so that no one was finished with their

prayerwalk until they had taken time to write down experiences from the day. So usually someone in the teamlet — that's what we call the pairs or trios that pray together — would spend an hour or less writing in the team journal and passing it on to the next teamlet. By the end of the day everyone's insights were written down. After a day passes, memories fade. Our team's prayer journal became very valuable in planning future prayer efforts and in forming a report about the city and its spiritual dynamics.

— *Katie Watson, of Denver, Colorado. Katie has coordinated aspects of several prayer journeys in Asia and the Middle East.*

• **Take care of relationships.** The shared adventures and sheer hard work engenders a rare sense of camaraderie. Praying together with such intensity can forge lasting friendships. Or the tensions can drive you apart, neutralizing your effectiveness.

Imagine how silly it would be to pray through Christless cities, trying to agree in prayer about the kingdom coming, but being angry inside because we couldn't agree on the schedule for using the shower that morning. Ridiculous things happen with relationships. We've learned to pay attention to team friendships in order to be stronger on the street. We've even gone to the point of asking someone to stay at home base on a day of prayerwalking if they can't get a matter resolved in forgiveness.

— *Timothy Younger, of Houston, Texas. Timothy has led several teams on prayer journeys in Asia.*

After the Journey: Reporting

• **Share the vision.** Before you leave home, arrange time to give a short report with friends and small groups after you return. When such reporting times are scheduled months ahead of time, anticipation builds and interest is more likely to follow you throughout the expedition. Prepare one-minute stories which can be told quickly. When you return, you may know the city you just visited better than your own hometown. You may even feel as if you cannot ever fully describe what you have seen or experienced. However, your goal is to move others to pray for the people you have just walked among by inviting them to join you for brief prayer sessions. Be gentle but persistent in playing the role of a mobilizing advocate for the people of the city you visited.

Handle wisely the insights team members believe they have received from God. Not everything should be shared, but some things can be useful to bolster the faith of local church leaders and missionaries in the host country and certainly of some of the folks at home. Some of your insights will be impressional knowledge that should not be presented as if it were verifiable, eyewitness fact. You can always give a report about the kind of prayers you prayed, where you sensed God's hand at work in a special way, or what promises or prophetic actions encouraged you.

- **Continue to prayerwalk.** Surprisingly, many prayer journey participants fail to continue prayerwalking when they return home. Although team disciplines and daily rhythms are different, make room in your schedule for on-site intercession. Why not invite a few others to prayerwalk a nearby neighborhood and see where it leads?

> After two months of intensive prayerwalking in a city of the Middle East many times the size of Austin, I came back to Austin realizing that I knew that distant city better than I knew my own hometown. I knew it better because I had prayed along the cobbled streets and crowded lanes of that place. I realized then that I had always looked at Austin through the grid of the church I pastored. I had been thinking of Austin as a breeding ground for people who could come to my church. I had failed to see Austin as God might view it. When we returned, my wife and I ventured into Austin to do the same kind of prayer we had done in the Middle East. We walked with a sense of holy compulsion. We've never been the same. The church hasn't been the same either.
>
> —*Dan Davis, a pastor of Hope Chapel, Austin, Texas*

13

PRAYER EXPEDITIONS: ACROSS TERRITORIES

Today many prayerwalkers are venturing on long-distance prayerwalks called prayer expeditions, which cross entire territories. They aim at waging needed spiritual warfare and establishing the blessing of God throughout whole regions.

The styles and goals are incredibly diverse, but almost every prayer expedition will be helped by applying the basic guidelines given in the previous chapter dealing with prayer journeys.

Different Types of Prayer Expeditions

We've noticed four main types.

1. Point-to-point expeditions usually trace a significant route. Sometimes the route can be historically meaningful.

> Just after we completed the long walk from London to Berlin, as a prophetic linking between our nations, I stood at the Brandenburg Gates, and I sensed that the German people could walk on from this point to Moscow and extend the reconciliation further. German leaders accepted the idea and are planning to set out this summer to cross the Polish border on the very date that the Germans invaded Poland in the second world war. We are going to follow — as far as we possibly can — the routes that the German army took into Poland and Russia. Symbolic acts are being planned. Germans will carry flags from the fifteen counties of Germany and lower them when crossing the Polish and Russian borders as a symbol of lowering pride and nationalism.
>
> — *John Pressdee, of Ichthus Christian Fellowship in London*

Dave Cape of South Africa emphasizes service along the routes he walks across Africa. Everywhere he goes on a prayer expedition, Dave carries a bowl used for foot washing. The bowl is attached to a large cross. He explains, "One day while I was praying, the Lord gave me a picture of my cross and bowl as it now looks. I just felt that the bowl needed to be mounted on a cross so that people were under no illusions as to why I was there." Dave has prayerwalked along a five-hundred-kilometer route across Zambia from Victoria Falls to the capital city, Lusaka. He's covered the three thousand miles from Victoria to Cape Town. He was also able to prayerwalk much of the Iraqi border during the Gulf War.

2. Border-to-border expeditions aim at praying for general spiritual awakening upon an entire region. The route encompasses the region by traversing across the face of it. Routing usually connects a few significant sites along the way, but the most important feature is spanning the geographical extremities in prayer.

> The walk from the northernmost to the southernmost point [of Great Britain] came first, in 1991. The next year we crossed the country from east to west. It was an act of prophetic symbolism. The two walks effectively formed a cross. We were stating in a physical as well as a spiritual way that the cross of Jesus should reign over the islands of Great Britain. When we reached the halfway point on the second walk and crossed the path we had traced the year before, we had a vision of a cross being poured out in molten pewter — very hard, shiny metal. What we had done was not transient and ethereal but was actually something set firm in the heavenlies. We're believing God for the outworking of that. I think we saw, too, that many people have been stimulated to prayer as a result of those walks.
>
> —*John Houghton, leading pastor of Hailsham Christian Fellowship, Hailsham, Great Britain*

Women's Aglow Fellowship launched a concentrated prayer thrust in late August 1992. They called it "Cast a Net of Prayer." Hundreds of Aglow women leaders were mobilized to cover the United States in prayer. Every state was covered in prayer in a single three-day period using several creative ways to cover their assigned territories. Routes were covered by land, sea and air. Because of the long distances and the short time frame, most prayer teams drove together in cars, but many walked significant routes. From Mount Denali in Alaska to the Atlantic shores of New Jersey, yellow ribbons were tied to cars or worn as arm bands as a symbol of Christ's love.

They sealed their prayers with a symbolic act. According to Doris Eaker, vice president of prayer ministry for Aglow, "We asked each state prayer coordinator to pray with a team on the final day at their state capital. We asked them to discreetly plant the words of Joshua 1:3 on the capitol grounds in a legal way that was not harmful." These words — telling how God granted his people every place where they put the soles of their feet — sealed the net of prayer that hundreds of women had extended around their states.

3. Surrounding expeditions seek to encircle an entire region or country.

> It's just about all our people talk about. New people will come into the church, and the people here will start talking about the march. It's become the focal point of what we're doing as a church.
>
> —*Jim Files, pastor of Windsor Park Baptist Church in Fort Smith, Arkansas. Once a year his church takes a week-long "Jericho march" around the perimeters of Fort Smith, a distance of about fifty miles. From 9:00* A.M. *to 4:30* P.M. *they walk, pray and worship, and then at night they camp out. They first marched around the city in 1990 with a plan to do it once yearly for seven years. Anywhere from fifty to two hundred people participate, many from other churches.*

A young woman named Verena Birchler initiated the idea of a prayerwalk through the border regions of Switzerland along the periphery of the entire country. They offered prayer seminars on Saturday mornings as part of their invitation to local people to join them for a day or two. Peter Hohn of Campus Crusade for Christ in Switzerland reported: "A small core team marched the whole way. We were joined by Christians from seventeen different denominations. There were sometimes fifty people, but the average was about eight people walking together. We feel it was a small beginning of a movement of prayer going on now. We hope to establish city prayer efforts all over Switzerland."

4. Relay expeditions cover entire regions, but the main feature seems to be the linkage of prayerwalkers. In a relay expedition, prayerwalkers pray through a preassigned portion of a larger route and symbolically hand over the prayer responsibility to another team of prayerwalkers who are primed to cover the next sector of the entire route.

The most well-known relay expedition has been the Torch Run. The Torch Run was instigated by Youth With A Mission but has been carried on by thousands of believers linked with many missions and many hundreds of churches. The first torch was lit on Easter Sunday morning, 1988, on the Mount of Ascension. Other torches were ignited from that flame. These torches have been carried by runners and prayerwalkers in organized, relay fashion the length and breadth of every continent. In fact, offshoot flames of the original torch are still being carried prayerfully in countless places across the globe today.

Mary Lance Sisk, of Charlotte, North Carolina, gives leadership to many intercession efforts. She reports:

> When I served as the national coordinator of Lydia Fellowship in the United States, we organized seventeen teams to pray along U.S. Highway 1, along the whole East Coast from south to north. Walking was involved, but we primarily used cars, praying the whole way from Key West, Florida, through Maine, to the Canadian border. It was a tremendous time of intercession and prayer and claiming and making decrees over the land. We took a large rock and painted the Ten Commandments on it. The first team started in the Florida keys. We would drive to a point and hand the rock to another team. We prayed there with that team. Each team had studied the area they were going to be driving through, and they would plan appropriate prayer — all the way to Canada.

Before the Expedition: Preparing

Expeditions are more complicated than prayer journeys. Any point of preparation helpful for prayer journeys will be even more essential for prayer expeditions.

• **Seek God's leading for times and ways.** More so than with any other sort of prayerwalk, God needs to be the initiator of prayer expeditions. Seek God's guidance seriously about every aspect, but especially about timing.

> We had the vision to prayerwalk old Crusade routes for some time. But we haven't felt a release in our spirits to do so yet. When God brings the fullness of time about, that's when this will happen. It's the kind of thing that could happen in a couple of years or maybe later in our lifetimes. We're talking about some politically difficult areas to cross, so the Lord will have to prepare the way. We want to make sure it's the Lord's timetable. I don't want to create my own mess without his blessing and timing.
>
> *— Duane Blackburn, an American pastor training to serve as*

a missionary. Duane hopes someday to lead a prayer expedition from Istanbul, Turkey, to Jerusalem in order to touch the routes of the Crusades with a spirit of repentance.

The classic way to carry out a prayer expedition is to walk every step of the way. While walking, the surrounding scenes envelop all the senses. This exposure gives God's Spirit more room to impress us with the subtle perceptions which are key to vital prayer expeditions.

If at all possible, physically walk. Constraints of time and terrain may cause you to consider using vehicles. Seek God's leading as to your mode of travel. Intercessors have often been led directly by God to pray while aboard boats, aloft in aircraft or at bullet-speed in cars or trains.

Some of the benefits of walking long distances are intangible. If passing over the route is the only point, why not zoom along the highway in a vehicle? Some of the advantages of marching long distances can be compared to the benefits of fasting. There's no special merit to the costly effort of fasting, but long fasts carry an intangible premium of effectiveness. We can be sure that God is not manipulated by self-deprivation, as if fasting were a hunger strike. Instead fasting consecrates the pray-er in seeking God. Extended fasting necessarily involves the whole person, from the most basic physical urges to the most fanciful thoughts. Everyday cycles of life and nutrition are interrupted to set the season apart as a special time of seeking God and receiving from him whatever authority he may grant to pray. In the same way, lengthy prayer expeditions focus the whole person. Most experienced long-distance prayerwalkers feel that physical walking yields enormous benefits. It's to be done, as is extended fasting, by God's guidance and with wisdom of senior leaders.

• **Seek God's leadership.** The significant physical and spiritual challenges call for solid leadership and pastoral oversight. Good administration is essential because expeditions involve large amounts of money and correspondence.

Everything went fine. I attribute that not only to the blessing of the Lord but to the advance preparation we did.

—*Dan Ball, pastor of First Assembly of God in Ashtabula, Ohio, who prepared for three months before a prayer expedition around the circumference of Ashtabula County. Each of the fifty participating churches took responsibility for prayerwalking a three-mile segment of a 150-mile route on the same day. On the day of the walk, the larger groups, some up to 350 people, received police escort.*

• **Select strong team members.** Physical demands are great, so select team members who can endure long walks. If you do recruit physically weaker members, make sure they are spiritually mature. You don't want to have walkers complaining throughout the trip about their physical weaknesses, because the enemy can compound these areas into overall spiritual weaknesses for the team. Try not to establish policies which may needlessly exclude strong participants.

> The joy of praying with people of all different nations and languages was something I can't express. The Holy Spirit sealed our prayer.
>
> —*Charles Simpson, of Ichthus Christian Fellowship. Charles spent five weeks in 1992 walking the entire route from London to Berlin, a distance of around eight hundred miles. At the time Charles was seventy-eight years old.*

• **Enlist local involvement.** In most cases you should try to engage the cooperation of local churches on the route. They can help you understand the spiritual situation of their locality. Some prayer expeditions arrange for nightly prayer rallies in towns along the way. This works well in certain lands, but do not assume that such rallies are always essential or desirable. While generating wonderful support, such gatherings can demand even more ministry exertion and exhaust the team.

• **Publicity and security.** Some prayer expeditions have taken place in regions highly favorable to Christians. Support vehicles openly declare the purpose and destination of walkers. Whenever such a form of testimony is advisable, declare yourselves!

In other countries, open publicity may not be suitable. Wisdom may require you to keep a lower profile. You will need to decide how much of your goal is to accomplish matters of prayer or to give clear testimony. How well do posters, T-shirts and banners testify to God's love in the land you are walking? Local leaders can give you important guidance.

Christian symbols such as large crosses are considered by some to be essential equipment and can indeed help in specific occasions. Yet in some countries such symbols can backfire by being interpreted as intrusive or as emblems of conquest (hearkening back to the days of the Crusades).

Be ready for the media even when the climate is favorable to Christians. Have a press release prepared ahead of time which gives the basic facts of the expedition. Decide ahead of time who will handle interviews.

• **Planning the route.** Plan the route with each day's march in mind.

That means more than marking a trail of significant prayer sites and breaking it into fifteen-mile sections. Balance logistical factors such as transportation to and from the end points of daily walks and your accommodations for the night. Some churches along the way may agree to host you. Be considerate of the schedule and restrictions your host may face.

Try to measure the route accurately by driving the whole length of it beforehand. "Guess-timations" derived from maps can prove disappointing at the end of a grueling day. Some prayerwalkers plan for up to twenty miles a day. Others set a limit of ten to fifteen miles daily.

Try various relay techniques. A team's daily mileage can be doubled by dividing the team to cover adjoining sectors along the same road. Some groups have devised elaborate relay techniques in which several teams surround an area at the same time.

Routes may need to be planned with the advice of local police forces. Wherever possible, avoid the speed and noise of main roads. Some narrow, twisting lanes can also be hazardous. You can sometimes opt for the welcome change of walking along farm paths and trails where there is no traffic.

• **Plan logistics.** Try to anticipate practical matters before the team leaves. Even the best prepared teams learn new dimensions of the word *flexibility*. Prayer expeditions cannot be managed from a distance. The homeside support team can help channel communications, but on-site administration is a must. On the road, designate a leader to make decisions regarding accommodations, budget, daily schedule and pace.

Do the best you can to plan and budget accommodations for the team. You may use hotels and guest houses or perhaps motor homes and camping equipment of all sorts. Arrangements can sometimes be made with local Christians. Make your needs precisely clear (such as meals, baths, laundry, bedding, privacy, transportation, length of stay and daily schedule) before accepting offers of hospitality. Be ready to cover the costs of your stay in a sensitive way.

If possible the team should have control of its own catering. But this may be less realistic in cross-cultural situations where advanced planning is difficult. Finding a steady source of pure drinking water may be the greatest challenge in some regions. Do not underestimate the importance of proper food and fluids on such a demanding exercise. Stand ready to spend what it may cost to eat well to stay healthy.

In general, the same equipment, clothing and medical supplies are needed in prayer expeditions as are required in long-distance hiking. Consult references in any good bookstore for helpful guidelines regarding extensive outdoor walks. The most useful piece of equipment is some sort of support vehicle. Some prayer expeditions have found that they required as many as three vehicles alongside a group of twenty prayerwalkers.

Some expeditions have enjoyed being outfitted with radio equipment. Check the legalities of radios in your host countries. In some areas a radio might wrongly bring you under suspicion as foreign intelligence agents!

During the Expedition: Praying

Developing a daily rhythm provides a source of external strength for the entire team. Most prayer expeditions aim to set out fairly early in the day after a short briefing and time of worship. Conclude the day's prayerwalking by mid-afternoon. Prayerwalking along highways by night is out of the question, but some evening hours can be well-spent interceding at select sites. An evening briefing can be of great value.

Some prayer expeditions have evening prayer rallies. You may want to encourage only part of the team members to attend such gatherings on any given evening so that each participant has some evenings filled with rest. In fact, it's wise to build entire days of rest into the schedule.

After the Expedition: Celebrating

A prayer expedition needs a suitable destination. Do more than just arrive somewhere. Conclude the expedition with a celebration. Better than planning your own party is to try to coordinate the finish of the prayerwalk with an already planned conference or festivity. Prayer expeditions have found that the March for Jesus is always a fitting culmination. One of the many destinations of the Torch Run was Lausanne II in the city of Manila in the Philippines in the summer of 1989. Thousands of Christian mission and church leaders were gathered from many countries of the world. As the torch came in the room where they were gathered, the warm reception affirmed the faith of every footstep of every runner who had prayed all the way from Jerusalem.

> After we finished the prayerwalks around the county, we wrapped things up with a worship and prayer rally. We had about fifteen hundred people attend. More people attended the prayer rally than came to the prayerwalk. In all, about fifty churches participated.
>
> —*Dan Ball, pastor of First Assembly of God in Ashtabula, Ohio*

> I felt symbolically the prayer expeditionary force was walking

on behalf of the body of Christ, as if we were the legs of the body for a time.

When the German leaders washed our feet at the end of our journey with five thousand people from all over Germany looking on, it was almost like a lowering of their national pride. But it was more of an exaltation of the body of Christ.

—*John Pressdee, of Ichthus Christian Fellowship, London, England, describing the concluding ceremony of a prayerwalk from London to Berlin in the summer of 1992. The expedition was timed so that the British, American, French and German prayerwalking teams could join sixty thousand other Germans for a national March for Jesus event on the day after their arrival in Berlin.*

14

"In Every Place to Pray"

Paul charged the church to accomplish a task of utmost priority: to get the entire world prayed for, person by person.

"First of all, then, I urge that entreaties and prayers, petitions and thanksgivings, be made *on behalf of all men*, for kings and all who are in authority, in order that we may lead a tranquil and quiet life in all godliness and dignity. This is *good and acceptable in the sight of God our Savior, who desires all men to be saved* and to come to the knowledge of the truth" (1 Tim. 2:1-4, italics added).

Paul gives us two reasons why the church is to pray for every person as a "first-of-all" matter of urgency. The first is God's desire to save people. Only comprehensive, systematic prayer for all people will begin to match God's ocean-deep desire for all people.

The second reason for planet-wide prayer is the real bottom line: God's joy. As comprehensive prayers are answered, the church grows to reflect God's character to the rest of the world ("in all godliness and dignity," 1 Tim. 2:2). As the glory of God's character is displayed to the world, Paul declares that it is "good and acceptable in the sight of God" (1 Tim. 2:3; the word *acceptable* could easily be rendered "pleasing").

Every-Person Prayer

The needed intercession is not expressed in general, superficial prayers such as "Watch over the people of Australia." Paul lists some of the specific kinds of prayer required to adequately pray for the world: "entreaties and prayers, petitions and thanksgivings" (1 Tim. 2:1).

How did Paul intend for such specific prayer to be made for every human being? Such detailed "every-person" prayer would require an enterprise thoroughly encompassing entire nations, family by family and town by town. Paul's simple plan is to call for Christians "in every place to pray."

> Therefore I want the men *in every place to pray*, lifting up holy hands, without wrath and dissension (1 Tim. 2:8, italics added).

Every-Place Prayer

Every-person prayer can only be accomplished by every-place prayer. The *mandate* of 1 Timothy 2:1 is fulfilled by the *method* of verse 8.

While verse 8 does not directly command us to range far beyond our own community, the geographic dimension is unmistakable. Paul may not call for prayerwalking exactly as we have described it in this book, but keep in mind that in Paul's day, travel to distant places was an extravagance possible to only a few. Paul would have envisioned a prayed-for world in light of his hope that there would soon be praying Christian families in every locale on earth. Today's inexpensive travel means that cities or neighborhoods still lacking a movement of families faithful to Christ need not go untouched by detailed, on-site prayer.

The Urgency of Every-Person Prayer

> For there is one God and one mediator between God and men, the man Christ Jesus, who gave Himself as a ransom for all, the testimony borne at the proper time (1 Tim. 2:5-6).

Christ forever mediates the gap between God and people. But there is yet another gap. It is the gap between the desire of the Father to be known and the fact that many peoples of the world have yet to come to "a knowledge of the truth" (1 Tim. 2:4).

God assigns messengers to fill the witness gap by carrying the "testimony" of the one Mediator "at the proper time." The testimony is released "in its times" (a literal reading of the original language). The word *times* is a plural form of the Greek word *kairos*, which means "a decisive moment" or what we might call a window of opportunity rather than the clock-ticking sequence of minutes and hours.

Paul knew that God had appointed his day as a critical juncture for the advance of the Word of God throughout the world. For that special hour he had been appointed as a messenger, as a church-establisher and as a disciple-trainer (to paraphrase his list: "a preacher and an apostle...[and] as a teacher" [1 Tim. 2:7]). Paul thought it hard to believe that God would appoint him to fill all of these roles (thus he states, "I am telling the truth, I am not lying") since God usually spreads out such entrustments to different people. But Paul knew that he couldn't do it alone. God's appointment of the time and his assignment of missionaries wasn't enough to assure that God's people would fully meet the moment. What was needed? Paul knew that the moment in history required the most comprehensive prayer effort ever called for in biblical history. "Therefore I want the men in every place to pray...for all people" (1 Tim. 2:8).

Many believe that God is appointing this present hour as a unique *kairos* hour of opportunity for the completion of world evangelization. If we follow Paul's line of thought, we'll recognize that opportune times and assigned missionaries won't be enough. To meet the moment, it's going to require every family within God's people to pray for every person in every place.

Holy Hands Praying for the Whole World (1 Tim. 2:8)

Paul draws attention to the hands of the family of God instead of their marching feet. The lifting of holy hands is a clear gesture of worship and intercession. Paul isn't merely recommending a good moral handwashing before coming to church. Holy hands are sanctified, priestly hands. Every believer has a praying place among God's "kingdom of priests" (Ex. 19:6; reiterated by 1 Pet. 2:5-9 and Rev. 1:6).

The biblical priests were commissioned into their work by a ceremony which "filled [their] hands" (2 Chron. 29:31). Hands were literally laden with offerings for God and figuratively consecrated and cleansed to be used in the service of prayer. Of the first priests, God said, "You shall anoint them and *fill their hand* and consecrate them, that they may serve me" (a literal rendering of Ex. 28:41, italics added).*

David invited the entire nation to serve God in building the temple by asking, "Who then is willing to *fill his hand* this day to the Lord?" (1 Chron. 29:5, literal translation). Leaders from every family "offered willingly" (29:6). When the temple was complete, Solomon opened the celebration with the most basic gesture of priestly prayer. "He stood before the altar of the Lord in the presence of all the assembly of Israel and spread out his hands...toward heaven" (2 Chron. 6:12-13).

---

* Note the association of filled hands with anointing and a pure consecration to serve God in prayer. The Hebrew phrase *filling of the hands* is usually translated with words such as *ordain* or *dedicate*. The first sacrificial "ram of ordination" (literally: "ram of filling") ended up ceremonially placed "in the hands of Aaron and on the hands of his sons" (Lev. 8:22-27; compare Ex. 29:24-25). Other references to the "filling of hands" as a commissioning to priestly service: Ex. 29:9,29,33,35, 32:29; Lev. 8:33, 16:32; Num. 3:3; and 2 Chron. 29:31 among several others.

Priestly hands are "holy hands," sanctified for a double purpose: to bring faithfully to God the offered treasures of the people (Lev. 1-3) and to signal the bestowing of God's blessing powerfully by extending upraised hands (Lev. 9:22).

Paul understands every believing family to share in this rich heritage of upraised, consecrated hands before God amidst the nations. Paul makes it clear in 1 Timothy 2:8-10 that God desires that the church go public with its devotion to Jesus and its prayerful concern for the world.

The purpose of every-person prayer lies in God's desire that his church would truly shine by the radiant godliness of their lives (1 Tim. 2:2,10) so that every person would have inexcusable exposure to the truth (1 Tim. 2:4-7).

"First of All" Means Soon

If every-person prayer is supposed to be "first of all," then it really can't wait. We have rightly given ourselves for centuries to the task of communicating the gospel to every person. Every person is to be told the gospel. Paul tells us of something more primary that leads to completed world evangelization: that every person in the world be prayed for.

Imagine God's joy in beholding a world in which every person alive is specifically blessed in priestly prayer every day. Let us use our feet to fill and subdue the earth, but as we do, let us use sanctified hands in priestly prayer to lift intercession and worship amidst every community, on behalf of every family, every man, woman and child.

APPENDIX A

A SHORT COURSE IN PRAYERWALKING

This appendix may be photocopied and distributed as an introduction to prayerwalking.

In hundreds of cities across the globe, ordinary believers are prayerwalking through the streets of their communities. They pray while walking, with eyes open for the spiritual awakening God is bringing.

We define prayerwalking as "praying on-site with insight." There is no set pattern or proven formula. Prayerwalkers have set out with every imaginable style. There's nothing magic at all in the footsteps. God's Spirit is simply helping us to pray with persistent spontaneity in the midst of the very settings in which we expect him to answer our prayers. We instinctively draw near to those for whom we pray.

Getting up close to the community focuses our prayer. We sharpen our prayers by concentrating on specific homes and families. But we enlarge our praying as well, crying out for entire communities to know God's healing presence.

Quiet prayerwalks complement more high-profile praise marches and prayer rallies. Worship and warfare blend with intercession that Christ would be welcomed as Lord by many throughout the entire city.

Prayerwalks give us a simple way to continually fill our streets with prayer. Many are praying city-size prayers while ranging throughout their towns with disciplined regularity in small bands of two or three. Thus prayerwalkers keep near their neighbors in order to touch our cities with the gospel and transforming service. Quiet triumphs often follow as God changes the city day by day and house by house.

How to Get Started Prayerwalking

• **Join with other believers.** Join your faith with others to help prayer flow in an engaging conversational style. Large groups sometimes fail to give everyone a chance to participate. Pairs and triplets work best.

• **Set aside time.** Allowing one or two full hours gives prayerwalkers a good chance to manage preliminaries and follow-up discussions, although much can be done in less time.

• **Choose an area.** Ask God to guide you. It's best by far to learn the joys of prayerwalking in unfamiliar neighborhoods. You'll return quickly to your own neighborhood with fresh vision. Centers of commerce and religion are fascinating, but there's nothing like touching families, schools and churches in residential areas. Use elevated points to pray over a panorama. Linger at specific sites which seem to be key.

• **Pray with insight.** Pray for the people you see. As you do, you might find the Spirit of God recalibrating your heart with his own sensitivities. Enhance these responsive insights with research done beforehand. Use knowledge of past events and current trends to enrich intercession. Above all, pray Scripture. If you have no clear place to begin praying, select just about any of the biblical prayers, and you will find that they almost pray themselves.

• **Focus on God.** Make God's promises rather than Satan's schemes the highlight of your prayer. Your discernment of evil powers may at times exceed God's specific guidance to engage them in direct combat. Consider the simplicity of first making direct appeal to the throne of God before attempting to pick street fights with demonic powers. Seek a restraining order from heaven upon evil so that God's empowered people may bring forth God's intended blessings on the city.

• **Regather and report.** Share what you have experienced and prayed. Expressing something of your insights and faith will encourage others — as well as yourself. Set plans for further prayerwalking.

• **Coordinate efforts.** Enlist other praying people to join with friends to cover special areas. Give leadership by forming and mixing prayer bands. Seek to collect written notes recording which areas have been covered and what kinds of prayers have been prayed. Pool your insights to ascertain whether God is prompting a repeated focus on particular areas. Eventually aim to cover your entire town or city, unless God guides otherwise.

Themes for Prayerwalking

Attempt to keep every prayer pertinent to the specific community you pass through. As you do, you will find prayers naturally progress to the nation and to the world.

Use a theme passage of Scripture. Unless God guides you to use another, try 1 Timothy 2:1-10. Many have found it to be a useful launching point for prayerwalking. Verse 8 speaks of the important territorial dimension to prayer connected with God's desire that all people be saved. "I want the men *in every place* to pray" (italics added).

Copy this and other passages in a format easy to read aloud several times during your walk. Each of the following prayer points emerges from this passage.

- **Concerning Christ:** Proclaim him afresh to be the one Mediator and the ransom for all. Name him Lord of the neighborhood and of the lives you see.
- **Concerning leaders:** Pray for people responsible in any position of authority — for teachers, police, administrators and parents.
- **Concerning peace:** Cry out for the godliness and holiness of God's people to increase into substantial peace. Pray for new churches to be established.
- **Concerning truth:** Declare openly the bedrock reality that there is one God. Celebrate the faithful revelation of his truth to all peoples through ordinary people (1 Tim. 2:8). Pray that the eyes of minds would cease to be blinded by Satan so that they could come to a knowledge of the truth.
- **Concerning the gospel:** Praise God for his heart's desire that all people be saved. Ask that heaven would designate this year as a "proper time" for the testimony of Christ to be given afresh with simple power (1 Tim. 2:6). Name specific people.
- **Concerning the blessing of God:** Thanksgivings are to be made on behalf of all people. Give God the explicit thanks he deserves for the goodness he constantly bestows on the homes you pass by. Ask to see the city with his eyes, that you might sense what is good and pleasing in his sight as well as what things grieve him deeply. Ask God to bring forth an enduring spiritual awakening.
- **Concerning the church:** Ask for healing in relationships, that there be no wrath or dissension among God's people. Ask that God would make his people, men and women alike, expressive in worship with the substance of radiant, relational holiness. Ask that our worship would be adorned with the confirming power of saints doing good in our communities.

Excerpted from Prayerwalking *by Steve Hawthorne and Graham Kendrick (Creation House, 1993).*

APPENDIX B

MORE RESOURCES ON PRAYER AND SPIRITUAL WARFARE

Since this book has such a narrow focus on on-site intercession, it's wise to widen your exposure and deepen your thinking by using the hundreds of wonderful resources now available on prayer. We hesitate even to begin listing books. For every resource listed, there may be a dozen nearly as good or better.

Christians are exploring the area of spiritual warfare so enthusiastically that new issues are being raised. Viewpoints may differ, but there is a sense that God is leading every part of the church to a clearer understanding of our part as overcomers in the spiritual battle with Christ. You shouldn't expect to find a complete agreement between the views stated in this book and the books mentioned below.

A Vision for Prayer

In the Gap: What It Means to Be a World Christian, by David Bryant (Regal Books, Ventura, Calif., 1984).

This classic tool helps Christians grow in a vision for God's global purposes coming to completion. Bryant lays a practical foundation for visionary prayer.

Concerts of Prayer: Christians Join for Spiritual Awakening and World Evangelization, by David Bryant (Regal Books, Ventura, Calif., 1984).

A vision for community-wide gatherings of prayer to seek God. Much of the seasoned wisdom is helpful for prayerwalks involving several churches praying together.

Public Praise: Celebrating Jesus on the Streets of the World, by Graham

Kendrick (Creation House, Orlando, Fla., 1992; published outside the United States under the title *Shine, Jesus, Shine*, Word Books, 1993).

Public Praise recounts the surprising emergence of the movement of public processional worship called March for Jesus. A rich exploration of the biblical joy of citywide celebrations which fill the streets with praise.

Learning to Worship as a Way of Life, by Graham Kendrick (Bethany House, Minneapolis, Minn., 1984).

A vision for worship, as practical as it is profound.

Operation World, by Patrick Johnstone (OMLIT Publishing, Waynesboro, Ga., fourth edition, 1986).

Summary information from every nation, arranged as a practical help for the praying Christian. Painstakingly researched, practical tips, a tool of incredible value to help prayerwalkers turn their attention to the nations.

Taking Our Cities for God, by John Dawson (Creation House, Orlando, Fla., 1989).

Excellent vision for redeeming cities to God. A proven resource. This book has probably stimulated more prayerwalking than any other book.

More Practical Guides for Prayerwalking

Prayerwalking: A New Approach to Spiritual Warfare, by Graham Kendrick and John Houghton (Kingsway Publications, Eastbourne, U.K., 1990).

A short, illustrated, opening guide to prayerwalking. It is filled with practical ideas and helpful details for long-range prayerwalks or impromptu efforts.

Manual of Participatory Missionary Prayer, by John Huffman (Latin America Mission, P.O. Box 52-7900, Miami, FL 33152).

Brief instructions for fourteen-, ten- and seven-day plans for on-site intercession as some of the first steps of church planting and evangelism efforts in specific neighborhoods.

A Sampler on Spiritual War

The School of Victorious Warfare: Twelve Lessons on How to Pray Victoriously for the Unevangelized, by Dick Eastman (Every Home for Christ, P.O. Box 35930, Colorado Springs, CO 80935, 1993).

The Believer's Guide to Spiritual Warfare, by Tom White (Vine Books, Ann Arbor, Mich., 1990).

Engaging the Enemy, edited by C. Peter Wagner (Regal Books, Ventura, Calif., 1991).

The Prayer Warrior Series, by C. Peter Wagner (Regal Books, Ventura, Calif., 1992 and 1993).

Book I: *Warfare Prayer: How to Seek God's Power and Protections in the Battle to Build His Kingdom*

Book II: *Prayer Shield: How to Intercede for Pastors, Christian Leaders, and Others on the Spiritual Frontlines*

Book III: *Breaking Strongholds in Your City: How to Use Spiritual Mapping to Make Your Prayers More Strategic, Effective, and Targeted*

Book IV: *Churches That Pray*

The Last of the Giants, by George Otis Jr. (Chosen Books, Tarrytown, N.Y., 1991).

Possessing the Gates of the Enemy, by Cindy Jacobs (Baker Book House/Revell, Grand Rapids, Mich., reprinted 1991).

Spiritual Warfare for Every Christian: How to Live in Victory and Retake the Land, by Dean Sherman (Frontline Communications, Seattle, Wash., 1990).

Victor or Victim: A Fresh Look at Spiritual Warfare, by Greg Mira (Grace! Publishing, 12416 Grandview Rd., Grandview, MO 64030, 1992).

Powers of Darkness, by Clinton E. Arnold (InterVarsity Press, Downers Grove, Ill., 1992).

Help for International Ventures

Stepping Out: A Guide to Short-Term Missions, edited by Steve Hawthorne, Tim Gibson, Richard Krekel and Ken Moy (YWAM Publishing, P.O. Box 55787, Seattle, Wash. 98155, 1992).

APPENDIX C

HOW PRAYERWALKING RELATES TO MARCH FOR JESUS

March for Jesus praise processions are a growing grass-roots expression of living Christianity. They are spreading worldwide as Christians of different nations, church backgrounds and cultures come together to celebrate Jesus with extravagant public praise.

March for Jesus is not a protest march, nor does it represent political issues. The purpose is simply to glorify Jesus openly before heaven and earth. March for Jesus creates a climate for evangelism and helps build healthy relationships and unity among churches.

A march of fifteen thousand Christians in London, England, in 1987 led to a march of fifty-five thousand and then two hundred thousand in 1990 and again in 1991. March for Jesus helped revitalize churches in England and created a climate for evangelism and church planting. In March of 1991, two successful marches of more than twenty thousand people were held in Austin and Houston, Texas, and built the groundwork for March for Jesus USA.

On May 23, 1992, 300,000 Christians in 142 American cities and 300,000 Christians in more than 25 European cities united as they marched through their cities singing, praying and exalting Christ as March for Jesus was internationally linked for the first time.

March for Jesus has helped break the caricatures of Christianity that exist in people's minds and reintroduce them to the church as a joyful company of people, full of life and color, with a message relevant to today's world.

On June 12, 1993, more than a million people in hundreds of cities around the world will unite and joyfully proclaim, "The earth is the Lord's, and the fulness thereof; the world, and all they that dwell therein" (Ps. 24:1, KJV).

On June 25, 1994, there will be a March for Jesus that circles the globe, encompassing major cities in numerous countries of the world, with Christians walking in praise processions in every time zone. The result could be twenty-four hours of continuous praise and prayer from followers of Jesus all over the earth.

The Relationship of Prayerwalking and March for Jesus

Prayerwalking and praise marching are similar, but distinct, prayer efforts. Each is best done in conjunction with the other, but both emerge with their own integrity.

A Common Task

Prayer is central to both endeavors. Both prayerwalking and the March for Jesus appeal to God to subdue evil forces and draw more people to himself. Both efforts openly proclaim the truth of God with praise. Both seek God's face for outpourings of his goodness upon whole cities and nations.

Complementary Pursuits

They are twin efforts, requiring each other to succeed. Prayerwalking prepares the way for praise marching. On the other hand, the March for Jesus has introduced many believers to the potency of prayer on the streets. The praise march releases thousands of potential prayerwalkers back to their neighborhoods with a different impression of God's impending presence on their city.

A Different Profile

Prayerwalking is a more flexible, wide-ranging affair than the March for Jesus events. Prayerwalking includes just about any sort of on-site intercessory prayer. Prayerwalkers usually go at their task without recognition in countless variations of praise-filled intercession almost anywhere and at anytime.

A March for Jesus is a more elaborate, high-profile gathering of believers, requiring a much sharper focus than prayerwalking. It is not an overgrown prayerwalk. In order for the March for Jesus movements to mature with a potent integrity for the entire Christian community throughout a city or nation, the paramount focus must be on worshipping Jesus. As Christ is glorified in explicit worship, God's people celebrate the common essentials of historic, biblical Christianity, and thus enjoy a tangible sense of unity. In processions with Christ, Christians often experience a growing identity before the Lord that they are God's servants to their city.

A Different Direction

The March for Jesus can be defined biblically as a procession up to Jerusalem. God's people from many tribes together draw near to his dwelling place, celebrating in a special festival. They give their Lord the glory of which he is worthy. Urgent prayers blend confidently with needed expressions of repentance. Their declaration of God's truth is energized with heartfelt thanksgiving for what he has already done for them. Like Israel's feasts of old, the March for Jesus has an expectant sincerity, as if it were a rehearsal of an anticipated gathering yet to come.

Prayerwalking, on the other hand, can be described biblically as a walk around Jericho, in contrast to a procession up to Jerusalem. Prayerwalkers wage spiritual war in their neighborhoods in order that God might draw their neighbors into the family of God. Prayerwalking helps believers to step into the place of serving and healing in the communities that God is granting to them. By exercising this servant role in the midst of their cities, Christians begin to express a fulfillment of God's promise to give his people a land and a family as an inheritance. Thus prayerwalking becomes a sojourn toward the home and family God is giving Christians to inhabit, and, ultimately, to inherit.

Both are needed. The joyful abandon of the March for Jesus may become possible because some of the necessary warfare will have already been accomplished by diligent prayerwalkers beforehand. Thus the actual celebration of the March for Jesus can be left uncluttered by excessive bombast against God's enemies. Christ's supreme lordship shines as the sole focus of attention. Spiritual warfare may actually modulate to a greater plane during the March for Jesus in keeping with the magnitude of God's deliverance described in Exodus 15 and Psalm 68. This is no lesser foray into enemy territory. God's enemies retreat as he arises in his magnificent processional presence during the march.

A biblical vision for the March for Jesus has been set forth in the book *Public Praise* (by Graham Kendrick, Creation House, 1992. The same book is published in the United Kingdom under the title *Shine, Jesus, Shine*, Word Books, 1993).

To participate in a March for Jesus
in or near a city in the United States or Canada, contact:

March for Jesus, USA
P.O. Box 3216
Austin, TX 78764
(512) 416-0066
Fax: (512) 445-5393

Inquiries from other countries
should be directed to:

March for Jesus
P.O. Box 39
Sunbury-on-Thames
Middlesex, TW16 6PP
United Kingdom
Telephone: (0932) 789681
Fax: (0932) 789691

ABOUT THE AUTHORS

Steve Hawthorne

Steve Hawthorne is best known as the designer of "Perspectives on the World Christian Movement," a popular mission vision course that is taught around the country. Hawthorne began his prayerwalking experience in 1985 while leading a team doing exploratory research for church-planting efforts in a Middle Eastern city. He has been part of several mission ventures in Asia and the Middle East, involving on-site prayer. He has helped train prayerwalkers in ten countries.

Hawthorne has also been involved in prayerwalking in his home city of Austin, Texas. At this writing, Austin has been comprehensively prayerwalked twice, involving believers from many churches.

In the summer of 1992 both Hawthorne and Kendrick joined a team of prayerwalkers for portions of a special prayer expedition in which intercessors walked from London to Berlin.

Graham Kendrick

Graham Kendrick is one of the world's most respected worship leaders today. His well-known song "Shine, Jesus, Shine" was designed to help believers from many churches break out of their buildings in massive displays of worship in the view of their cities.

Kendrick first encountered prayerwalking in specific areas of London where his church, Ichthus Fellowship, was hoping to plant new congregations. Prayerwalking is regarded by Ichthus Fellowship leadership to be a key element in their efforts to evangelize, plant churches and bring a measure of Christ's healing justice to the community.

Kendrick has played a key part in the March for Jesus movement, which emerged alongside prayerwalks in greater London. The music he wrote for an early praise march popularized the vision of taking the church onto the streets in praise and worship. Shortly afterward Kendrick found himself among a handful of leaders who had independently received a vision to instigate a long-range prayerwalk. This walk traversed the entire expanse of England in 1989, from the northernmost point to the southernmost point. A year later he joined yet another team walking across England from west to east.

SHARE YOUR PRAYER — YOUR REPORTS ARE WELCOME!

Your experiences in prayerwalking may encourage others as future resources are designed. The authors welcome you to send reports of your prayerwalking efforts, particularly if this book has been helpful to you. Which parts have been helpful and why? Perhaps the anecdotes of your experiences could prove valuable for future endeavors of prayer.

If you send a report, you may want to answer questions such as: How did God guide you to begin prayerwalking? How many people have been prayerwalking with you? With what kind of regularity? And for how long? What churches were involved? What areas or routes have you pursued? What were the dates of your prayer journey or prayer expedition? Where did you go? What prayers were prayed there? Have you seen answers to your prayers?

Please include your name and address. We will make contact before using your communication in any way. Please alert us if you describe situations where we need to be sensitive about security, such as events in the so-called "closed" countries.

We regret that we lack the staff and structure to be able to respond to your reports. It's likely that concerns and questions about the particulars of spiritual war and prayer in your city can be addressed best by Christian leaders near you.

Thank you!

From the U.S.A. or Canada, write:

Prayerwalking
c/o March for Jesus, USA
P.O. Box 3216
Austin, TX 78764

From other countries, write:

Prayerwalking
c/o March for Jesus
P.O. Box 39
Sunbury-on-Thames
Middlesex, TW16 6PP
United Kingdom

269.2
LINCOLN CHRISTIAN COLLEGE AND SEMINARY 112840
H399

3 4711 00177 2534